HONOR THE EARTH

HONOR THE EARTH

INDIGENOUS RESPONSES TO ENVIRONMENTAL DEGRADATION IN THE GREAT LAKES

Edited by Phil Bellfy

Ziibi Press

Published in the United States by Ziiibi Press <ziibi.org> through CreateSpace.

ISBN-13: 978-1497487253

ISBN-10: 1497487250

TABLE OF CONTENTS

PREFACE

Aki: The Spirit of the Land is in Our Language

Maaganiit Noodin

Shkaakaamikwe / Mazikaamikwe Ezhi-ni'gikenimaanaan
Miigwetch kina gwaya gii bi dagoshinoyeg miinwa bizindawiyeg.

Biindigeg,
  Come in
Enji-Anishinaabemong
  Where Anishinaabemowin is spoken
Enji-manjimendaming
  Where there is remembering
Enji-gikendaasong
  A place of knowing
Enji-zaagi'iding
  A place of love

Bizandamog,
  Listen
Enendamowinan zhaabobideg ode'ng
  Ideas run through hearts
Bawaajigewinan waasa izhaamigag
  Dreams go far
Anamejig niimiwag dibishkoo mewenzha
  Those who pray dance like long ago
Kina bimaadizijig miinwaa wesiiyag owaabandaanaawaa bidaasigemigog
  All the people and animals see it, the light coming

Bimaadizig
  Live

Nisawayi'iing misko-biidaabang idash ni misko-pangishimag
  Between the red dawn and the red sunset
Nisawayi'iing giizis idash ni niibaadibikad'giizis
  Between the sun (or the month) and the full moon (time passing)
Nisawayi'iing manidoog idash wiindigoog
  Between the spirits we love and the ones who devour
Nisawayi'iing awanong idash ankwadong mii ji-mikaman gdo'ojichaakam
  Between the fog and the clouds you can find your soul

Biindigeg, weweni bizindamog, minobimaadizig
  Come in, carefully listen, live well.

"Biindigeg, weweni bizindamog, minobimaadizig,"

I write these words as an invitation to understand our relationship with "aki / land." She is the center of existence; the source of life, to know her is to understand the universe. To know her requires the quiet acts of listening, dreaming and believing. To know her also requires that we walk, we move across her surface, through days and nights, springs and winters, witnessing and protecting all that she is. Our relationship with her is one of science, politics, art, ecology, health, and in my case, language, especially as it rearranges itself in songs and poetry.

It is imperative that we preserve the language that allows us to better understand the Anishinaabe relationship with aki. It is equally as important that we celebrate aki by using that language, keeping that way of knowing flowing like the rivers to the oceans, because that rhythm of motion between the land and the language is one of the things that keeps us alive.

Although there are undoubtedly innumerable examples I have yet to discover, there are a few that appear most striking to me: the word "aki" and some of its relatives; the names used to talk about the life-giver Aki; and the way we talk about what we do with her gift of life.

Aki is such a small word and yet, many language teachers believe that the smallest, simplest pieces of meaning are possibly the oldest. Aki is certainly one of the first terms Anishinaabeg must have needed to begin speaking of who, where and why we are. The aadisokaanag / stories are long and beautifully complex, but many begin with the belief that Gizhemanido had a vision which led to the creation of the universe including the rock, water, fire and wind that become Aki who in these old stories she is often called by one of two names, Shkaakaamikwe or Mazikaamikwe.

Although I can only make intelligent guesses about the roots of these words it is important to note that neither of them are as simply as "Gashwan Aki." To call her by her name in Anishinaabemowin implies much more than the ground personified. Both Shkaakaamikwe and Mazikaamikwe end with "ikwe," the term for woman, so she must be considered a representation of that force we know as one half of human construction, but used in this way, that little word-part is used more for balance and identity, not the creation of a stereotype.

One of the beautiful aspects of the old ways is that, like the language itself, there is no constant designation of he or she, but rather a mention of inini (man) or (ikwe) woman, male or female, only as needed, most often in names, and always after the action has been described. In fact, it

viii

is in akiwenzii, the word for old man that we find aki, perhaps to remind us that he too, is our partner in protecting and producing life with our mother.

The two names, Shkaakaamikwe and Mazikaamikwe, differ significantly and may simply be names without assigned meanings, but Anishinaabemowin words are often poems unto themselves, strings of meaning that create a mosaic of understanding. In these words I hear what I know she does, "mazi" is a piece of language often used to speak about something made into an image: "mazinaadin" is to make an image, "mazinibii" to draw, "mazinaabidoo'an" to bead on a loom, "mazina'igan" a page or book.

Speakers must consciously or unconsciously think of these creative images when they hear or say Mazikaamikwe. Shkaakaamikwe is less obvious, but in it, I hear "zhakaa" which is a piece of meaning added to indicate something is soft and damp, like snow or a bog. One could also consider the phrase "oshki ogimaa kwe," which roughly translates to the "new leading woman." And when we think of where old stories (and now science) tell us life began, I think both may be related to the concept.

These are the names for aki, the earth, the one we know as a mother. I think of them when we sing our song for her, and her daughters of the four directions who rise each morning and walk in the four directions across her landscape, her body, and our souls.

Shkaakaamikwe,
Mazikaamikwe,
G'daanisag bmosewag
Giiwedinong
Waabanong
Zhowaanong
Epangishimag

I added Anishinaabe lyrics to a song by Brenda MacIntyre who says "this song came to help heal the people." I could think of no better way to honor our connection to Aki than to sing of her and her daughters, the four sisters, who protect the processes of birth and death, the cycle of seasons and journey of our souls.

We call this journey, "minobimaadiziwin." This is significant in thinking about our mother, the earth, when we recognize the rhythm of bmode, bmose, bmpato, bmise, bgizo. Akina goya (all of us) living on earth crawl, or walk, or run, or fly, or swim. These words are like a song sung in our hearts as we move and live with Aki. It is she who allows us to do these things and it is our language that allows us to connect them in our minds with life, movement, well-being. We are the "aki" in "akina goya."

We are part of this waawii'ok bimaadiziwin (this circle of life). G'gii niigimin miidash ombigiying miidash ininiwiying maage ikwewiying. (We are born and then grow up as men and women.) What we must remember is: Gego banaajtooken ezhi-bimaadziying neyaab g'daa biidoomin Anishinaabe-bimaadiziying. (Don't break the way of life, we need to bring back the Anishinaabe way of living.) We need to honor the old ways of knowing and understanding our world and ourselves.

As we strive to blend ancient philosophy, theology and ecological beliefs with a modern world, I am inspired by those who have gone before me and those who lead me know. In particular, I think of the women who began the Mother Earth Waterwalk in 2007 to raise awareness about our water. These women continue to remind us, "water is precious and sacred. . . it is one of the basic elements needed for all life to exist."

They have circled, Superior, Michigan, Huron, Ontario and Erie, all of which we call Chigaming. These gentle women are some of the daughters of the Earth I admire most. They are not presidents of countries or companies, they are not rock stars or billionaires, but they are living vessels of water and spirit and I am certain that as Gizhemanido looks down upon the earth, they shine more brightly than anything that has been made by humanity. I know Nokomis Nibaagiizis will be with them night and day, as will many of us in spirit.

Another Mother that I must mention when speaking of those who artfully balanced the demands of motherhood, bimaadiziwin, and rapidly changing times on this earth, is Jane Johnston Schoolcraft. Although she lived over 100 years ago, her concerns and beliefs are still a useful mirror for our times. She knew many worlds and lived successfully in several. And she should be recognized as the mother of modern Anishinaabe poetry. Although she could write like Poe or Longfellow in elegant and flowing English, it is her simple works in Anishinaabemowin that I like the most.

Robert Dale Parker published a book that carves for her a rightful place in the literature of American letters. In cooperation and response to these efforts, John Nichols gave readers a treasure when he re-transcribed one of her poems making it clear it was most likely written as a song sung to her children when she made the difficult choice to leave them at school.

The title she chose was simply, "Nindinendam (I am thinking)" and the most frequent word used is, not surprisingly, "endanakiiyaan" (my homeland), a combination of endayaan and akii that reflects what this land can and should mean to all of us, kina goya. Her verses are simple and clear.

Nyaa nindinendam	Oh I am thinking
Mekawiyaanin	I am reminded
Endanakiiyaan	Of my homeland

X

| Waasawekamig | A faraway place |
| Endanakiiyaan | My homeland |

Nidaanisens e	My little daughter
Nigwizisens e	My little son
Ishe naganagwaa	I leave them far behind
Waasawekamig	A faraway place
Endanakiiyaan	My homeland

Zhigwa gosha wiin	Now
Beshowad e we	It is near
Ninzhike we ya	I am alone
Ishe izhayaan	As I go
Endanakiiyaan	My homeland

Endanakiiyaan	My homeland
Ninzhike we ya	I am alone
Ishe giiweyaan	I am going home
Nyaa nigashkendam	Oh I am sad
Endanakiiyaan	My homeland

And when I sing this song now, gathering strength to face a new day, I add these lines to mark the way I long for my own daughters, now growing into their own lives, sometimes separated from me as I work on recovering the sound of the widening space we call home together. I sing it and wonder about the way love opens even as it is spilled. G'zaaginim n'daanisag miinwaa pane giizis zaagiaasiged pii zoongide-zagajigabawiying.

N'daanisensag	My daughters
Ikwesensag	My girls
nd'gikendamin	we know it
kchi'zaaginagog	I love you so much
zaagiyeg gaye.	and you both love me too.

May this book be a Anishinaabe love song to Aki from all her sons and daughters.

◊ ◊ ◊ ◊ ◊ ◊

Maaganiit Noodin received an MFA in Creative Writing and a PhD in English and Linguistics from the University of Minnesota. She is Assistant Professor in English and American Indian Studies and at the University of Wisconsin-Milwaukee. Her book *Bwaajimo: A Dialect of Dreams in Anishinaabe* explores the Anishinaabe language in literature. She has published poetry in numerous journals and magazines and sings with Miskwaasining Nagamojig (the Swamp Singers) a women's hand drum group whose lyrics are all in Anishinaabemowin. It is as a daughter, and for her daughters, that she continues to connect sounds in this space of Great Lakes.

ACKNOWLEDGEMENTS

This volume grew out of a conference that was held on "Earth Day" weekend in April of 2007 on the campus of Michigan State University, East Lansing, Michigan. All of the essays that appear in this book have been reviewed and updated by the authors.

The Earth Day conference and this book could not have happened without the generous support of the Canadian Embassy in Washington, DC, and the Canadian Consulate in Detroit. Dennis Moore, of the Detroit Consulate, deserves special miigwetch, merci, and thanks for his unwavering support.

The conference was also supported by the Canadian Studies Centre, at Michigan State University, under the Acting Directorship, in 2007, of Phil Handricks,.

Conference organizers would also like to thank these additional sponsors for their support: MSU College of Arts and Letters, MSU American Indian Studies Program, and the MSU North American Indigenous Faculty and Staff Association.

The conference was organized by the *Center for the Study of Indigenous Border Issues (CSIBI)*. CSIBI Co-directors are: Phil Bellfy (Professor Emeritus of American Indian Studies, Michigan State University, East Lansing, Michigan), Karl Hele (Associate Professor and Director of First Peoples Studies, School of Community and Public Affairs, Concordia University, Montreal), and David McNab (Associate Professor of Indigenous Thought and Canadian Studies, Departments of Equity Studies and Humanities, Faculty of Liberal Arts and Professional Studies at York University, Toronto;). CSIBI's publishing arm is the *Ziibi Press*. This volume is published under that imprint.

More information on CSIBI and the Ziibi Press can be found at: csibi.org.

INTRODUCTION

Honor The Earth

Phil Bellfy

The Great Lakes were first visited by Europeans over four hundred years ago, and since then, the Lakes' environs have been severely altered. The evidence can be seen everywhere—massive multi-lane highways, huge mega-cities, large-scale technological "improvements" that have altered vast landscapes, mines, power-plants, nuclear generating stations, paper mills, steel smelters, water diversion projects—the list goes on and on. In technology's wake, we see pollution of our air, our water, our land, and even our own bodies.

But, if you look hard enough, you can find some areas that appear to be untouched by the Westerners' hand. The North Shore of Lake Superior is one of those places. Here you will find immense rock out-croppings covered in forest, lakes teeming with fish, moose and deer and bear foraging seemingly everywhere. You will also find ancient pictographs along the shore, and "pukaskwas" –small holes dug out of the huge boulder "beaches" found along the shoreline of Lake Superior. These boulder beaches are often found a mile or so inland from the existing shoreline, marking the shoreline of an earlier "Lake Superior" which was more vast and deeper than the lake of today.

Imagine a sloping field of boulders covering perhaps an area as large as a football field or larger. The boulders vary in size, from the smallest being perhaps the size of a softball, the largest, beach-ball size. The "surface" of this boulder beach is rather smooth, even though inclined, sloping down toward the lake. Within this landscape (rockscape, would be a better term) you may notice an occasional "depression," an area where the rocks have been "excavated," heaped up along the ridge of the hole that is being created. The hole itself may be no deeper than three feet; the boulders moved in its creation may number no more than a few dozen.

It is claimed that no one knows why the ancient people of the region created these pukaskwa holes –they seem to serve no purpose that we can decipher. They're too small to have served as shelter; besides, shelter would have been more readily obtained in the forests that surround these boulder beaches. They certainly aren't "mines" in the sense that we might imagine people "excavating" in these boulder beaches for some thing of value –there's nothing but boulders everywhere (in fact, what now passes for "forest" is simply a bunch of trees growing on top of even more "boulder-beach," now covered with a thin layer of soil after who knows how many millennia).

In the case of the pictographs, we can at least see some cultural reason for their creation, as they often depict human figures, Thunderbirds, or Misshupeshu, the Spirit of the lake. But not so for the pukaskwa "holes."

Of course, we (those of us alive today) are not completely ignorant about those who inhabited these areas long ago –those we may call the Ancient Ones. If you will allow me a little speculation: we know that the pictographs served to depict events and spirits of the places where the Ancient Ones painted them on those rock faces millennia ago. We know that these practices formed just one element of the Ancient Ones "cosmology" –that "body of knowledge" which constituted their ancient Way of Life. Some of those ancient ways have come down to us today as elements of what many may call "Indian religion."

So, based on what we know today, and basing our speculation on that knowledge, I think that it's safe to assume that the pukaskwa holes served—in whatever capacity—as elements of the relationship that the Great Lakes' ancient peoples had with their environment, in whatever spiritual configuration that image may conjure up in your own imagination. And, we can be sure that whatever visible form that sacred relationship may have taken –pictographs, pukaskwa holes—we can be certain that the relationship was based on respect for the natural landscape, pure and simple.

It was through this respectful relationship, developed over the millennia, that the "original people" of this area not only maintained their lives, they thrived within the natural boundaries established by their relationship with the natural world. In today's vocabulary, it may be something as simple as an understanding that if human beings take care of the environment, the environment will take care of them. The entire relationship can be summarized as "harmony and balance, based on respect."

Of course, here we are today, in the Third Millennium, struggling to maintain our "way of life."

As "technological people," we have destroyed much of our environment, and those of us in the Great Lakes cannot escape from the responsibility for much of our actions. We are told to not eat too many fish caught in the Great Lakes; often, in our cities, old people and infants are told to remain indoors as the air is too befouled to be breathed; asthma is reaching epidemic proportions; occasionally, beaches are closed to swimming due to an increased risk of bacterial infection; sometimes people die from drinking contaminated water, others "just" get sick; the same is true of our food supply –many get sick and some die; our bodies often become ravaged by cancer and other environmentally-induced diseases, which often kill us; and, in what is to me the most revealing caution, we are told to "stay out of the sun" as the danger of skin cancer lurks in every ray.

xviii

Don't breathe the air, don't eat the food, don't drink the water, don't even stand outside in the daylight. This is the state of "modern civilization" and the state of "modern" humans –"living" within the confines of a polluted world, surrounded by a multitude of "things." This is doubly true for us in the Great Lakes region –home of the "rust belt" and its attendant environmental ills. Our Lakes are polluted, as are our rivers, many of us are sick, we are battling "invasive species" which are taking an additional toll on our resources, devastating our "indigenous" flora and fauna.

But many of us are not sitting idly by watching our TVs and waiting for the "final episode" to be aired; many of us have become "environmental activists" simply because to be otherwise would be to acquiesce in our own destruction. Many Native people of the Great Lakes have, too, become "environmentalists," although they may have been living that Way of Life long before it became "trendy" to be so called. It goes back to those Ancient Ones, those who came long before us, those who lived their lives in harmony and balance with the Natural World, aided in this relationship by mutual respect.

There is also something to be said for living close to the natural world, as Native people have been "restricted" to "reservations" which are often "out of the way" places that were considered to be of "no use" to the early Europeans. It is also true that these "natural areas" are those with no mineral "wealth" or other resources held in high regard by the dominant culture today. Hence, simply by history, and out of necessity, Native people live "close to the land."

Even though they live far from the "benefits" of "civilization," Native people have also been among those most affected by "modern" pollution. If they eat their "natural" diet, rich in the bounty of the lakes and rivers, they are in danger of consuming amounts of mercury and carcinogenic substances far in excess of "allowable" standards. As we shall see in some of the essays which comprise this book, they often live "down-stream" from factories that discharge industrial pollution.

I encourage the readers of this volume to keep in mind that Ancient dictum –live in harmony and balance with the natural world, and do so ever mindful of the respect that that natural world deserves. We shall attempt to trace that relationship throughout these essays, and give you at least a slight glimpse back into an earlier time, spend some time on the conditions of the present, and a short vision of a possible future.

The Preface, which you have already read, sets the stage for what follows. It gives us (all of us, Native and non-Native) the underlying "philosophy" of respect –it's built into the language of Great Lakes' Indigenous people, and, consequently, it comprises the foundation of our worldview.

The next section, "Environmental Destruction and Indigenous Responsibility," presents a few essays that expand on Maaganiit Noodin's Preface, exploring the foundations of Indigenous Identity and responsibility and our relationship to the environment.

We then move into an examination of some Great Lakes environmental history through the eyes of some historical figures and observations in the section titled "Environmental Indigenous Imagery," The "Traditional Knowledge and Western Science" section details how "Indigenous ways of Knowing" relate to "traditional" western science and the implications of "science" on the lives of all of us (again, Native and non-Native).

The next section of these Proceedings, "Environmental Degradation and the Indigenous Response: the Great Lakes and Beyond," deals with some "(Sweet)grass-roots" action –specific examples of environmental destruction and how some Indigenous groups have chosen to work toward a future that reflects Indigenous values, and does so in the hope that the "harmony and balance," mentioned at the beginning of this volume, can be, once again, brought into force here in the Great Lakes.

This volume ends with a brief description of the Traditional Knowledge Revival Pathways project of the Aboriginal people of Australia. And, finally, I present a "vision for the future" of the Indigenous Great Lakes, based on the environmental work that I am currently engaged in. Every bit of what I write is echoed in the essays and the commitment of "All Our Relations," and the vision presented by each and every one of our committed and competent contributors.

◊ ◊ ◊ ◊ ◊ ◊

PART I -- ENVIRONMENTAL DESTRUCTION AND INDIGENOUS RESPONSIBILITY

Decolonization: A Key to the Survival of Native North America

Ward Churchill

> The Europeans who began taking over the New World in the sixteenth and seventeenth centuries were not ecologists. Although they were compelled to realize that the Americas were not quite uninhabited, they were not prepared to recognize that these new lands were, in an ecological sense, much more than "sparsely" inhabited. This second hemisphere was, in fact, essentially "full."
> --William Catton -- *Overshoot*

The standard Euroamerican depiction of "precontact" Native North Americans has long been that the relative handful of us who existed wandered about perpetually in scattered bands, grubbing out the most marginal subsistence by hunting and gathering, never developing writing or serious appreciations of art, science, mathematics, governance, and so on. Aside from our utilization of furs and hides for clothing, the manufacture of stone implements, use of fire, and domestication of the dog, there is little in this view to distinguish us from the higher orders of mammalian life surrounding us in the "American wilderness."(1)

The conclusions reached by those who claim to idealize "Indianness" are little different at base from the findings of those who openly denigrate it: Native people were able to inhabit the hemisphere for tens of thousands of years without causing appreciable ecological disruption only because we lacked the intellectual capacity to create social forms and technologies that would substantially alter our physical environment. In effect, a sort of sociocultural retardation on the part of Indians is typically held to be responsible for the pristine quality of the Americas at the point of their "discovery" by Europeans.(2)

In contrast to this perspective, it has recently been demonstrated that, far from living hand-to-mouth, "Stone Age" Indians adhered to an economic structure that not only met their immediate needs but provided considerable surpluses of both material goods and leisure time.(3) It has also been established that most traditional native economies were based in agriculture rather than hunting and gathering—a clear indication of a stationary, not nomadic, way of life—until the European invasion dislocated the indigenous populations of North America.(4)

It is also argued that native peoples' longterm coexistence with our environment was possible only because of our extremely low population density. Serious historians and demographers have lately documented how estimates of precontact indigenous population levels were

3

deliberately lowered during the nineteenth and early twentieth centuries in order to lessen the implications of genocide bound up in the policies of the U.S., Canada and their colonial antecedents.(5) A noted ecologist has also recently determined that, rather than being dramatically underpopulated, North America was in fact saturated with people in 1500. The feasible carrying capacity of the continent was, moreover, outstripped by the European influx by 1840, despite massive reductions of native populations and numerous species of large mammals.(6)

Another myth is contained in the suggestion that indigenous forms of government were less refined than those of their European counterparts. The lie is put to this notion, however, when it is considered that the enlightened republicanism established by the United States during the late 1700s—usually considered an advance over then-prevailing European norms—was lifted directly from the model of the currently still functioning Haudenosaunee (Iroquois) confederacy.(7) In many ways the Haudenosaunee were indicative of political arrangements throughout Native North America.(8) American Indians evidenced similar achievements in preventative medicine, mathematics, astronomy, architecture and engineering, all without engendering appreciable environmental disruption.(9) Such a juxtaposition of advanced sociocultural matrices and sustained ecological equilibrium is inexplicable from the vantage point of conventional Euroderivative assumptions.

Unlike Europeans, Native Americans long ago attained a profound intellectual apprehension that human progress must be measured as an integral aspect of the natural order, rather than as something apart from and superior to it. Within this body of knowledge, elaborated and perfected through oral tradition and codified as "law" in ceremonial/ritual forms, the indigenous peoples of this hemisphere lived comfortably and in harmony with the environment, the health of which was recognized as an absolute requirement for our continued existence.(10)

In simplest terms, the American Indian world view may be this: Human beings are free—indeed, encouraged—to develop our innate capabilities, but only in ways that do not infringe upon other elements—called "relations," in the fullest dialectical sense of the word—of nature. Any activity going beyond this is considered as "imbalance," a transgression, and is strictly prohibited. Engineering, for example, was and is permissible, but only insofar as it does not permanently alter the earth itself. Similarly, agriculture was widespread, but only within parameters that did not supplant natural vegetation.(11)

Key to the indigenous American outlook is a firm acknowledgment that the human population may expand only to the point, determined by natural geographic and environmental circumstances, where it begins to displace other animal species and requires the permanent substitution of cropland for normal vegetation in any area. North America's aboriginal

4

populations never entered into a trajectory of excessive growth, and, even today, many native societies practice a self-regulation of population size that allows the substance of our traditional worldviews with their interactive environmental relationships to remain viable.(12)

Cultural Imperialism

> They came for our land, for what grew or could be grown on it, for the resources in it, and for our clean air and pure water. They stole these things from us, and in the taking they also stole our free ways and the best of our leaders, killed in battle or assassinated. And now, after all that, they've come for the very last of our possessions; now they want our pride, our history, our spiritual traditions. They want to rewrite and remake these things, to claim them for themselves. The lies and thefts just never end.
> --Margo Thunderbird -- 1988

Within the industrial wasteland of the early twenty-first century, such traditional perspectives are deformed right along with the physical dimensions of indigenous culture. Trivialized and coopted, they have been reduced to the stuff of the settler society's self-serving pop mythology, commercialized and exploited endlessly by everyone from the Hollywood moguls and hippie filmmakers who over the past 75 years have produced literally thousands of celluloid parodies not merely of our histories, but of our most sacred beliefs, to New Age yuppie airheads like Lynne Andrews who pen lucrative "feminist" fables of our spirituality, to the flabbily overprivileged denizens of the "Men's Movement" indulging themselves in their "Wildman Weekends," to pseudoacademic frauds like Carlos Castaneda who fabricate our traditions out of whole cloth, to "well-intentioned friends" like Jerry Mander who simply appropriate the real thing for their own purposes. The list might easily be extended for pages.(13)

Representative of the mentality is an oft-televised public service announcement featuring an aging Indian, clad in beads and buckskins, framed against a backdrop of smoking factory chimneys while picking his way carefully among the mounds of rusting junk along a well-polluted river. He concludes his walk through the modern world by shedding a tragic tear induced by the panorama of rampant devastation surrounding him. The use of an archaic Indian image in this connection is intended to stir the settler population's subliminal craving for absolution. "Having obliterated Native North America as a means of expropriating its landbase," the subtext reads, "Euroamerica is now obliged to 'make things right' by preserving and protecting what was stolen." Should it meet the challenge, presumably, not only will its forebears' unparalleled aggression at last be in some sense redeemed, but so too will the blood-drenched inheritance they bequeathed to their posterity be in that sense legitimated. The whole thing is of course a sham, a glib contrivance designed by and for the conquerors to promote

5

their sense of psychic reconciliation with the facts and fruits of the conquest.(14)

A primary purpose of this essay is to disturb—better yet, to destroy altogether—such self-serving and -satisfied tranquility. In doing so, its aim is to participate in restoring things Indian to the realm of reality. My hope is that it helps in the process to heal the disjuncture between the past, present and future of Native North American peoples which has been imposed by more than four centuries of unrelenting conquest, subjugation and dispossession on the part of Euroamerica's multitudinous invaders. This does not make for pleasant reading, nor should it, for my message is that there can be no absolution, no redemption of past crimes unless the outcomes are changed. So long as the aggressors' posterity continue to reap the benefits of that aggression, the crimes are merely replicated in the present. In effect, the aggression remains ongoing and, in that, there can be no legitimacy. Not now, not ever.

Contemporary Circumstances

> We are not ethnic groups. Ethnic groups run restaurants serving "exotic" foods. We are nations.
> -- Brooklyn Rivera - 1986

The current situation of the indigenous peoples of the United States and Canada is generally miscast as being that of ethnic/racial minorities. This is a fundamental misrepresentation in at least two ways. First, there is no given ethnicity which encompasses those who are indigenous to North America. Rather, there are several hundred distinctly different cultures— "ethnicities," in anthropological parlance—lumped together under the catch-all classification of "Native Americans" ("Aboriginals" in Canada). Similarly, at least three noticeably different "gene stocks"—the nomenclature of "race"—are encompassed by such designators. Biologically, "Amerinds" like the Cherokees and Ojibwes are as different from Inuits ("Eskimo-Aleuts") and such "Athabascan" ("Na-Dene") types as the Apaches and Navajos as Mongolians are from Swedes or Bantus.(15)

Secondly, all concepts of ethnic or racial minority status fail conspicuously to convey the sense of national identity by which most or all North American indigenous populations define ourselves. Nationality, not race or ethnicity, is the most important single factor in understanding the reality of Native North America today.(16) It is this sense of ourselves as comprising coherent and viable nations which lends substance and logic to the forms of struggle in which we have engaged over the past half-century and more.(17)

It is imperative when considering this point to realize that there is nothing rhetorical, metaphorical or symbolic at issue. On the contrary, a concrete and precise meaning is intended. The indigenous peoples of

North America—indeed, everywhere in the hemisphere—not only constituted but continue to constitute nations according to even the strictest definitions of the term. This can be asserted on the basis of two major legal premises, as well as a range of more material considerations. These can be taken in order.

• To begin with, there is a doctrine within modern international law known as the "right of inherent sovereignty" holding that a people constitutes a nation, and is thus entitled to exercise the rights of such, simply because it has done so "since time immemorial." That is, from the moment of its earliest contact with other nations the people in question have been known to possess a given territory, a means of providing their own subsistence (economy), a common language, a structure of governance and corresponding form of legality, and a means of determining membership/social composition. As was to some extent shown above, there can be no question but that Native North American peoples met each of these criteria at the point of initial contact with Europeans.(18)

• Second, it is a given of international law, custom and convention that treatymaking and treaty relations are entered into *only* by nations. This principle is constitutionally enshrined in both U.S. and Canadian domestic law. Article 1 of the U.S. Constitution, for instance, clearly restricts treatymaking prerogatives to the federal rather than, state, local or individual levels. In turn, the federal government itself is forbidden to enter into a treaty relationship with any entity aside from another fully sovereign nation (i.e., it is specifically disempowered from treating with provincial, state or local governments, or with corporations and individuals). It follows that the U.S. government's entry into some 400 ratified treaty relationships with North America's indigenous peoples— an even greater number prevail in Canada—abundantly corroborates our various claims to sovereign national standing.(19)

Officials in both North American settler states, as well as the bulk of the settler intelligentsia aligned with them, presently contend that, while native peoples may present an impeccable argument on moral grounds, and a technically valid legal case as well, pragmatic considerations in "the real world of the new millenium" precludes actualization of our national independence, autonomy, or any other manifestation of genuine self-determination. By their lights, indigenous peoples are too small, both in terms of our respective landbases/attendant resources and in population size(s), to survive either militarily or economically in the contemporary international context.(20)

At first glance, such thinking seems plausible enough, even humane. Delving a bit deeper, however, we find that it conveniently ignores the examples of such tiny European nations as San Marino, Monaco and Liechtenstein, which have survived for centuries amidst the greediest and most warlike continental setting in the history of the world. Further, it blinks the matter of comparably-sized nations in the Caribbean and

Pacific Basins whose sovereignty is not only acknowledged, but whose recent admissions to the United Nations have been endorsed by both Canada and the U.S. Plainly, each of these countries is at least as militarily vulnerable as any North American Indian people. The contradictions attending U.S./Canadian Indian policy are thus readily apparent to anyone willing to view the situation honestly. The truth is that the states' "humanitarianism" is in this connection no more than a gloss meant to disguise a very different set of goals, objectives and sensibilities.

Nor do arguments to the "intrinsic insolvency" of indigenous economies hold up to even minimal scrutiny. The Navajo Nation, for instance, possesses a landbase larger than those of Monaco, Fiji and Grenada combined. Within this area lies an estimated 150 billion tons of low sulfur coal, about forty percent of "U.S." uranium reserves and significant deposits of oil, natural gas, gold, silver, copper and gypsum, among other minerals. This is aside from a limited but very real grazing and agricultural capacity.(21) By any standard of conventional economic measure, the Navajos—or Diné, as they call themselves—have a relatively wealthy resource base as compared to many Third World nations and more than a few "developed" ones. To hold that the Navajo Nation could not survive economically in the modern world while admitting that Grenada, Monaco and Fiji can is to indulge in sheer absurdity (or duplicity).

While Navajo is probably the clearest illustration of the material basis for assertions of complete autonomy by Native North American nations, it is by no means the only one. The combined Lakota reservations in North and South Dakota yield an aggregate landbase even larger than that of the Diné and, while it exhibits a somewhat less spectacular range of mineral assets, this is largely offset by a greater agricultural/grazing capacity and smaller population size.(22) Other, smaller, indigenous nations possess landbases entirely adequate to support their populations and many are endowed with rich economic potentials which vary from minerals to timbering to ranching and farming to fishing and aquaculture. Smallscale manufacturing and even tourism also offer viable options in many instances.(23)

All this natural wealth exists within the currently-held native landbase ("reserves" in Canada, "reservations" in the U.S.). Nothing has been said thus far about the possibility that something approximating a just resolution might be effected concerning indigenous claims to vast territories retained by treaty—or to which title is held through unextinguished aboriginal right—all of which has been unlawfully expropriated by the two North American settler states.(24) Here, the Lakota Nation alone would stand to recover, on the basis of the still-binding 1868 Fort Laramie Treaty, some five percent of the U.S. 48 contiguous states area. The region includes the Black Hills, reputedly the 100 most mineral-rich square miles on the entire planet.(25) All told, naturalization of persons residing within the treaty areas—or those who might wish to relocate there for purposes of placing themselves under native rather than U.S./Canadian jurisdiction—would likely increase the citizenry of Native North America by several millions.(26)

In sum, just as the indigenous peoples of North America "once" possessed the requisite ingredients of nationhood, so too do we continue to possess them. This is true whether one uses as one's point(s) of reference the dimension of our territories, the basis of our economies, the size of our populations, or any other reasonable criteria. Perhaps most important in a legal sense, as well as in terms of ethics and morality, we continue to hold our inherent rights and standing as nations because, quite simply and undeniably, we have never voluntarily relinquished them. To argue otherwise, as so many settler officials and "scholars" are prone to do, is to argue the invalidity of the Law of Nations.(27)

Sharing the Land

There are several closely related matters which should be touched upon before wrapping this up. One has to do with the idea of self-determination. What is meant when indigenists demand an unrestricted exercise of self-determining rights by native peoples? Most nonindians, and even a lot of Indians, seem confused by this and want to know whether it's not the same as complete separation from the U.S., Canada, or whatever the colonizing power may be. The answer is, "not necessarily." The unqualified acknowledgement by the colonizer of the right of the colonized to total separation ("secession"), is the necessary point of departure for any exercise of self-determination. Decolonization means the colonized exercise the right in whole or in part, as we see fit, in accordance with our own customs, traditions and appreciations of our needs. We decide for ourselves what degree of autonomy we wish to enjoy, and thus the nature of our political and economic relationship(s), not only with our former colonizers, but with all other nations as well.(28)

My own inclination, which is in some ways an emotional preference, tends to run toward complete sovereign independence, but that's not the point. I have no more right to impose my preferences on indigenous nations than do the colonizing powers; each indigenous nation will choose for itself the exact manner and extent to which it expresses its autonomy, its sovereignty.(29) To be honest, I suspect very few would be inclined to adopt my sort of "go it alone" approach (and, actually, I must admit that part of my own insistence upon it often has more to do with forcing concession of the right from those who seek to deny it than it does with putting it into practice). In the event, I expect you'd see the hammering out of a number of sets of international relations in the "free association" vein, a welter of variations of commonwealth and home rule governance.(30)

The intent here is not, no matter how much it may be deserved in an abstract sense, to visit some sort of retribution, real or symbolic, upon the colonizing or former colonizing powers. It is to arrive at new sets of relationships between peoples which effectively put an end to the era of international domination. The need is to gradually replace the existing world order with one which is predicated in collaboration and cooperation between nations.(31) The only way to ever really accomplish that is to physically disassemble the gigantic state structures which evolved from the imperialist era, structures which are literally predicated in systematic intergroup domination and cannot in any sense exist without it.(32) A concomitant of this disassembly is the inculcation of voluntary, consensual interdependence between formerly dominated and dominating nations, and a redefinition of the word "nation" itself to conform to its original meaning: bodies of people bound together by their bioregional and other natural cultural affinities.(33)

This last point is, it seems to me, crucially important. Partly, that's because of the persistent question of who it is who gets to remain in Indian Country once land restoration and consolidation has occurred. The answer, I think, is anyone who wants to, up to a point. By "anyone who wants to," I mean anyone who wishes to apply for formal citizenship within an indigenous nation, thereby accepting the idea that s/he is placing him/herself under unrestricted Indian jurisdiction and will thus be required to abide by native law.(34)

Funny thing; I hear a lot of nonindians asserting that they reject nearly every aspect of U.S. law, but the idea of placing themselves under anyone else's jurisdiction seems to leave them pretty queasy. I have no idea how many nonindians might actually opt for citizenship in an Indian nation when push comes to shove, but I expect there will be some. And I suspect some Indians have been so indoctrinated by the dominant society that they'll elect to remain within it rather than availing themselves of their own citizenship. So there'll be a bit of a trade-off in this respect.

Now, there's the matter of the process working only "up to a point." That point is very real. It is defined, not by political or racial considerations, but by the carrying capacity of the land. The population of indigenous nations everywhere has always been determined by the number of people who could be sustained in a given environment or bioregion without overpowering and thereby destroying that environment.(35) A very carefully calculated balance—one which was calibrated to the fact that in order to enjoy certain sorts of material comfort, human population had to be kept at some level below saturation per se—was always maintained between the number of humans and the rest of the habitat. In order to accomplish this, Indians incorporated into the very core of their spiritual traditions the concept that all life forms and the earth itself possess rights equal to those enjoyed by humans.(36)

Rephrased, this means it would be a violation of a fundament of traditional Indian law to supplant or eradicate another species, whether animal or plant, in order to make way for some greater number of humans, or to increase the level of material comfort available to those who already exist. Conversely, it is a fundamental requirement of traditional law that each human accept his or her primary responsibility, that of maintaining the balance and harmony of the natural order as it is encountered.(37) One is essentially free to do anything one wants in an indigenous society so long as this cardinal rule is adhered to. The bottom line with regard to the maximum population limit of Indian Country as it has been sketched in this presentation is some very finite number. My best guess is that five million people would be pushing things right through the roof.(38) Whatever. Citizens can be admitted until that point has been reached, and no more. And the population cannot increase beyond that number over time, no matter at what rate. Carrying capacity is a fairly constant reality; it tends to change over thousands of years, when it changes at all.

Population and Environment

What I'm going to say next will probably startle a few people (as if what's been said already hasn't). I think this principle of population restraint is the single most important example Native North America can set for the rest of humanity. It is the thing which it is most crucial for others to emulate. Check it out. I recently heard that Japan, a small island nation which has so many people that they're literally tumbling into the sea, and which has exported about half again as many people as live on the home islands, is expressing "official concern" that its birth rate has declined very slightly over the last few years. The worry is that in thirty years there'll be fewer workers available to "produce," and thus to "consume" whatever it is that's produced.(39)

Ever ask yourself what it is that's used in "producing" something? Or what it is that's being "consumed"? Yeah. You got it. Nature is being consumed, and with it the ingredients which allow ongoing human existence. It's true that nature can replenish some of what's consumed, but only at a certain rate. That rate has been vastly exceeded, and the extent of excess is increasing by the moment. An overburgeoning humanity is killing the natural world, and thus itself. It's no more complicated than that.(40)

Here we are in the midst of a rapidly worsening environmental crisis of truly global proportions, every last bit of it attributable to a wildly accelerating human consumption of the planetary habitat, and you have one of the world's major offenders expressing grave concern that the rate at which it is able to consume might actually drop a notch or two. Think about it. I suggest that this attitude signifies nothing so much as stark, staring madness. It is insane: suicidally, homicidally, ecocidally, omnicidally insane. No, I'm not being rhetorical. I meant what I've just said in the most literal way possible,(41) but I don't want to convey the misimpression that the I see the Japanese as being in this respect unique. Rather, I intend them to serve as merely an illustration of a far broader

11

and quite virulent pathology called "industrialism"—or, lately, "postindustrialism"—a sickness centered in an utterly obsessive drive to dominate and destroy the natural order (words like "production," "consumption," "development" and "progress" are mere code words masking this reality).(42)

It's not only the industrialized countries which are afflicted with this disease. One by-product of the past five centuries of European expansionism and the resulting hegemony of eurocentric ideology is that the latter has been drummed into the consciousness of most peoples to the point where it is now subconsciously internalized. Everywhere, you find people thinking it "natural" to view themselves as the incarnation of god on earth—i.e., "created in the image of God"—and thus duty-bound to "exercise dominion over nature" in order that they can "multiply, grow plentiful, and populate the land" in ever increasing "abundance."(43)

The legacy of the forced labor of the *latifundia* and inculcation of Catholicism in Latin America is a tremendous overburden of population devoutly believing that "wealth" can be achieved (or is defined) by having ever more children.(44) The legacy of Mao's implementation of "reverse technology" policy—the official encouragement of breakneck childbearing rates in his already overpopulated country, solely as a means to deploy massive labor power to offset capitalism's "technological advantage" in production—resulted in a tripling of China's population in only two generations.(45) And then there is India…

Make absolutely no mistake about it. The planet was never designed to accommodate five billion human beings, much less the ten billion predicted to be here a mere forty years hence.(46)

If we are to be about turning power relations around between people, and between groups of people, we must also be about turning around the relationship between people and the rest of the natural order. If we don't, we'll die out as a species, just like any other species which irrevocably overshoots its habitat. The sheer numbers of humans on this planet needs to come down to about a quarter of what they are today, or maybe less, and the plain fact is that the bulk of these numbers are in the Third World.(47) So, I'll say this clearly: not only must the birth rate in the Third World come down, but the population levels of Asia, Latin America, and Africa must be reduced over the next few generations. The numbers must start to come down dramatically, beginning right now.

Of course, there's another dimension to the population issue, one which is in some ways even more important, and I want to get into it in a minute. But first I have to say something else. This is that I don't want a bunch of Third Worlders jumping up in my face screaming that I'm advocating "genocide." Get off that bullshit. It's genocide when some centralized state, or some colonizing power, imposes sterilization or abortion on target groups.(48) It's not genocide at all when we recognize that we have a problem, and take the logical steps ourselves to solve them. Voluntary sterilization is not a part of genocide. Voluntary abortion is not a part of genocide. And, most importantly, educating ourselves and our respective peoples to bring our birth rates under control through conscious resort to birth control measures is not a part of genocide.(49)

What it is, is part of taking responsibility for ourselves again, of taking responsibility for our destiny and our children's destiny. It's about rooting the ghost of the Vatican out of our collective psyches, along with the ghosts of Adam Smith and Karl Marx. It's about getting back in touch with our own ways, our own traditions, our own knowledge, and it's long past time we got out of our own way in this respect. We've got an awful lot to unlearn, and an awful lot to relearn, not much time in which we can afford the luxury of avoidance, and we need to get on with it.

The other aspect of population I wanted to take up is that there's another way of counting. One way, the way I just did it, and the way it's conventionally done, is to simply point to the number of bodies, or "people units." That's valid enough as far as it goes, so we need to look at it and act upon what we see, but it doesn't really go far enough. This brings up the second method, which is to count by differential rates of resource consumption—that is to say, the proportional degree of environmental impact per individual—and to extrapolate that into people units. Using this method, which is actually more accurate in ecological terms, we arrive at conclusions that are a little different than the usual notion that the most overpopulated regions on earth are in the Third World. The average resident of the United States, for example, consumes about thirty times the resources of the average Ugandan or Laotian. Since a lot of poor folk reside in the U.S., this translates into the average yuppie consuming about seventy times the resources of an average Third Worlder.(50)

Returning to the topic at hand, you have to multiply the U.S. population by a factor of thirty—a noticeably higher ratio than either western Europe or Japan—in order to figure out how many Third Worlders it would take to have the same environmental impact. I make that to be 7.5 billion U.S. people units. I think I can thus safely say the most overpopulated portion of the globe is the United States. Either the consumption rates really have to be cut in this country, most especially in the more privileged social sectors, or the number of people must be drastically reduced, or both. I advocate both. How much? That's a bit subjective, but I'll tentatively accept the calculations of William Catton, a respected ecological demographer. He was the guy who estimated that North America was thoroughly saturated with humans by 1840.(51) So we need to get both population and consumption levels down to what they were in that year, or preferably a little earlier. Alternatively, we need to bring population down to an even lower level in order to sustain a correspondingly higher level of consumption.

Here's where I think the reconstitution of indigenous territoriality and sovereignty in the West can be useful with regard to population. Land isn't just land, you see; it's also the resources within the land, things like coal, oil, natural gas, uranium, and maybe most important, water. How does that bear on U.S. overpopulation? Simple. Much of the population expansion in this country over the past quarter-century has been into the southwestern desert region. How many people have they got living in the valley down there at Phoenix, a locale that might be reasonably expected to support 500?(52) Look at the sprawl of greater LA: twenty million people where there ought to be maybe a few thousand.(53) How do they accomplish this? Well, for one thing, they've diverted the entire Colorado River from its natural purposes. They're siphoning off the Columbia River and piping it south.(54) They've even got a project underway to divert the Yukon River all the way down from Alaska to support southwestern urban growth, and to provide irrigation for the agribusiness in northern Sonora and Chihuahua called for by NAFTA.(55) Whole regions of our ecosphere are being destabilized in the process.

Okay, in the scenario I've described, the whole Colorado watershed will be in Indian Country, under Indian control. So will the source of the Columbia. And diversion of the Yukon would have to go right through Indian Country. Now, here's the deal. No more use of water to fill swimming pools and sprinkle golf courses in Phoenix and LA. No more watering Kentucky bluegrass lawns out on the yucca flats. No more drive-thru car washes in Tucumcari. No more "Big Surf" amusement parks in the middle of the desert. Drinking water and such for the whole population, yes, Indians should deliver that. But water for this other insanity? No way. I guarantee that'll stop the inflow of population cold. Hell, I'll guarantee it'll start a pretty substantial outflow. Most of these folks never wanted to live in the desert anyway. That's why they keep trying to make it look like Florida (another delicate environment which is buckling under the weight of population increases).(56)

And we can help move things along in other ways as well. Virtually all the electrical power for the southwestern urban sprawls comes from a combination of hydroelectric and coal-fired generation in the Four Corners region. This is smack-dab in the middle of Indian Country, along with all the uranium with which a "friendly atom" alternative might be attempted,(57) and most of the low sulfur coal. Goodbye, the neon glitter of Reno and Las Vegas. Adios to air conditioners in every room. Sorry about your hundred mile expanses of formerly street-lit expressway. Basic needs will be met, and that's it. Which means we can also start saying goodbye to western rivers being backed up like so many sewage lagoons behind massive dams. The Glen Canyon and Hoover Dams are coming down, boys and girls.(58) And we can begin to experience things like a reduction in the acidity of southwestern rain

14

water as facilities like the Four Corners Power Plant are cut back in generating time, and eventually eliminated altogether.(59)

What I'm saying probably sounds extraordinarily cruel to a lot of people, particularly those imbued with the belief that they hold a "god-given right" to play a round of golf on the well-watered green beneath the imported palm trees outside an air-conditioned casino at the base of the Superstition Mountains. Tough. Those days can be ended with neither hesitation nor apology. A much more legitimate concern rests in the fact that many people who've drifted into the Southwest have nowhere else to go to. The places they came from are crammed. In many cases, that's why they left.(60) To them, I say there's no need to panic; no one will abruptly pull the plug on you, or leave you to die of thirst. Nothing like that. But quantities of both water and power will be set at minimal levels. In order to have a surplus, you'll have to bring your number down to a more reasonable level over the next generation or two. As you do so, water and power availability will be steadily reduced, necessitating an ongoing population reduction. Arrival at a genuinely sustainable number of regional residents can thus be phased in over an extended period, several generations, if need be.

Provision of key items such as western water and coal should probably be negotiated on the basis of reductions in population/consumption by the U.S. as a whole rather than simply the region served—much like the U.S.-controlled World Bank and International Monetary Fund now dictate sweeping terms to Third World countries in exchange for relatively paltry investments, but for opposite reasons—in order to prevent population shifts being substituted for actual reductions. Any such negotiated arrangement should also include an agreement by the U.S. to alter its distribution of food surpluses and the like, so as to ease the transition to lower population and correspondingly greater self-sufficiency in destitute Third World areas.(61)

The objective inherent to every aspect of this process should be, and can be, to let everyone down as gently as possible from the long and intoxicating high that has beset so much of the human species in its hallucination that it, and it alone, is the only thing of value and importance in the universe. In doing so, and I believe *only* in doing so, can we fulfil our obligation to bequeath our grandchildren, and our grandchildren's grandchildren, a world which is fit (or even possible) to live in.(62)

I Am Indigenist

There are any number of other matters which by rights should be discussed, but they will of necessity have to await another occasion. What has been presented has been only the barest outline, a glimpse of what might be called an "indigenist vision." Hopefully, it provides enough shape and clarity to allow anyone who wishes to pursue the thinking further, to fill in at least some of the gaps I've not had time to address, and to arrive at insights and conclusions of their own. Once the main tenets have been advanced, and I think to some extent that's been accomplished, the perspective of indigenism is neither mystical nor mysterious.

In closing, I would like to turn again to the critics, the skeptics, those who will decry what has been said here as being "unrealistic," or even "crazy." On the former score, my reply is that so long as we define realism, or reality itself, in conventional terms, the terms imposed by the order of understanding in which we now live, we will be locked forever into the trajectory in which we presently find ourselves. (63) We will never break free, because any order, any structure, defines reality only in terms of itself. Consequently, allow me to echo the sentiments expressed in the French student revolt of 1968: "Be realistic, demand the impossible!"(64) If you read through a volume of American Indian oratory, and there are several available, you'll find that native people have been saying the same thing all along. (65)

As to my being crazy, I'd like to say, "Thanks for the compliment." Again, I follow my elders and my ancestors—and R.D. Laing, for that matter—in believing that when confronted with a society as obviously insane as this one, the only sane posture one can adopt is what that society would automatically designate as crazy. (66) I mean, it wasn't Indians who turned birthing into a religious fetish while butchering off a couple-hundred million people with weapons of mass destruction and systematically starving another billion or so to death. Indians never had a Grand Inquisition, and we never came up with a plumbing plan to reroute the water flow on the entire continent. Nor did we ever produce "leaders" of the caliber of George W. Bush, Dick Cheney, and Donald Rumsfeld. Hell, we never even figured out that turning prison construction into a major growth industry was an indication of social progress and enlightenment. (67) Maybe we were never so much crazy as we were congenitally retarded.

Whatever the reason, and you'll excuse me for suspecting it might be something other than craziness or retardation, I'm indescribably thankful that our cultures turned out to be so different, no matter how much abuse and sacrifice it's entailed. I'm proud to stand inside the heritage of native struggle. I'm proud to say I'm an unreconstructable indigenist. For me, there's no other reasonable or realistic way to look at the world. And I invite anyone who shares that viewpoint to come aboard, regardless of your race, creed or national origin. Maybe Chief Seattle said it best back in 1854: "Tribe follows tribe, and nation follows nation, like the waves of the sea. Your time of decay may be distant, but it will surely come, for even the white man whose god walked with him and talked with him as friend with friend, cannot be exempt from the common destiny. We may be brothers after all. We will see."(68)

16

◊ ◊ ◊ ◊ ◊ ◊

Ward Churchill (Keetoowah Cherokee) was, until his retirement in 2007, chair of the Department of Ethnic Studies and professor of American Indian Studies at the University of Colorado. A past member of the leadership council of Colorado AIM, he now resides in Atlanta. Among his more than 20 books are *Agents of Repression; The COINTELPRO Papers; Since Predator Came; From a Native Son; A Little Matter of Genocide; Acts of Rebellion; Kill the Indian, Save the Man;* and *On the Justice of Roosting Chickens.*

Notes

1. References in this regard are legion. In a canonical sense, the perfect representation may be found in a lengthy selection essays assembled by Margaret Mead and Ruth L. Bunzel and entitled *The Golden Age of American Anthropology: The Growth of the Science of Man on the North American Continent as Told by Those Who Laid the Foundations* (New York: George Braziller, 1960)
2. This was certainly true during the nineteenth century; see, e.g., Francis Paul Prucha, ed., *Americanizing the American Indian: Writings of the "Friends of the Indian," 1800-1900* (Lincoln: University of Nebraska Press, 1973). For contemporary counterpoint, see, e.g., Jerry Mander, *In the Absence of the Sacred: The Failure of Technology and Survival of the Indian Nations* (San Francisco: Sierra Club Books, 1991).
3. Marshall Sahlins, *Stone Age Economics* (Chicago: Aldine, 1972) pp. 1-40.
4. With respect to the approximately two-thirds of all vegetal foodstuffs currently consumed by humanity, and which were under cultivation in this hemisphere alone as of 1492, see Jack Weatherford's *Indian Givers: How the Indians of the Americas Transformed the World* (New York: Crown, 1988). Concerning agricultural forms and techniques, see the deeply flawed but nonetheless useful study by R. Douglas Hurt entitled *Indian Agriculture in America: Prehistory to the Present* (Lawrence: University Press of Kansas, 1987).
5. The apparently willful reductionist manipulation of demographic data pertaining to Native North America by historians such as John Gorman Palfrey and, subsequently, by anthropologists like James Mooney and Alfred L. Kroeber, is well-covered by Francis Jennings in his *The Invasion of America: Indians, Colonialism and the Cant of Conquest* (New York: W.W. Norton, 1976) pp. 15-31. As compared to the Mooney/Kroeber estimates of approximately one million people north of the Río Grande in 1492, a figure long enshrined as "truth" by the Smithsonian Institution, more reasonable/realistic assessments suggest a population 15-18 million. See, e.g., Henry F. Dobyns, *Their Number Become Thinned: Native American Population Dynamics on the Eastern Seaboard* (Knoxville: University of Tennessee Press, 1976) p.

42; Kirkpatrick Sale, *The Conquest of Paradise: Christopher Columbus and the Columbian Legacy* (New York: Alfred A. Knopf, 1990) p. 316.

6. William R. Catton, Jr., *Overshoot: The Ecological Basis for Revolutionary Change* (Urbana: University of Illinois Press, 1981).

7. For a detailed accounting of the Haudenosaunee influence on the Founding Fathers' construction of the U.S. Constitution, see Donald A. Grinde, Jr., and Bruce Johansen, *Exemplar of Liberty: Native America and the Founding of American Democracy* (Los Angeles: UCLA American Indian Studies Center, 1991). Also see Grinde's *The Iroquois and the Founding of the American Nation* (San Francisco: Indian Historian Press, 1977) and Johansen's *Forgotten Founders: How the American Indians Helped Shape Democracy* (Boston: Harvard Common Press, 1982).

8. A good survey of traditional indigenous forms of governance will be found in Rebecca Robbins' "Self-Determination and Subordination: The Past, Present and Future of American Indian Self-Governance," in M. Annette Jaimes, ed., *The State of Native America: Genocide, Colonization and Resistance* (Boston: South End Press, 1992) pp. 123-38.

9. The Maya of the Yucatan and present-day Guatemala, for example, had developed the concepts of zero and prime number extraction long before they were known in Europe; Charles Gallenkamp, *Maya: The Riddle and Rediscovery of a Lost Civilization* (New York: Viking, [3rd ed., 1985) pp. 79-80. A hemispheric overview is provided in Michael P. Closs, ed., *Native American Mathematics* (Austin: University of Texas Press, 1986). On the sophistication of indigenous medical practices, which included brain surgery at a time when Europe's doctors still believed that drawing off "bad blood" would cure illness, see Virgil Vogel, *American Indian Medicine* (Norman: University of Oklahoma Press, 1970) and Miguel Guzmá Peredo, *Medical Practices in Ancient America* (Mexico City: Ediciones Euroamericanas, 1985). Aspects of indigenous astronomy are covered in Guillermo Céspedes, *América Indígena* (Madrid: Alianza, 1985). On architecture, see Peter Nabokov and Robert Easton, *American Indian Architecture* (New York: Oxford University Press, 1988). Buddy Mays' *Ancient Cities of the Southwest* (San Francisco: Chronicle Books, 1982) covers the latter topic as well as engineering marvels such as the 400 miles of Hohokam irrigation canals which are still used by the city of Phoenix.

10. One example of this practice, that of the Haudenosaunee, is delineated in Paul A.W. Wallace's *The White Roots of Peace* (Philadelphia: University of Philadelphia Press, 1946).

11. For analysis and discussion, see the essays contained in Christopher Vecsey and Robert W. Venables, eds., *Native American Environments: Ecological Issues in American Indian History* (Syracuse, NY: Syracuse University Press, 1980).

12. See, e.g., Frank Waters, *The Book of the Hopi* (New York: Viking, 1963).

13. The examples listed, as well as a number of others, are discussed at length in my *Fantasies of the Master Race: Literature, Cinema and the Colonization of American Indians* (San Francisco: City Lights, [2nd ed.]

1998) and *Indians "R" Us? Culture and Genocide in Native North America* (Monroe, ME: Common Courage Press, 1994).

14. Such propagandistic manipulation of native imagery by the settler society has ample historical precedent; see, e.g., Robert F. Berkhofer, Jr., *The White Man's Indian: Images of the American Indian from Columbus to the Present* (New York: Alfred A. Knopf, 1978). On the specific image referenced, see the memoirs of the actor depicted; Iron Eyes Cody, *Iron Eyes: My Life as a Hollywood Indian* (New York: Everest House, 1982).

15. The three groupings are recognized by linguists and geneticists alike; Joseph H. Greenberg, *Language in the Americas* (Stanford, CA: Stanford University Press, 1988). Of the trio, Amerind is by far the oldest and most extensive, demonstrating a continuous presence in the hemisphere for at least 40,000 years—perhaps 70,000 years or longer—and encompassing most of the area from central Canada to Tierra del Fuego; L.S. Cressman, *Prehistory of the Far West: Homes of Vanquished Peoples* (Salt Lake City: University of Utah Press, 1977); Richard Wolkomir, "New Find Could Rewrite the Start of American History," *Smithsonian*, No. 21 (March 1991) pp. 130-44. The current argument that there may have been a fourth stock is well-made in Theodore Schurr, et al., "Amerindian Mitochondrial DNAs Have Rare Asian Mutations at High Frequencies, Suggesting They Derived from Four Primary Maternal Lineages," *American Journal of Human Genetics*, Vol. 46, No. 3 (April 1990) pp. 613-23; also see Satoshi Horai, et al., "Peopling of the Americas: Founded by Four Major Lineages of Mitochondrial DNA," *Molecular Biology of Evolution*, Vol. 10, No. 1 (1993) pp. 23-47.

16. The distinction is handled well in Louise Mandell, "Indians Nations: Not Minorities," *Les Cahiers de Droit*, Vol.. 27, No. 1 (March 1983) pp. 101-21.

17. For an interesting overview, see Troy Johnson, Joane Nagel and Duane Champagne, eds., *American Indian Activism: Alcatraz to the Longest Walk* (Urbana: University of Illinois Press, 1997). Also see Peter Matthiessen, *In the Spirit of Crazy Horse: The Story of Leonard Peltier* (New York: Viking, [2nd ed.] 1991); Rex Wyler, *Blood of the Land: The U.S. Government and Corporate War Against the American Indian Movement* (Philadelphia: New Society, [2nd ed.] 1992).

18. See, e.g., Felix S. Cohen, "Original Indian Title," in Lucy Cohen, ed., *The Legal Conscience: Selected Papers of Felix S. Cohen* (New Haven, CT: Yale University Press, 1960) pp. 273-304; Michael Asch, ed., *Aboriginal and Treaty Rights in Canada: Essays on Law, Equality, and Respect for Difference* (Vancouver: UBC Press, 1997). More broadly, see Gordon Bennett, *Aboriginal Rights in International Law* (London: Royal Institute, 1978). Oddly complimentary views are expressed in *Selections from V.I. Lenin and J.V. Stalin on the National Colonial Question* (Calcutta: Calcutta Book House, [2nd ed.] 1975).

19. The texts of 371 treaties with indigenous peoples ratified by the U.S. Senate between 1787 and 1871 are compiled in Charles J. Kappler's *Indian Treaties, 1778-1883* (New York: Interland, 1973). A further twenty valid treaties have been discovered more recently. See Vine

Deloria, Jr., and Raymond J. DeMallie. *Documents of American Indian Diplomacy: Treaties, Agreements, and Conventions, 1775-1979*, 2 vols. (Norman: University of Oklahoma Press, 1999) Vol. 1, pp. 181-232. As concerns Canada, the texts of some 480 treaties are compiled in *Canada: Indian Treaties and Surrenders from 1680 to 1890*, 3 vols. (Ottawa: Queen's Printer, 1891; reprinted by Coles [Toronto], 1971; reprinted by Fifth House [Saskatoon], 1992). The implications of formal recognition of indigenous nations are codified as law in the U.N. Charter and elsewhere; Cristeau Aurelieu, *The Historical and Current Development of the Right to Self-Determination on the Basis of the Charter of the United Nations and Other Instruments adopted by United Nations Organs, With Particular Reference to the Protection of Human Rights and Fundamental Freedoms* (U.N. Doc. E/CN.4/Sub.2/404, 2 June 1978). Also see Michla Pomerance, *Self-Determination in Law and Practice* (The Hague: Marinus Nijhoff, 1982).

20. For illustrative expression of such sentiments, see the quotations of various U.S. officials speaking before the U.N. Working Group on Indigenous Populations deployed by Jimmie Durham in his *Columbus Day* (Minneapolis: West End Press, 1983) pp. ???. The arguments are well-handled by Vine Deloria, Jr., in his *Behind the Trail of Broken Treaties: An American Indian Declaration of Independence* (Austin: University of Texas Press, [2nd ed.] 1985); excerpted as "The Size and Status of Nations," in Susan Lobo and Steve Talbot, eds., *Native American Voices: A Reader* (New York: Longman, 1998) pp. 457-65.

21. On Navajo landbase and demography, see Francis Paul Prucha, *Atlas of American Indian Affairs* (Lincoln: University of Nebraska Press, 1990). On resource distribution, see, e.g., U.S. Department of Justice, Commission on Civil Rights, *The Navajo Nation: An American Colony* (Washington, D.C.: U.S. Government Printing Office, 1975).

22. See, e.g., U.S. Department of Interior, BIA Report No. 12, *Status of Mineral Information on the Pine Ridge Reservation, South Dakota* (Washington, D.C.: U.S. Bureau of Indian Affairs, 1976).

23. Overall, see U.S. Department of Interior, Bureau of Indian Affairs, *Indian Lands Map: Oil, Gas and Minerals on Indian Reservations* (Washington, D.C.: U.S. Government Printing Office, 1978); Presidential Commission on Indian Reservation Economies, *Report and Recommendation to the President of the United States* (Washington, D.C.: U.S. Government Printing Office, Nov. 1984); Claudia Notzke, *Aboriginal Peoples and Natural Resources in Canada* (North York: Captus, 1994).

24. According to the federal government's Indian Claims Commission, which studied the question in exhaustive detail from 1947 through 1977, the United States holds no pretense of legal title to approximately 35 percent of its gross territoriality. This is exclusive of areas to which title may have been invalidated by virtue of fraudulent or coerced treaties, etc.; Indian Claims Commission, *Final Report* (Washington, D.C.: U.S. Government Printing Office, 1978). For analysis, see Russel Barsh, "Indian Land Claims Policy in the United States," *North Dakota Law Review*, No. 58 (1982) 21-???. Issues

of the same magnitude loom in Canada, especially in British Columbia, where no treaty cessions at all appear to have occurred; Brian Slattery, *The Land Rights of Indigenous Canadian Peoples* (Saskatoon: University of Saskatchewan Native Law Centre, 1979); Kent McNeil, *Common Law Aboriginal Title* (Oxford: Clarendon Press, 1989).

25. A good overview of the mineral wealth of the Black Hills is contained in Amelia Irvin's "Energy Development and the Effects of Mining on the Lakota Nation," *Journal of Ethnic Studies*, Vol. 10, No. 1 (Spring 1982) pp. 89-101. Also see Harvey Wasserman, "The Sioux's Last Fight for the Black Hills," *Rocky Mountain News*, Aug. 24, 1980.

26. It should be noted that, current colonialist preoccupations with "blood quantum" notwithstanding, naturalization is a traditional means of confirming member/citizens within many, or most, indigenous nations. See, e.g., Jack D. Forbes, "The Manipulation of Race, Caste and Identity: Classifying Afroamericans, Native Americans and Red-Black People," *Journal of Ethnic Studies*, Vol. 17, No. 4 (Winter 1990) pp. 1-52; Ward Churchill, "The Crucible of American Indian Identity: Native Tradition versus Colonial Imposition in Postconquest North America," *American Indian Culture and Research Journal*, Vol. 23, No. 1 (Spring 1999) pp. 39-67.

27. Voluntary relinquishment is the only legally valid means by which a nation may be divested of its sovereignty; Lawrence Oppenheim, *International Law* (London: Longman's, Green, [8th ed.] 1955), p. 120. Otherwise, "recognition once given is irrevocable unless the recognized [nation] ceases to exist or ceases to have the elements of nationhood"; Robert T. Coulter, "Contemporary Indian Sovereignty," in National Lawyers Guild, Committee on Native American Struggles, *Rethinking Indian Law* (New Haven, CT: Advocate Press, 1982) p. 117, citing M. Whitman, *Digest of International Law* §1 at 2 (1963).

28. For one elaboration of these principles, see Ved Nanda, "Self-Determination in International Law: Validity of Claims to Secede," *Case Western Reserve Journal of International Law*, No. 13 (1981) pp. 257-80. Also see Lee C. Buchheit, *Secession: The Legitimacy of Self-Determination* (New Haven, CT: Yale University Press, 1978) and Maivan Clech Lam, At the Edge of the State: Indigenous Peoples and Self-Determination (Ardsley, NY: Transnational, 2000) esp. pp. 112-42.

29. A clear delineation of the available options will be found in Hannum Hurst's *Autonomy, Sovereignty, and Self-Determination* (Philadelphia: University of Pennsylvania Press, 1990).

30. A prototype for this sort of arrangement exists between Greenland (populated mainly by Inuits) and Denmark. See, e.g., Gudmundur Alfredsson, "Greenland and the Law of Political Decolonization," *German Yearbook on International Law*, No. 25 (1982) pp. 290-308.

31. This is essentially the idea advanced by Richard Falk in an essay titled "Anarchism and World Order," in his *End of World Order: Essays on Normative International Relations* (New York: Holmes & Meier, 1983) pp. 277-98. Also see Bernard Neitschmann, The Fourth

World: Nations versus States, in George J. Demko and William B. Wood, eds., *Reordering the World: Geopolitical Perspectives on the 21st Century* (Boulder, CO: Westview Press, 1994) pp. 225-42.

32. A good argument as to why megastates will "inevitably fall apart" is made by Martin Van Creveld in his *The Rise and Decline of the State* (Cambridge, UK: Cambridge University Press, 1999).

33. Barth, *Ethnic Boundaries*; Connor, *Ethnonationalism*; John Hutcheson, *The Dynamics of Cultural Nationalism* (New York: HarperCollins, [2nd ed.] 1994); Kirkpatrick Sale, *Dwellers in the Land: The Bioregional Vision* (Philadelphia: New Society, 1991).

34. This is the basic idea set forth in "TREATY." Also see Reinhard Bendix, *Nation-Building and Citizenship* (Berkeley: University of California Press, 1964).

35. The concepts at issue here are brought out very well in Catton, *Overshoot*.

36. Such ideas have even caught on, at least as questions, among some Euroamerican legal practitioners; see Christopher D. Stone, *Should Trees Have Standing? Towards Legal Rights for Natural Objects* (Los Altos, CA: William Kaufman, 1972).

37. For further elaboration, see Vine Deloria, Jr., *God Is Red* (New York: Delta, 1973), and "Native American Spirituality," in his *For This Land: Writings on Religion in America* (New York: Routledge, 1999) pp. 130-4.

38. I base my estimate in large part upon the regional preinvasion demographic estimates extrapolated by Dobyns in *Their Number Become Thinned*.

39. CNN "Dollars and Cents" reportage, May 27, 1992. Interestingly, the same sort of thinking has marked the analyses of marxists with regard to the "developmental problems" confronting Africa; see, e.g., Gérard Chaliand, *Revolution in the Third World: Myths and Prospects* (New York: Viking, 1977) p. 114.

40. The idea is developed in detail in Jeremy Rifkin's *Entropy: A New World View* (New York: Viking, 1980). It should be noted, however, that the worldview in question is hardly "new," since indigenous peoples have held it all along; see, e.g., Russell Means, "The Same Old Song," in my *Marxism and Native Americans* (Boston: South End Press, 1983) p. 22.

41. See the "controversial" definition of insanity offered by R. D. Laing in his *The Politics of Experience* (New York: Ballantine, 1967).

42. One good summary of this, utilizing extensive native sources—albeit many of them go unattributed—is Mander's *In the Absence of the Sacred*.

43. If this sounds a bit scriptural, it is meant to. A number of us see a direct line of continuity from the core imperatives of judeochristian theology, through the capitalist secularization of church doctrine and its alleged marxian antithesis, right on through to the burgeoning technotopianism of today. This is a major conceptual cornerstone of what indigenists view as eurocentrism (a virulently anthropocentric outlook in its essence); see Vine Deloria, Jr., "Secularism, Civil

Religion, and the Religious Freedom of American Indians," in his *For This Land*, pp. 218-28.

44. The information is in André Gunder Frank's *Capitalism and Underdevelopment in Latin America: Historical Studies of Chile and Brazil* (New York: Monthly Review Press, 1967), but the conclusion is avoided.

45. See generally, Jerome Ch'en, *Mao and the Chinese Revolution* (New York: Oxford University Press, 1967); Alice Goldstein, ed., *China: The Many Facets of Demographic Change* (Boulder, CO: Westview Press, 1996). Also see Kuttan Mahadevan, Chi-Hsien Tuan, Jing-Yuan Yu and P. Kishnan, *Differential Development and Demographic Dilemma: Perspectives from China and India* (New Delhi: South Asia, 1994).

46. Paul R. Ehrlich and Anne H. Ehrlich, *The Population Explosion* (New York: Simon and Schuster, 1990); Michael Tobias, *World War III: Population and the Biosphere at the End of the Millennium* (New York: Continuum, 1998); United Nations, *World Population Prospects: A Report* (New York: United Nations, 2000).

47. I am extrapolating from the calculations of Catton in Overshoot.

48. This consideration, unfortunately, may have a certain bearing in China; see Song Jian, Chi-Hsien Tuan and Jing-Yuan Yu, *Population Control in China: Theory and Applications* (Westport, CT: Greenwood, 1985); H. Yuan Tien, *China's Strategic Demographic Initiative* (New York: Praeger, 1991); United Nations, *Case Studies in Population Policy: China* (New York: United Nations, 1991). It also has bearing in the U.S., however; see Brint Dillingham, "Indian Women and IHS Sterilization Practices, *American Indian Journal*, Vol. 3, No. 1, 1977; Committee for Abortion Rights and against Sterilization Abuse, *Women Under Attack: Abortion, Sterilization Abuse, and Reproductive Freedom* (New York: CARASA, 1979); Margarita Ostalaza, *Politica Sexual y Socialización Politica de la Mujer Puertorriqueña la Consolidación de Bloque Histórico Colonial de Puerto Rico* (Río Piedras, PR: Ediciones Huracán, 1989).

49. Sound arguments to this effect are advanced in Paul R. Ehrlich and Anne H. Ehrlich, *Population/Resources/Environment* (San Francisco: W. H. Freeman, 1970).

50. Paul R. Ehrlich and Anne H. Ehrlich, from their book *Healing the Earth*, quoted in CNN series *The Population Bomb*, May 1992.

51. This would be about fifty million, or about one-sixth of the present U.S. population; Catton, *Overshoot*, p. 53.

52. G. Wesley Johnson, Jr., ed. *Phoenix in the Twentieth Century: Essays in Community History* (Norman: University of Oklahoma Press, 1993).

53. Both the environmental and the social costs attending the LA catastrophe have been staggering. See Mike Davis, *City of Quartz: Excavating the Future in Los Angeles* (London: Verso, 1990); *Ecology of Fear: Los Angeles and the Imagination of Disaster* (New York: Henry Holt, 1998).

54. See, e.g., Mark Reisner, *Cadillac Desert: The American West and Its Disappearing Water* (New York: Viking, 1986).

55. See the essay entitled "The Water Plot: Hydrological Rape in Northern Canada," in my *Struggle for the Land: Native North American*

Resistance to Genocide, Ecocide, and Colonization (San Francisco: City Lights, [2nd ed.]2002) pp. 292-323.

56. Ronald L. Myers, ed., *Ecosystems of Florida* (Gainesville: University of Florida Press, 1990); John Ogden and Steve Davis, eds., *Everglades: The Ecosystem and Its Restoration* (Washington, D.C.: CRC Press, 1994).

57. See the essay titled "A Breach of Trust: The Radioactive Colonization of Native North America," in my *Acts of Rebellion: The Ward Churchill Reader* (New York: Routledge, 2003), pp. 111-40.

58. On the human as well as environmental costs attending coal stripping in the Four Corners region, see the essay titled "Genocide in Arizona: The 'Navajo-Hopi Land Dispute' in Perspective," in my *Struggle for the Land*, pp. 135-72. Also see Thayer Scudder, et al., *No Place to Go: Effects of Compulsory Relocation on Navajos* (Philadelphia: Institute for the Study of Human Issues, 1982).

60. See generally, U.S. Department of Commerce, Bureau of the Census, Economics and Statistics Division, *U.S. Census of Population: General Population Characteristics, United States* (Washington, D.C.: U.S. GPO, 1990). For background, see Kirkpatrick Sale, *Power Shift: The Rise of the Southern Rim and Its Challenge to the Eastern Establishment* (New York: Random House, 1975). For more recent contextualization, see Davis, *City of Quartz* and *Ecology of Fear*. A good deal of the impact could also be offset by implementing the ideas contained in John Todd and George Tukel, *Reinhabiting Cities and Towns: Designing for Sustainability* (San Francisco: Planet Drum Foundation, 1981). Also see Sale, *Dwellers in the Land*.

61. For purposes of comparison, see *Funding Ecological and Social Destruction: The World Bank and International Monetary Fund* (Washington, D.C.: Bank Information Center, 1990). By contrast, the principle I advocate might be described as "Demanding Ecological and Social Preservation." For the extent to which this is an issue, see Paul Harrison, *Inside the Third World: The Anatomy of Poverty* (New York: Penguin, [3rd ed.] 1993).

62. Many indigenous peoples take the position that all social policies should be entered into only after consideration of their likely implications, both environmentally and culturally, for our posterity seven generations in the future. Consequently, a number of seemingly good ideas for solving short-run problems are never entered into because no one can reasonably predict their longer-term effects; see Sylvester M. Morey, ed., *Can the Red Man Help the White Man? A Denver Conference with Indian Elders* (New York: Myrin Institute, 1970). Also see the concluding chapter of Deloria, *God Is Red*.

63. For an analogous argument, see Thomas Kuhn's *The Structure of Scientific Revolutions* (Chicago: University of Chicago Press, [3rd ed.] 1996).

64. Although the slogan probably originated with Ché Guevara, it is most commonly associated with the May 1968 student uprising in France. Ample contextualization will be found in George Katsiaficas'

The Imagination of the New Left: A Global Analysis of 1968 (Boston: South End Press, 1987).

65. See, e.g., Virginia Irving Armstrong, ed., *I Have Spoken: American History Through the Voices of the Indians* (Chicago: Swallow Press, 1971).

66. Laing, *Politics of Experience*. Also see R.D. Laing, *The Divided Self: An Existential Study of Sanity and Madness* (New York: Routledge, 1999).

67. See generally, Daniel Burton-Rose, Dan Pens, and Paul Wright, eds., *The Celling of America: An Inside Look at the U.S. Prison Industry* (Monroe, ME: Common Courage Press, 1998).

68. Armstrong, *I Have Spoken*, p. 79.

◊ ◊ ◊ ◊ ◊

Dreaming Amongst the Trees:
Ceremony as Indigenous Education

Renée E. Bédard

As a professor of Indigenous Studies, I am often asked the following questions: What is Indigenous ceremony? Why is ceremony important to Indigenous people? These are significant questions worth further inquiry. Ceremonial processes are a vital source of identity formation, knowledge creation and connection to the land. According to Paula Gunn Allen,

> Because of the basic assumption of the wholeness of unity of the universe, our natural and necessary relationship to all life is evident; all phenomena we witness within or "outside" ourselves are, like us, intelligent manifestations of the intelligent universe from which they arise, as do all things of the earth and the cosmos beyond. (1)

As Paula Gunn-Allen points out above, Indigenous people manifest their relationships to everything around them and ground their sense-of-self through ceremony. Indigenous people learn their roles and responsibilities as human beings in relation to the cosmos by undergoing unique education contexts found in various ceremonies. Through these ceremonial customs, an Indigenous person develops connections to their heritage, culture and territories.

This paper is an examination of the contexts that define ceremony as Indigenous education. It is written from an Indigenous point of view and directly written for an Indigenous audience, but is open to anyone to explore and seek understanding about the nature of ceremony in the lives of Indigenous people. Indigenous people need more allies and friends who understand our views of the world, so as to better understand why we fight to protect our languages, lands, people and cultures so vigorously. This paper is not a 'how-to-manual' or a 'tell-all' on the specifics of conducting ceremony. There are no step-by-step instructions on building fasting lodges, sweats or tipis. Using written literature and personal narrative, this paper will explore the philosophies, ideologies and issues relating to Indigenous ceremonies. Surveying the discussions by Indigenous scholars and non-Indigenous observers who have documented Indigenous ceremonial customs, I will begin to offer a vision of why it is important to discuss the context of ceremony in Indigenous cultures as a form of education. I will conclude with a brief summary of my own thoughts and recollections of past attendance at ceremonies.

> When I was a boy I went out to an Island to fast. My father paddled me there. For several nights I dreamed of an *ógǐmě* (chief, superior person). Finally he said to me, "Grandson. I think you are now ready to go with me". Then *ógǐmě* began dancing around me as I sat there on a rock and when I happened to glance down at my body I noticed that I had grown feathers. Soon I felt just like a bird, a golden eagle (*kǐniu*). *Ógǐmě* had turned into an eagle also and off he flew towards the south. I spread my wings and flew after him in the same direction. After a while we arrived at a place where there were lots of tents and lots of "people". It was the home of the Summer Birds...(After returning north again the boy was left at their starting point after the guardian spirit had promised help whenever he wanted it. The boy's father came for him and took him home again. (3)

Indigenous people have been undergoing ceremonies as a means of teaching and learning for thousands of years. Throughout the generations ceremonies were refined and developed to be uniquely suited to not only the lived contexts but also the environmental contexts of the people so that they could learn how to survive on the land. The process of ceremony connects participants to the natural environment, as well as their family, community, and nation. Ceremony also serves as the foundation of Indigenous spiritual knowledge, identity and culture, connecting us to land, time and space in ways unique to each Indigenous culture. For many Indigenous peoples, education begins first in ceremony, such as that described in the above quote about a boy on his fast.

Basil Johnston (Ojibwe) notes that Indigenous ceremonies arose out of the need to consult, interact, and learn about the world. As Johnston explains that:

> In private, hunters, and fisherman sought the patronage and the pardon of the manitous (mysteries) who presided over the animals and the birds; and medicine men and women invoked the mysteries to confer curative powers upon the herbs that were used in their preparations. In public, the people conducted rituals and ceremonies to foster upright living; petitioned Kitche Manitou and the deities for blessing; or offered thanksgiving for game and abundant harvest. From the origin and form of these ceremonies, and from the substance of the chants and prayers, the Ojibway-speaking peoples' understanding and interpretation of moral order can be discovered. (4)

In order to understand life and how best to live within Indigenous contexts, Indigenous people conducted spiritual experiments and research or what we now call ceremonies in order to gain knowledge.

28

Each generation added to the reservoir of information in order to develop what we know call our sacred and traditional knowledge. The ancestors refined and developed these procedures of learning and exploration, which were then passed down through the generations, from the young to the old. Indigenous nations developed varying ceremonies designed from living within specific ecologies.

To understand ceremony as a form of Indigenous education also requires that we understand that the Western dualist vision of the world is incomplete. Concepts such as either/or, good/bad and light/dark used to teach rational conscious Western thought leaves no room for Indigenous understanding that the world is full of spirit, movement, rhythm, and transformation. According to Anishinaabe Elder Jim Dumont (Ojibwe), an individual's participation in ceremony grounds that person in two worlds, ordinary and non-ordinary (5), natural and supernatural, or the profane and the sacred. Jeanette Armstrong cites her own experience in coming to a similar insight:

> It was after I went on a long ceremonial fast that it all came together. It was as if I had two separate bubbles of perception, which suddenly came together into one bubble of perception twice as large. I could see that there were not two separate realities but a oneness of a broader reality. I have to watch at all times so that I don't lose that. (6)

Indigenous learning practices are not like western-style educational methods with their reliance on written literacy serving as the measure for knowledge and experience. Rather, the whole of the cosmos both outside and inside our minds is the original Indigenous classroom, with ceremony being the vehicle or tool for facilitating the process of learning. This way of seeing education is holistic, circular and interactive.

In Hallowell's account, a young boy takes part in an important pubescent ceremony requiring him to go out and fast on the land. This particular ceremony is referred to as the "dream-fast," (7) but it is also a coming-of-age custom, where children transition into adulthood and begin to learn adult responsibilities. The boy is sent to enter into the "adult" phase of his life through both the ordinary world and the non-ordinary world. He embarks on a personal journey, where he is to fast solitarily from food and water. On his journey, a spirit in the body of a man visits him and ultimately the boy learns that this is his guardian spirit. The event did occur for the boy and he experienced extra-ordinary events that changed the way he would forever interact with the world. Indigenous ceremonies, such as the boy's fast, are important parts of Indigenous cultural learning techniques and processes for gaining knowledge of what it means to be Indigenous. Accumulation of such knowledge informs culture and key aspects of a person's identity. Knowledge generated during ceremony can ultimately aid a person in making choices, decisions and actions in their daily life.

Ceremony also reveals that Indigenous education operates on multiple levels of reality. Dumont refers to this type of learning mechanism as, "the Native's way of 'seeing'." (8) Indigenous cultural teachers use ceremony to usher their pupils into experiences that will offer them knowledge for both the ordinary reality of the everyday and the non-ordinary reality of the spirit world. They 'learn about' as well as 'participate in' multiple realities. Learning on multiple plains of existence marks Indigenous education as a unique process. People participate in creating their own learning environment by constructing ceremonial rituals that will help them to bridge the spiritual realm and find information that would not be found in 'everyday' reality. Ceremony becomes the educational tool used to teach Indigenous people information they can use to help them on their life's path.

The pedagogy of learning within ceremonial instruction is based on what Dumont refers to as a "primal way of *seeing*," meaning the ability to see and interact with multiple dimensions. (9) Indigenous worldviews are therefore grounded in "a three-hundred-and-sixty-degree-vision"(10) of the world. The Indigenous student's mind is instructed during ceremony to first-and-foremost begin to see with a sense of a circular view or a "total way of seeing, which encompasses the essential elements of ordinary reality and seeks out the all-important manifestations of a non-ordinary reality." (11) Dumont contends this way of seeing is unique to Indigenous people. This form of learning is refined through 'actual lived experiences' in other realities using ceremonial events, prayers, songs, and so on. He defines three-hundred-and-sixty-degree-vision using the following story from a Midéwiwin medicine man from Minnesota who expressed how this "vision" came to all Indigenous peoples of North America or "Red Man" as he refers to them:

> In the beginning, while the races still lived together as one, each of the races had to come to a decision as to what direction he would choose. During this time White Man and Red Man found themselves walking together along the same road. At some point in their journey they came to a division in their path. One of the two possible roads before them offered knowledge and growth through accumulation and mounting of all that could be seen ahead (a one-hundred-and-eighty-degree-vision). This is what White Man chose and he has developed in this "linear" and accumulative fashion ever since. The other road appeared less attractive materially and quantitatively, but offered a whole and comprehensive vision that entailed not only vision before but also vision behind (a three-hundred-and-sixty-degree-vision). This was a circular vision that sought to perceive and understand the whole nature of an object or event – its physical reality as well as its soul. The Red Man chose this road and he has developed in this circular and holistic way ever since. (12)

In this account of the medicine man, Dumont highlights the point that learning in the Indigenous manner is an experiential process involving all "six" senses, the five sensual ways of knowing the world, as well as the 'spirit' sense or mind's-eye. Recognizing that, "There is another level of reality which is concurrent with everyday reality" (13) is the initial step into beginning the learning exercise. Ceremonial education begins with this recognition of reality as something more than what we witness everyday of our lives in the ordinary world. In essence, this recognition is a "cerebral exercise" (14) or first lesson among many to follow, but which first establishes the right mindset to begin learning from an Indigenous context.

Once the right frame of mind is established, other lessons begin with participating in ceremonial explorations or journeys into the non-ordinary world beyond this physical realm of the everyday. The mind must "participate" and go into another set of realities in order to make contact and learn in the spirit realm. Another important occurrence in the Hallowell's account is this idea of spirit-transitioning. Spirit transition is participation in the ceremonial experience. During ceremonial transitioning into other realities can take the form of metaphysically crossing-over, travel, transportation, transformation and metamorphosis. In the Hallowell account, the Ogīmĕ appeared to the boy as a regular man, but then changed into an eagle and flew away south. The boy also experienced this ability to transform himself, "[When] I happened to glance down at my body I noticed that I had grown feathers..." (15) The boy became a bird and flew off like the Ogīmĕ or eagle in the same manner southwards. There came a moment when reality shifted for the boy and the ordinary world gave way to the non-ordinary world. In ceremonial situations, such as what the young boy underwent in his ceremonial fast, a special condition occurred where his everyday mind decided to participate in the spirit world. This moment of belief or acceptance gave way for the non-ordinary to take over the mind's experiences. Therefore, it is possible for supernatural or other-than-ordinary experiences to occur, to interact with the other beings of that realm and to gather information those experiences manifest. Dumont says that once the mind enters this understanding, "human beings also can realize their own ability to be transformed or to transform themselves." (16)

Another way to better appreciate this experience is to understand the transition a person goes through when falling asleep or entering the dream-state. Sometimes we are conscious of the transition between consciousness and unconsciousness, or the waking world and the dream world, but sometimes we are not always aware, we just drift. Both worlds touch in that moment and continue to run concurrently with our physical selves in the ordinary world, but our spiritual selves are off exploring another reality. Dumont suggests,

> this reality that we experience (perhaps most readily in dreams) is constantly intersecting with what we know as everyday reality. We are most aware of it when we are not so intensely focused in the everyday reality. The levels of reality are concurrent and have equal

credibility. They provide "true" experiences to which we must respond. (17)

With this transition, the ordinary reality steps aside as time and space take on their animate features, shifting along with the experience.

During the boy's fast, several events unfold in the new found animate temporal and spatial dimensions. He was both fasting for several days and yet spending months away. He was both in his physical body while he underwent the fasting ceremony, yet he also then transformed and flew away as a bird to a far off land. Both events happened concurrently to each other, simultaneously putting the boy in different time and space. Such is the nature of the education for the boy. He experiences that time and space move to aid him in his participation in learning.

Willie Ermine (Cree) notes that with many cultures of the world, spiritual leaders, "holy people and philosophers" as he refers to them (and Indigenous people among them) explore inner space of 'self' using ceremony as their vehicle of transportation. He says,

> In their quest to find meaning in the outer-space, Aboriginal people turned to the inner space. This inner space is that universe of being within each person that is synonymous with the soul, the spirit, the self, or the being. The priceless core with each of us and the process of touching that essence is what Kierkegaard called 'inwardness'. Aboriginal people found a wholeness that permeated inwardness and that also extended into the outer space. Their fundamental insight was that all existence was connected and that the whole enmeshed the being in its inclusiveness. (18)

Within this space of the inner mind, soul and spirit, the rules of the everyday do not apply. Once the Indigenous mind grasps this, even a boy can fly as an eagle.

According to Ermine, ceremony taps into a, "mysterious force that connects the totality of existence – the forms, energies, or concepts that constitute the outer and inner worlds." (19) Joseph Couture (Cree/Métis) further contends that this way of being and seeing is altogether possible because Indigenous knowing is what he refers to as "a non-dualistic process." (20) He suggests that the mode of Indigenous knowing about the world, "transcends the usual oppositions between rational knowledge and intuition, spiritual insight and physical behaviour." (21) Further, he describes this immanence as "the pervasive, encompassing reality of the life force, manifest in laws – the laws of nature, the laws of energy, or the laws of light." (22) For our Indigenous ancestors, the potential and implications of such forms of exploration, travel and participation in the non-ordinary reality were physically transformative. Willie Ermine writes that, "With this 'force,' knowing becomes possible." (23)

From this 'force,' that Ermine references, our ancestors as explorers brought back knowledge of the world, and all manner of experiential ways of knowing that are both physical and metaphysical. With that knowledge, the lives of Indigenous peoples could be made better, life courses changed and decisions made.

We now use these modes of knowing to access those other realities, to travel ourselves as contemporary Indigenous peoples, into those inner spaces of mind and spirit. Ermine further suggests that we need to promote such exploration and learning, so that we to can continue to learn and grow. Indigenous communities across North America have different ceremonies based on a variety of needs, circumstances and reasons for being, but all come back to one reason for their existence – to aid in educating the Indigenous mind.

Ceremonial Teachers: Elders as Cultural Experts

In ceremony, learning is best facilitated when there are knowledgeable and qualified teachers. Ceremonial teachers include various people with different kinds of spiritual and cultural expertise. In essence, the old saying, 'it takes a village to raise a child' is in fact the heart of Indigenous teaching practices. Everyone in Indigenous families and communities tend to help teach. Yet, in the context of ceremonial events, cultural teachers are generally Elders and other spiritual experts, such as medicine persons or healers and ceremonial practitioners. For the purpose of this paper, however, I will focus the discussion mainly on Elders.

Elders are named to the position of 'Elderhood' in Indigenous communities based not merely on their older age, but on their vast amount of cultural knowledge and spiritual experience with ceremonies. The role of Elders is to teach the younger generation traditional knowledge, customs and other cultural/spiritual practices in order to ensure that information is perpetuated. In this way, Elders are important educational instructors in spirituality and cultural practices relating to the participation in ceremonial customs.

Elders as teachers are held up to high cultural and spiritual standards because they are in charge of the well-being of Indigenous adults, youth and children's cultural and spiritual identities. Ojibwe Elder Alex Skead explains how he regards the role of Elder as highly important. He says, "I feel that love for young people [and] that they should learn a little bit, whatever we can share." (24) Skead also adds that Elders should be highly trained individuals. He says that, "If you don't know what you are talking about never mind being a teacher or an Elder. You may be an Elder, but you can't teach nothing." (25) The knowledge, experience and training Elders undergo over their lifetimes makes them 'cultural-memory-banks' of information for Indigenous families, communities and nations.

Therefore, to learn from an Elder is a very important opportunity and a gift. To be the recipient of a lifetime worth of knowledge and experience about the world is a great honour and accordingly deserve respect, as well as reverence. Couture notes that, "[o]ne learns about Elders by learning from them over a long period of time, by becoming comfortable with a learning-by-doing model. Their counseling and teaching focus on learning from one's experience." (26) Thus, an Elder's time, knowledge and teaching practices are priceless to Indigenous communities.

Within many Indigenous communities today, Elders have become the most frequently relied on as cultural and spiritual 'trained' experts in ceremonial practices. Couture describes them as,

> ...*evidence that Natives know a way to high human development*, to a degree greater than generally suspected. Their qualities of mind (intuition, intellect, memory, imagination) and emotion, their profound and refined moral sense manifest in an exquisite sense of humor, in a sense of caring and communication finesse in *teaching* and counseling, together with a high level of spiritual and psychic attainment, are perceived as clear behavioral indicators, deserving careful attention, if not compelling emulation. (27)

Further, Elders are considered to be trained in the philosophies, histories and cosmologies of Indigenous relationships to land, sky, water and the universe. Couture notes that, "they are trained in the lessons of how the very nature of our being is in at-one-ment with the cosmo-genesis. And so, they hold to the land, ceremony, medicine, linked to the past, in Spirit." (28) The *Gathering Strength* volume of the *Report of the Royal Commission on Aboriginal Peoples* (RCAP) (1996) reaffirmed that Elders are of utmost importance to consult in learning Indigenous knowledge. RCAP states that they are the: "Keepers of tradition, guardians of culture, the wise people, the teachers. While most of those who are wise in traditional ways are old, not all old people are elders, and not all elders are old." (29) Their wisdom is not only personally learned, but also comes from the shared knowledge and experiences of their ancestors, spirit-helpers and their Elders, which is described by Pam Colorado (Oneida) as a "collective effort to know throughout time." (30)

Couture notes that in Indigenous cultures we look to Elders as keys to understanding culture, as guides to take us on explorations of the cosmos and mentors to learn how to be good human beings. He gladly applauds them saying,

> We look to Elders for the way words are used, for the structural devices they employ, for the teaching and counselling approaches they utilize, for the philosophical and spiritual perspectives of the world, experienced and envisioned.... (31)

Colorado refers to these ways of learning as procedures of "Native Science." (32) She defines the teaching by Elders as a holistic and

34

spiritual process, which "gathers information from the mental, physical, social and cultural/historical realms". (33) Traditional teaching tools of Elder instructions or apprenticeship, as she refers to it, includes feelings, history, prayer and relations. Colorado explains that: "Elders guide us through our experiences, usually by identifying appropriate rituals or processes so that we gain insight and understanding of ourselves, the universe and our place in it. (34) The guidance of Elders determines the learning processes, type and amount of knowledge each person should be exposed to at specific times. Elders know how much knowledge, the training needed and when to teach each individual certain aspects of culture and spiritual.

As Joseph Couture points out, the teaching methods expressed by Elders guide the learner to live in balance in relationships with all other living things:

> There is an observable Elder "psychology" implicit in what they do and say, Elders, as highly aware persons, and as carriers of oral tradition, are the exemplars, the standing reference points. When guided by Elders, the apprentice learns to perceive and understand something of such dimensions as the nature itself of the knowledge, of the centrality of primal experiences, of the "laws of Nature," as this in Elder sayings...Evolved Elders arrive at and preserve a sense-rooted thinking which knows the world as a spiritual reality. He who "knows," experiences a spiritual nature in the perceived world. Reality is experienced by entering deeply into the inner being of the mind, and not by attempting to break through the outer world to a beyond. This positions the Native person in "communion," within the living reality of all things. His "communion" is his experience of the ideas within, concentric with reality without. Thus, to "know," to "cognize," is experiential, direct knowing. (35)

In short, ceremony is not just something that's out there for anyone to go out and experience without proper aid, guidance and instruction. Ceremonial teachers like Elders guide these forms of traditional research in order to ensure that the experiences the person undergoes are authentic to that of their past ancestors and also accordingly, to the future generations that will follow in the footsteps of present day practitioners.

The Land, Ceremonial Grounds, Sacred Places

Indigenous education begins on the land, and the land forms the foundation for ceremony as it instructs people how to live on it season by season. It is for this reason that many Indigenous nations across North America recognize the land as Mother Earth or Mother the Earth, the first and most important teacher. In Ojibwe, Mother Earth is referred to as *Eshkakimig-kwe*. (36) Ojibwe people will often say, 'Go sit on the lap of your real mother, your first mother!' when referring to the land. When ceremonies are held, generally they are performed outside so that individuals can walk on, sit on and touch the land.

The Creation story is one of the first stories people learnt about how their culture came to be, it details how the land and waters took their shape, and how culture is a direct emanation of this creation. Edward Benton-Banai (Ojibwe) explains that the first human beings created many of the ceremonies as they participated and learned lessons from all the territorial, aquatic, aerial and celestial movements that gifted the Anishinaabe with life. These original ceremonies were in turn handed down through countless generations. So, in the southern and western parts of North America there are Sundance ceremonies, in the northeastern part of continent there are the Three Sister ceremonies for corn, bean, squash. In the northern and central regions there are sweetwater ceremonies for the maple sap and strawberry ceremonies that run throughout in the spring and early summer. All these different ceremonies are not only seasonal, but are regional and place specific.

According to Vine Deloria (Standing Rock Sioux), when Indigenous tribes were given land by "higher powers," they in turn took up "ceremonial duties" which he says needed to be performed for as long as the people occupied and used that land. Deloria continues, "Removing an Indian tribe from its aboriginal territory, therefore, results in the destruction of ceremonial life and much of the cultural structure which has many ceremony and ritual significance [sic]." (38) Land in this sense encompasses all terrestrial, aquatic and aerial species, features and formations, and is not confined solely to the place where one stands, and is not defined as the square or rectangular property of an individual stakeholder. In an Indigenous context, land is defined more by the way one relates and engages with it as the source of all life.

The ceremonial duties Indigenous people have to the land are a manifestation of how they reaffirm and re-enact their relationships to environment on a regular basis. Deloria notes that, "[o]bligations demanded by the lands upon which people lived were part of their understanding of the world; indeed, their view of life was grounded in the knowledge of these responsibilities. Tribal ritual life was intimately related to the seasons of the year." (39) Deloria further acknowledges that Indigenous people share the land with these other species and have come to see them as their relations, family and kin. Living in the same environment, humans and these other species began to follow the same rhythms of the seasons. In the case of human beings, these other species were needed for survival: food, shelter, and clothing. He explains, that "the people perceived that a social contract existed between men and the other animals. The human ceremonial life confirmed the existence of this equality." (40) Therefore, the land is acknowledged as an important relation and indeed a necessary participant in the ceremonial duties of each nation.

Ceremony is the natural rhythm developed between Indigenous people and the land as they enact and re-enact many of the ceremonies performed by their ancestors. Jeanette Armstrong believes that, "The individual in harmony with the natural world celebrates and exquisitely experiences its magnificence. The colors continuously changing, the vastness, the songs of the living, the breath of the earth moving in continuous cycles are all cherished and made totally meaningful to one's existence." (41) She further notes that this relationship is centuries old with the natural world, refined and defined by trial and error. She writes that,

> [o]ver the centuries of seeking to live cooperatively within the natural world, Native peoples evolved a body of knowledge contained in the various ceremonies, which facilitated the individual learning process. Such ceremonies seek to unite, acquaint and remind the participants of the underlying principles of creation." (42)

Ceremony is the physical expression of continuous deliberate focus on enacting the relationship between humans and the natural world. Indigenous people choose to participate in that relationship with the land when they choose to do ceremony.

Indigenous people also have physical reminders of valuable spirit-journeys taken through ceremonies and recorded on the land. The rock petroglyphs and pictographs across the Great Lakes region are important conceptualizations of ceremonial education. In Peterborough, Ontario, one can walk up to the carvings created by Anishinaabe people who conducted ceremonies and rituals. They recorded their spirit-journeys, visions and quests onto the face of the soft marble rock, which have endured the rigors of time, weather and discovery by western anthropologists in the 1960s, as well as the countless tourists. (43) Images of boats, women, men, animals, strange and wonderful beings, all stare back at us today as reminders of past ceremonies that brought human beings into the spirit-world. Further, our stories, legends and histories are filled with knowledge of the ancestral explorers of inner space.

Art Historian Gerald McMaster (Plains Cree) argues that this site is a source of inspiration, spirituality, truth, understanding and wonder for both the Anishinaabe who reside on the territory, but also to those who come to visit these sacred grounds. He says,

> ...it is part of a vast number of similar sites across North America that continue to provide aboriginal people with important connections to the land. Not dissimilar to the way churches function for Christians, these sites are persistent reminders for aboriginal people of the mysteries of the land. And, like the artists commissioned by the church, the people who conceived of these images were no doubt acutely aware of the magnitude of this space. Other local residents sought special connections to this space on a regular basis rather than on specific "days of the week." These profound images are mediators between two worlds, yet

contemporary people can appreciate them for their beauty without understanding their spiritual significance. What they do continue to signify is the importance of the land in the aboriginal consciousness. (44)

To this day, seasonal ceremonies are held at the petroglyphs for fall and spring fasters, as well as other smaller ceremonies, thus perpetuating the role of the rocks as visual mediators between the physical and spiritual worlds.

The petroglyphs speak of past explorations into the spirit world, revealing a specific type of education derived from introspection of the mind, spirit and soul. They illuminate the process of self-discovery, self-growth and what Willie Ermine calls, "the first door to mystery." (45) The classroom becomes the 'unknown' world of the inner-self. This educational process developed from many journeys to these sacred sites where knowledge would be gathered from the beings in the stone. The repetition of this journey over countless generations subsequently contributed more stories to these places, eventually transforming the land into a place of higher learning for all Anishinaabe people. Ermine describes this process as "the accumulation and synthesis of insights and tribal understandings acquired through inwardness, and the juxtaposition of knowledge on the physical plane as culture and community, is the task of Aboriginal education" (46). The fact that we still seek more and more knowledge about the world of the unseen, mystery and the spirit world, speaks of our unfinished exploration of 'inner space.' In fact, Ermine argues that we are compelled to travel to this space by our own human desire to learn. These sacred sites, he says, are the "calculated trajectories to the world within" (47) ourselves.

Just like family photos hanging on the walls of a home, the petroglyphs are living reminders of our ancestors' inner musings of a universe discovered in the spirit realm. The petroglyph carvings show our ancestor's experiences with the metaphysics and mystery of the inner space. They reveal insight into the human experience in that environment and the connectedness to the spirit realm. Our ancestors documented their experiences in stone, and it was only by sharing what they had learned that we can fully understand the importance of perpetuating spirit journeys among the Anishinaabe today.

Many Indigenous nations have physical reminders of how the ancestors achieved access to the spiritual realms. As Anishinaabe, we have our oral stories, words in our language that denote spiritual meanings, the petroglyphs and other rock carvings left behind by people who went on quests, visions and dreaming-journeys, as well as birch-bark scrolls. Many of these are records of times when our peoples were actively exploring the spirit world using ceremony.

Ermine argues that the clues still survive on the lands of Indigenous peoples. In describing the medicine wheels of the Indigenous peoples of the prairies and plains of the United States he passionately describes them,

> The outcrops of stone and rock known as medicine wheels survive from a time when our people were actively exploring the inner space. These wheels convey concepts derived from introspection and illustrate the pathways to self-discovery, the first door to mystery. They speak, in the silence of the unknown, about the progressive growth of self through a cyclical journey of repetition, experience, and constitution of meaning. The wheels mirror the cosmology of the inner space. These stones circles and the indestructible fragments constituting the whole wheel infuse us with thoughts of a universe depicting the wholeness found in the inner space. They give us insight into our common humanity and our connectedness. The ancient ones recorded their findings in the inner space in simple stone, and it is only by analyzing and synthesizing the truths of inner space that we can fully decipher the messages of the wheels. (48)

The physical objects, carvings and drawings of our ancestors of their time in inner space act as guides to us today, as well as reminders of the potential knowledge that comes from journeying into the mind's inner corners.

Teachers Big and Small: Animal Stewards, Guides and Helpers

In Indigenous cultures, observing the cycles, patterns and behaviors of plants and animals is significant to the learning process. Ermine notes that animals and plants are also teachers. In ceremony, their role is to act as facilitators, guides and stewards to human beings through to certain parts of inner space. He remarks, "There are also the people of the animal and plant world who steward certain doors to knowledge of the inner space. The Old Ones and the keepers of the earth among our people tell of the rich information about the inner space contained in these life forms." (49) Those who take part in ceremonies on the land are often reminded and given strict instructions to harm none of the creatures that come to visit. To harm an animal, insect, plant or any living thing while in ceremony is considered a grave trespass. Those animals and even plants that you might sit down beside are all considered ' spirit helpers' that might have something important to teach. In reference the role of plant-life, Pam Colorado notes that the Elders speak of the, "great peace, the still, electrifying awareness of experience in the deep words." (50)

Human interactions with earth, the animals and plants can be one of the most powerful teacher-student relationships. The stillness, flow and movement of the land synchronizes the human mind with the inner world. Deloria suggests:

Here, power and place are dominant concepts – power being the living energy that inhibits and/or composes the universe, and place being the relationship of things to each other...put into a simple equation: power and place produce personality. This equation simply means that the universe is alive, but it also contains within it the very important suggestions that the universe is personal, and, therefore, must be approached in a personal manner. The personal nature of the universe demands that each and every entity in it seek and sustain personal relationships. (51)

It is for this reason that I argue it is not just the aspects of ceremony itself that teach, but those helpers a person meets and interacts with along the way that also reveal the mystery of the cosmos. It is significant to recognize the importance of the entire process and that might simply come from listening to a chickadee's song. Finding guides is a key part of the process, as well as finding appropriate teachers and helpers.

The animal and plant guides to this inner space act as a, "vital nexus in comprehending the sophisticated directional maps into the metaphysical." (52) Like navigators of spiritual geography, these guides in the form of cultural experts act as compasses on where to go, what to watch and how to get to inner space. They speak for us, guard and protect those individuals who seek ceremony as their educational path.

Language

Language is also an important aspect to ceremonial Indigenous education. It taps into specific ways of seeing, reading and interacting with the world. The ancestors left their descendants instructions in the words used today. Language can describe spiritual thoughts, descriptions and actions that only relate to the context of ceremony. Without those words, Indigenous ceremony might not hold many of the original meanings intended by the ancestors. How to contextualize and interpret ceremony as an Indigenous educational process was imbedded in the languages. Without traditional Indigenous languages, teaching as well as the learning processes might be lost forever because they do not necessary translate easily into other languages like English, French or Spanish. For example, the Anishinaabe word for stone in Ojibwe is sin (53), which can be either animate or inanimate depending on whether or not the word is used in context with ceremonial practices. In ceremony, a stone can be considered a spirit being, which is often referenced to as Grandfather or Grandmother. There are many other Ojibwe words that show us how and when to do things in ceremony. Language in conjunction with ceremony, thus provide a tapestry of meanings for the spiritual components of Indigenous learning. Ermine reminds us that:

The language of the people provides another valuable indication of an inner space. The word for 'mystery' usually refers to a higher power and also connotes our own deeper selves as a humble connection with the higher mystery. In conceptualizing this existence of 'ponderable' mysteries, our languages reveal a very high level of rationality that can only come from an earlier insight into power. Our languages suggest inwardness, where real power lies. It is this space within the individual that, for the Aboriginal, has become the last great frontier and the most challenging one of all. (54)

This quote refers to the fact that our knowledge of inner space is embedded in the languages. Indigenous languages capture ways of knowing originating from the land, the stories shared amongst our families, and the traditions passed down in our communities and within our nations.

According to Basil Johnston, Indigenous education begins even before we are born, while we swim as fetuses in our mother's wombs. We hear the words of our mother and the outside world echoing through its dark waters. We begin to understand on a psychic level that language is more than just sounds, but a way to identify the world we know. From there we are born, ready to become receptive to knowing language. He notes,

I think that children learn easily and readily because they listen and give wholeheartedly of themselves to sound. Even while they are yet fetal beings, without any means of knowing the world outside the womb, it is said, and I believe, that children can hear. If that is so, then hearing may well be regarded as prior to and even more essential than are the other senses in learning. And hearing remains the principal means by which children get to know the world and the other beings in it during the first few months of their lives. For infants there is little else but sound and touch; they can only listen. (55)

As a child listens to the words of their ancestors language, first from the womb and then nurtured amongst family, they are ushered into Indigenous ways of seeing the world that begin to open the pathways for each individual to have the potential to access inner space.

Couture says, "Native traditional mind is openly and sharply impressed, in my view, by sensory qualities of relationships, all perceived as inherently meaningful." (56) Elders, he explains, are our teachers, instructors and facilitators to the learning journey. Indigenous books are represented by physical and spiritual experience: seeing, hearing, touching, tasting, smell and the sixth sense of psychic awareness. Couture offers that, "Elder teaching of concepts is therefore characteristically and understandably directly visual or 'pictorial.'" (57) He argues that Indigenous languages use symbols, related to the natural world to teach how everything is structured. Couture notes that where we learn is as important as what we learn. He believes that:

Native ceremonies are the primary oral literature, and remain the main traditional source of psychic energy for thinking, for identity development and control, for survival and its enhancement. The oral literate mind displays a capacity to integrate, to form patterns, a process that penetrates and transforms the experiences obtained in and through a dynamic, non-print environment. (58)

From our oral literature as Indigenous peoples we learn the language of spirit and the sacred. In the Anishinaabe language, we learn to talk and introduce ourselves to all of Creation. We are named in traditional languages, given animal clans and are told which nation we belong. Then we learn to state our names, our clans, where we come from and declare ourselves to the world that we are Anishinaabe, maybe Mohawk or Cree, and so on. The simple task of learning to introduce oneself through the language is in fact a ceremony among the Anishinaabe. Introductions can open up relations with the plant world and allow a person to find much need medicines. A person must explain first who they are and then why they seek to conduct ceremony. All this is information exchanged through language. Language and ceremony are closely connected and intertwined. The languages of all Indigenous peoples across North America were formed and molded through interactions with the world around us and from our journey's into inner space through ceremony.

Without language, the ceremonies we use today might not have come about in the manner we now practice them and without traditional language in the future, ceremonies might not have the same meaning they did for our ancestors. How will our children know how to connect and talk to the plant world, the animal world, the spirit world and the cosmos, if they do not speak in the language of their ancestors? Indigenous languages were formed from listening to the wind, hearing the water flow of the rocks in a stream or seeing the colors of a sunset. Language helps us communicate with the natural world in a language that the physical and spirit worlds recognize and respond. Those words of Indigenous languages have the metaphysical power to connect with the cosmos, the land, animals, plants, the spirits and the Great Mystery. Without that language as a bridge between these two worlds the connection is broken.

For this reason, language revitalization amongst young people is vitally important, particularly in families, with individuals and inside Indigenous communities that have suffered from loss of language. As Indigenous peoples, we need to move to restore the language in order to ensure the knowledge imbedded in the languages and dialects of specific regions are not lost or forgotten. The responsibility of the current generation is to restore that which was stolen from our parents and grandparents, to have pride is speaking the language of our ancestors. *Mzinegiizhigo-kwe ndizhinikaaz. Dokis ndonjibaa. Anishinaabe-kwe ndaw. Ndo-Ojibwem.*

Coming Home: Our Collective Healing Journey

The ceremonies conducted today in our Indigenous communities, amongst our family, friends and communities are allowing many of us as Indigenous people to heal the hurts in our lives and find peace. Our communities have a lot of healing work to do in order to survive this time period as we try to come to terms with the damage done by Residential Schools, Indian Act policies, violence, abuse, drugs, alcohol and much more. There is a lot of good work being done in the communities, thanks to our Elders, cultural experts and community members who are speaking out and bringing back the old ways to heal the communities through education of ceremonial customs. People are returning to the lodges, the Sundances, the tipis, to the songs and prayers of their ancestors. They are learning all manner of ceremonies that had at one time gone underground to hide from the colonization.

For my people, the Anishinaabeg, many years were spent without ceremony in our communities. We had put them away to keep them safe and to keep ourselves safe from outsiders. Many of our people went through a 'wandering stage' of not knowing their culture, identity or beliefs. They are coming back now to their language, customs and ways of living on the land. Odawa Elder Liza Mosher describes this time in her life where she reconnected to her culture:

> For me, I've never known my home yet, because I went through that wandering stage, I wandered all over looking and searching, it wasn't until I walked into that Lodge that I found what I was looking for and then I finally came home because that Lodge is my home. And that's were my teachings are for my life and for the first time, hearing the teachings. I was raised in a Catholic home but I never could feel anything, it was prayers, you'd memorize those prayers but they don't mean nothing. But when you go into the Lodge, when you talk to the Creator, just like I'm talking to you. You feel good because it's coming from the heart, not from the mind, you don't memorize, when you memorize there is no feeling, there's no connection, but for me to talk to the Creator from the heart because feelings come with that, the tears come of happiness, of joy, of peace of mind and the respect of all creation at all times. (59)

For many Indigenous people ceremony is like *coming home*. Going to ceremony, taking part in ceremony can be a place where an individual learns purpose, identity and a sense of self-confidence. Mosher offers that ceremony is where she found herself. She explains that, "[b]y finding our identity, by going to ceremonies, going to Sweats, going to fast. For me, fasting is where most of my teachings are. Going out there and sitting with my Mother (the Earth)." (60)

Ceremonies have become the means to restore spiritual balance within one's self and with the world. Jeanette Armstrong refers to this process as "World renewal." (61) The concept is expressed through ceremonial processes, such as vision quests, fasts and sweats, to mention only a few examples. She writes, "The seasonal or annual practice to ceremonially and collectively incorporate the continuous new realities into the principles of harmony with the natural world is a spiritual journey for each individual." (62) Ceremony is used to bring harmony back into the lives of those who undergo the process, for multiple reasons. Today, as contemporary Indigenous people our minds are of two worldviews or two cultures and this can be very unbalancing.

> Our ancestors had different things to contend with on a yearly basis. In contemporary contexts, the Indigenous person has one mind that belongs to our Indigenous culture, our traditions and languages. The second mind-set is that which has been educated in western culture, beliefs and traditions. Indigenous people can no longer hide from the fact that western culture has greatly contributed to globalization, mass consumption, and a throw-away society that disregards any negative effects to the earth. Leroy Little Bear (Blackfoot) explains that the impact of westernization on the Indigenous consciousness is a fragmentary perceptive of the world, which he refers to as "jagged worldviews." (63)

Little Bear explains that he sees worldviews colliding in the minds of Indigenous people. Contemporary Indigenous people face life in urban environments, other cultures and foreign languages. More specifically, a *diasporic* feeling of disconnect to the land, customs, community and heritage that is rapidly spreading across Indigenous communities. Little Bear feels that colonization disrupted the Indigenous views of the world and introduced European-Western perspectives on the world, thus creating a 'jigsaw puzzle' in each person's mind. Thus, no contemporary Indigenous person can possibly have a complete Indigenous worldview, instead it is a fragmented lens. He notes,

> No one has a pure worldview that is 100 percent Indigenous or Eurocentric; rather, everyone has an integrated mind, a fluxing and ambidextrous consciousness, a pre-colonized consciousness that flows into a colonized consciousness and back again. It is this clash of worldviews that is at the heart of many current difficulties with effective means of social control in postcolonial North America. It is also this clash that suppresses diversity in choices and denies Aboriginal people harmony in their daily lives. (64)

With many Indigenous people returning to ceremony and educating themselves on their culture, often for the first time, they are attempting to restore themselves to a more balanced state of consciousness. At the very least, many are trying to come to terms with the damage done by colonization and asking themselves important questions about identity, culture and history.

Douglas Cardinal (Blackfoot) describes how he was educated through ceremony to dismantle the 'jigsaw puzzle' he had in his mind. He writes:

I had to be taken to medicine man Chief Smallboy's camp at a time when I was very ill. At the camp a lot of time was spent helping me become balanced internally. They healed me with their ceremonies. I was told that the world I had created in my mind was destroying me. I wasn't in harmony with who I was. In the ceremonies, to seek harmony within myself, I had to deal with the things inside that were destructive to me. (65)

Individuals searching for the sort of balance Cardinal received during his ceremonial experiences are vulnerable and need great regard, care and respect. Ceremony can teach these people their human worth in this world. As Indigenous people, ceremony offers us a reminder of our humanity in a world that is often inhumane when it comes to issues involving the rights of Indigenous peoples worldwide, the state of poverty, violence, starvation and poor water conditions. As Indigenous people, each of us is on our own journey of learning life's lessons as we move through this world till the day we pass over into the spirit world and join our ancestors.

Concluding Thoughts: Preparing for Autumn Ceremonies

Basil Johnston explains that,

Twice annually, in some rare cases four times, the Anishnabeg celebrated thanksgiving in ceremony. This did not replace the private acts of thanksgiving...In autumn just before the Anishnabeg went to their isolated wintering quarters there was a thanksgiving in spirit and form like that of the spring. Only the theme was different. (66)

As the summer ends and the fall season or *dgwaagi* in Ojibwe comes upon us, the land is transforming, changing as it prepares for the blanket of snow that will cover Mother the Earth in the next few months. The smell of the air seems a little bit fresher and crisper. The sounds of the trees is picking up as the fall storms prepare to arrive. The birds are beginning to gather to fly south, the small animals are running around searching for warm homes and the plants are dying back. Everything is preparing for that time of year when Mother Earth puts on her most beautiful dress of fall colours: reds, oranges, yellows and browns. That western wind *e-bngishmog* is starting to blow our way and we beginning to think about the fall ceremonies, which is a time that we give thanks for all the land has given us this past summer.

Ojibwe Elder Alex Skead has said that it is part of the Anishinaabe culture to give thanks. Learning to give thanks teaches us of our place in Creation, that it from Creation that we come from and should be thankful. Skead says,

...you look outside and that's our culture, and then there's time that you have to have thanksgiving. Like the change of the season, like it is going to be winter pretty soon and there is going to be snow and ice on the lake. And then the fall, like in the fall we have leaves that are falling. Everything is changing into colours. So that's why we have to give some thanksgiving. And before the hibernation, some of the animals are hibernating like the bear, and the chipmunks and snakes, what have you in this living world. (67)

I have good memories of attending ceremonial sweats and fasts for myself during the fall season and also being a helper for those going to fast during the fall. I recall one year when I was preparing for a ceremony and I went to the store the other day to purchase some a few small household things. Memories of being bombarded by sights and sounds of mothers with their children yelling at each other over shopping carts heaped with back-to-school supplies still remain with me. While those are typical fall activities we all witness every years, one year specifically stays will me. It was 2008 and I was going out to sweat and fall.

I recall the feelings that fall is surely here because aisles were filled with Halloween and Thanksgiving decorations of paper turkeys and brightly colored children's costumes. Both holidays flowing from Indigenous traditions of honoring our deceased ancestors, our family, friends, communities and the bounty harvested from the land in preparation for the winter. While I looked for tarps for my fall fasting lodge and some warm socks, I became overwhelmed by the noise of fighting families and the hurried carts flashing by me in a race for the next open cash register. As I reflected on my surroundings, I felt saddened by the commercialization of what essentially should be a time to slow down, reflect and honor what the land has given us. All you have to do is go to your local farmer's market throughout the months of spring to fall and see the bounty of food that land has produced or watch a fishermen carry their stringers of fish from the lakes and rivers or watch the hunters throughout the fall with their kills of deer, moose, duck and partridges to understand that we are blessed by the land. That particular year I felt the particular need to reconnect with the land and what it meant to have a relationship with nature and my identity as an Anishinaabe woman.

Americans and Canadians were not the first people in North America to have thanksgiving holidays. Although traditionally most Indigenous peoples of North America never had an *official* holiday marking a specific time or day to give thanks as we all now practice on our pre-scheduled Canadian and American Thanksgiving days. Yet fall is one of those traditional times of year to honour and renew our relationship with the natural world.

Most Indigenous peoples, however, tend to give thanks for life, food, family and friends all year long whenever we do our daily prayers to the Creator. Most Anishinaabe who observe and follow traditions get up in the morning, lay down their tobacco for the spirits and give thanks. Yet, we as Anishinaabe also mark the fall season with important feasts to celebrate the harvest from the land and preparation for winter.

In the fall of 2008 I was busily getting ready for that time when I would go out on the land to sit quietly with Mother the Earth, as well as give thanks for both water and food by fasting from both for several days. I prepared first by gathering my give-away gifts, tarps to construct my lodge, blankets, warm clothes to stay outdoors and my bundle. I always take joy in returning to the land, to dream amongst the trees and spend time with the tiny creatures that come to visit my lodge. That year I rejoiced in those moments that I drank my first sips of water and first bites of food after my fast was complete. I looked forward to seeing family and friends who feasted the conclusion of my fasting time and celebrated the abundance of food this year has brought us. After my ceremony I was filled with a new awareness of self, many new teachings and the renewal of my cultural connections to my people and the land. This is what ceremonial education means to a contemporary Anishinaabe.

To conclude this paper I offer the following poem by Basil Johnston, entitled, "Autumn Thanksgiving":

> The roses
> Enflamed the meadows
> With whites and scarlets.
>
> The robins
> Filled the summer days
> With their songs.
>
> The whitefish
> Flashed their silvered tails
> In lakes and streams.
>
> The corn
> Waxed firm and tall
> In sun and rain
>
> The deer
> Grew sleek and fat
> Upon the grasses.
>
> Our stories are full
> Our medicines are strong
> Our weapons are worn
> Our spirits are glad
> Kitche Manitou has been kind. (68)

In writing this paper, my goal was to share the importance of ceremony in the lives of Indigenous peoples in North America. I have utilized a variety of sources to illustrate how various scholars describe the dynamic nature of Indigenous ceremonies in the education, learning and knowledge gathering experiences of Indigenous people. It is critical that we as Indigenous people celebrate our identities and culture as the original peoples of Turtle Island. Further, we need to acknowledge that our people still practice the old ways, so that our children and our children's children can perform those same ceremonies generations after we have left this world for the spirit realm. As Willie Ermine explains, we still have those traditions and we are meant to pass them on to our children:

> The rituals and ceremonial observances still practiced by our Old ones in our tribal communities compel us to make more inward journeys. Tribal rituals are the calculated trajectories to the world within and any such journeys can only be propelled by the collective energy of a people ordained to explore that domain. The tribal ceremonies display with vivid multidimensional clarity the entries and pathways into this inner world of exciting mystery that has been touched by only the few who have become explorers of sacred knowing. Rituals and ceremonies are corporeal sacred acts that give rise to holy manifestations in the metaphysical world. Conversely, it is the metaphysical that constructs meaning in the corporeal. *Continuation of rituals and ceremonies will enable the children of those early spiritual explorers to advance the synthesized understanding of inner space.* (69)

◊ ◊ ◊ ◊ ◊ ◊

Renee E. Bedard is an Anishinaabe-kwe (Ojibwe) and a member of the Dokis First Nation. She currently is an assistant professor at Brock University in the Faculty of Education and works out of the Tecumseh Centre for Aboriginal Research and Education.

Notes

(1) Paula Gunn-Allen. The Sacred Hoop: Recovering the Feminine in American Indian Traditions. (Boston: Beacon Hill Press, 1992), 61.
(2) The term 360° vision comes from Jim Dumont, "Journey to Daylight-Land: Through Ojibwa Eyes" in Laurentian Review, (1976), 11.-23.
(3) Irving A. Hallowell, Culture & Experience (Schocken Paperback, 1967), 178.
(4) Basil Johnston. Ojibway Ceremonies. Toronto: McClelland & Stewart Inc., 1982, vii.
(5) Dumont. "Journey to Daylight-Land: Through Ojibwa Eyes" in Laurentian Review (1976), 35.

(6) Douglas Cardinal and Jeannette Armstrong. The Native Creative Process: A Collaborative Discourse between Douglas Cardinal and Jeanette Armstrong, (Penticton, British Columbia: Theytus Books, 1991), 49.

(7) Jim Dumont, 1976, 32.

(8) Jim Dumont, 1976, 35.

(9) Jim Dumont. 1976, 31.

(10) Jim Dumont. 1976, 31-32.

(11) Jim Dumont. 1976, 40.

(12) Jim Dumont, 1976, 31-32.

(13) Jim Dumont, 1976, 33.

(14) Jim Dumont, 1976, 33.

(15) Irving A. Hallowell, 1967, 178.

(16) Jim Dumont, 1976, 33.

(17) Jim Dumont, 1976, 33.

(18) Willie Ermine, "Aboriginal Epistemology." in First Nations Education in Canada: The Circle Unfolds, ed. Marie Battiste and Jean Barman. Vancouver: UBC Press, 1995, 103; Søren Kierkegaard. "Truth in subjectivity," in Reality, man and existence: Essential works of existentialism, ed.,H.J. Blackham. Revised (London, ON: Bantam, [1846] 1965).

(19) Willie Ermine, 1995, 103.

(20) Joseph Couture, "Explorations in Native Knowing," in The Cultural Maze: Complex Questions on Native Destiny in Western Canada, ed. John W. Friesen, (Calgary: Detselig, 1991) 57.

(21) Joseph Couture, "Explorations in Native Knowing,"1991, 57.

(22) Joseph Couture, "The Role of Native Elders: Emergent Issues," in The Cultural Maze: Complex Questions on Native Destiny in Western Canada, ed. John W. Friesen, (Calgary: Detselig, 1991), 1991, 208.

(23) Willie Ermine, 1995, 104.

(24) Peter Kulchyski, Don McCaskill and David Newhouse, eds. "Alex Skead (Ojibwe)," in In the Words of Elders: Aboriginal Cultures in Transition. (Toronto: University of Toronto Press, 1999), 182.

(25) Peter Kulchyski, et al., 1999, 182.

(26) Joseph Couture, "The Role of Native Elders: Emergent Issues," 1991, 208.

(27) Joseph Couture, "The Role of Native Elders: Emergent Issues," 1991, 207-208. Emphasis Added.

(28) Joseph Couture, "The Role of Native Elders: Emergent Issues," 1991, 208.

(29) Canada, Royal Commission on Aboriginal Peoples: Report of the Royal Commission on Aboriginal Peoples. Volume 3, Gathering Strength, (Ottawa: Canada Communications Group, 1996), 527.

(30) Pam Colorodo, "Bridging Native Science and Western Science," in Convergence, Vol. XXI, Number 2/3, (1988), 58.

(31) Joseph Couture, "The Role of Native Elders: Emergent Issues," 1991, 213.

(32) Colorado, 1988, 50.

(33) Colorado, 1988, 57.

(34) Colorado, 1988, 56.

(35) Joseph Couture, "Explorations in Native Knowing,"1991, 61.

(36) Shirley Williams, Eshkintam Nishinaabemang Mzinagan: Introduction to Nishinaabewin. (Wikwemikong, Ontario: Neganigwane Company, 1996), 55.

(37) Edward Benton-Banai. The Mishomis Book: The Voice of the Ojibway. Hayward, Wisonsin: Indian Country Communications Inc., 1988, 16.

(38) Vine Deloria, Jr. For This Land: Writings on Religion in America, ed. James Treat, (New York and London: Routledge, 1999), 244-245.

(39) Vine Deloria, 1999, 245.

(40) Vine Deloria, 1999, 245.

(41) Douglas Cardinal and Jeannette Armstrong, 1991, 42.

(42) Douglas Cardinal and Jeannette Armstrong, 1991, 58.

(43) Gerald McMaster, "Towards and Aboriginal Art History," in Native American Art in the Twentieth Century, ed. W. Jackson Rushing III, (London: Routledge, 1999), 88.

(44) Gerald McMaster, 1999, 88.

(45) Willie Ermine,1995, 106.

(46) Willie Ermine, 1995, 105.

(47) Willie Ermine, 1995, 105.

(48) Willie Ermine,1995, 106.

(49) Willie Ermine,1995, 106.

(50) Pam Colorodo, 1988, 52.

(51) Vine Deloria, "Power and Place: Equal Personality," in Indian Education in America, ed. Vine Deloria. (Boulder, Colorado: American Indian Science and Engineering Society, 1991).

(52) Willie Ermine,1995, 107.

(53) Shirley Williams, 1996, 59.

(54) Willie Ermine,1995, 107.

(55) Basil Johnston, "How do we learn language? What do we learn?" in Talking on the Page: Editing Aboriginal Oral Texts, eds. Laura J. Murray and Keren Rice, (Toronto: University of Toronto Press, 1999), 44.

(56) Joseph E. Couture, "Explorations in Native Knowing," 1991, 59.

(57) Joseph E. Couture, "Explorations in Native Knowing," 1991, 59.

(58) Joseph E. Couture, "Explorations in Native Knowing," 1991, 59.

(59) Peter Kulchyski, et al., "Liza Mosher (Odawa)." in In the Words of Elders: Aboriginal Cultures in Transition. (Toronto: University of Toronto Press, 1999), 145-146.

(60) Peter Kulchyski, et al., 1999, 146.

(61) Douglas Cardinal and Jeannette Armstrong, 1991, 54.

(62) Douglas Cardinal and Jeannette Armstrong, 1991, 54.

(63) Leroy Little Bear, "Jagged Worldviews Colliding," in Reclaiming Indigenous Voice and Vision, ed. Marie Battiste. (Vancouver: UBC Press, 2000), 84-85.

(64) Leroy Little Bear, 2000, 85.

(65) Douglas Cardinal and Jeannette Armstrong, 1991, 54.

(66) Basil Johnston, 1976, 144.

(67) Peter Kulchyski, et al., "Alex Shead (Ojibwe)," 1999, 185.

References

Benton-Banai, Edward. The Mishomis Book: The Voice of the Ojibway. Hayward, Wisonsin: Indian Country Communications Inc., 1988.

Canada, Royal Commission on Aboriginal Peoples: Report of the Royal Commission on Aboriginal Peoples. Volume 3, Gathering Strength, (Ottawa: Canada Communications Group, 1996).

Cardinal, Douglas and Jeannette Armstrong, The Native Creative Process: A Collaborative Discourse between Douglas Cardinal and Jeanette Armstrong, (Penticton, British Columbia: Theytus Books, 1991).

Colorodo, Pam, "Bridging Native Science and Western Science," in Convergence, Vol. XXI, Number 2/3, (1988): 101-112.

Couture, Joseph, "Explorations in Native Knowing," in The Cultural Maze: Complex Questions on Native Destiny in Western Canada, ed. John W. Friesen, (Calgary: Detselig, 1991), 53-73.

—. "The Role of Native Elders: Emergent Issues," in The Cultural Maze: Complex Questions on Native Destiny in Western Canada, ed. John W. Friesen, (Calgary: Detselig, 1991), 201-217.

Deloria Jr., Vine, For This Land: Writings on Religion in America, ed. James Treat, (New York and London: Routledge, 1999).

Dumont, Jim, "Journey to Daylight-Land: Through Ojibwa Eyes" in Laurentian Review, (1976):11-23.

Ermine, Willie, "Aboriginal Epistemology." in First Nations Education in Canada: The Circle Unfolds, ed. Marie Battiste and Jean Barman. (Vancouver: UBC Press, 1995), 101-112.

Gunn-Allen, Paula, The Sacred Hoop: Recovering the Feminine in American Indian Traditions. (Boston: Beacon Hill Press, 1992).

Hallowell, Irving A., Culture & Experience. (Schocken Paperback, 1967).

Johnston, Basil, "How do we learn language? What do we learn?" in Talking on the Page: Editing Aboriginal Oral Texts, eds. Laura J. Murray and Keren Rice, (Toronto: University of Toronto Press, 1999.

Kierkegaard, Søren, "Truth in subjectivity," in Reality, man and existence: Essential works of existentialism, ed.,H.J. Blackham. Revised. (London, ON: Bantam, [1846] 1965).

Kulchyski, Peter, Don McCaskill and David Newhouse, eds. "Alex Skead (Ojibwe)," in In the Words of Elders: Aboriginal Cultures in Transition. (Toronto: University of Toronto Press, 1999), 141-167.

—. Liza Mosher (Odawa). "In the Words of Elders: Aboriginal Cultures in Transition." (Toronto: University of Toronto Press, 1999), 145-146.

Little Bear, Leroy, "Jagged Worldviews Colliding," in Reclaiming Indigenous Voice and Vision, ed. Marie Battiste. (Vancouver: UBC Press, 2000), 77-85.

McMaster, Gerald, "Towards and Aboriginal Art History," in Native American Art in the Twentieth Century, ed. W. Jackson Rushing III, (London: Routledge, 1999), 81-96.

Williams Shirley, Eshkintam Nishinaabemang Mzinagan: Introduction to Nishinaabewin. (Wikwemikong, Ontario: Neganigwane Company, 1996).

Grassroots Indigenous Epistemologies: Native Non-Governmental Organizations and the Environment.

María Cristina Manzano-Munguía

.... We cannot preserve our nations unless we take action to restore pride in our traditions, achieve economic self-sufficiency, develop independence of mind, and display courage in defence of our lands and rights. Only by committing ourselves to these goals can we hope to look into the future and see ourselves re-emerging as peoples ready to take our rightful places in the world. The path to self-determination is uphill and strewn with obstacles, but we must take it; the threat to our existence as indigenous people is so immediate that we cannot afford not to. The only way we can survive is to recover our strength, our wisdom, and our solidarity by honouring and revitalizing the core of our traditional teachings.... (Taiaiake Alfred 1999: xii).

Over the past three decades there has been an increasing interest on curriculum design and implementation of First Nations or Native American environmental programs at universities and colleges across Canada and the United States (see for instance the work of Rice 2013). However, the vast majority of the academia and program designers are reluctant to accept environmental Indigenous epistemologies and still the top-down model of either the "Western episteme"(Escobar 1995: 7) or the Euro-Western environmental content (Peat 1994; Rice 2013) dominates the learning process in North America. Here the battle for truth (Foucault 1980) entails the acceptance and practice of Indigenous "nature-based and environmental sustaining philosophies from Elders" (Rice 2013: 67) and not from Western academic authorities who did not have to give up their land, ideals, dreams, culture, history and freedom (see Churchill 2003; Escobar 1997; Esteva 1997; Manuel and Posluns 1974; Thayer 2000).

Despite this dreadful scenario, Native non-governmental organizations (NNGOs) not only strive to meet the changing needs of their service community, but also revive the practice of Indigenous knowledge and traditions in urban areas across Canada (Chester Langille Interview 2007; Manzano-Munguía 2007). This chapter explores how environmental Indigenous knowledge is being deployed through the work of Elders who are being housed at Native non-governmental organization in urban centres. Specifically, I will focus on a Native organization located in London, Ontario. In doing so, I will rely on my fieldwork experience (2003-2007) while conducting my doctoral research (see Manzano-Munguía 2009). Even though it was not the thematic of my research it emphasizes grassroots constructions of knowledge on environment, which gives force and saliency to Indigenous epistemologies.

In the last five decades, an increasing number of Western scholars such as cultural anthropologists, archaeologists, and historians have been challenging the authenticity of Indigenous traditions and knowledge (e.g., Briggs 1996; Gill 1987; Haley & Wilcoxon 1997; Linnekin 1991). These scholars are oblivious of Elders' knowledge and advice, which are view as "bodies of knowledge and corresponding codes of value" (Churchill 2003a:276; see also Alfred 1999, 2005 and Deloria 1995). Moreover, Elders' oral history is valuable and there is no need to search for its' authenticity. Cruickshank (1990) and Basso's (1996) pioneer work on Elders oral history and Indigenous grassroots constructions of knowledge is inspiring and ignited the path for acknowledging and giving relevance to grassroots construed epistemologies. For example, Chinua Achebe (2001) sees himself as a deconstructionist of colonial images and writings about Africa and Africans. Based on his personal experience and from a native point of view, Achebe's critique to colonialism creates the foundation for an African epistemology, which is difficult to achieve due to the internal and external constraints that imperialist nations imposed upon African intelligentsia. He describes three inducements for becoming a writer and an activist: the overpowering urge to tell a story; his experience of having a unique story to tell; and the process of getting in trouble (2001: 39).

Following Achebe, I feel the urge to tell a story about the grassroots epistemologies that Native non-governmental organizations (NNGOs) are encouraging and reviving on issues pertaining to Indigenous environment. Drawing from Elder's stories and advice this knowledge is being deployed in multiple settings across the urban sprawl. In doing so, I will first give a general overview of these organizations in Canada, specifically in London, Ontario. Second, I specifically address the teaching of environmental Indigenous epistemologies by looking at one case study within an NNGO, which illustrates the work achieved at the grassroots level in deconstructing Euro-Western epistemologies.

Native Non-governmental Organizations from the Ground-Up

Over the last three decades there has been an increasing academic interest in the myriad types of organizations labelled as non-governmental (see Edwards and Hulme 1996; Fisher 1997; Markowitz 2001; Martens 2002). This broad category encompasses a wide range of NGOs studies that look at community or government-based structures, grass-roots development programs, the defence of human rights and social justice programs, and pro-environment conservation initiatives and programs in local, national, and transnational contexts. Despite earlier attempts to consolidate NGOs, this category remained unclear and ambivalent. As Martens (2002) puts it: "…many studies fail(ed) to offer any definition of the term NGO as if the components and the understanding of the phrase [were of] common knowledge" (2002: 272). Coined in 1945 by the United Nations (UN) the term "non-governmental organization" related to international bodies accredited for consulting purposes (Martens 2002: 271) but NGOs proliferated outside the UN context in industrialized, developing, and third world countries.

By the 1980s these organizations proliferated and engaged in community-based initiatives mostly funded through government aid agencies (Edwards and Hulme 2002). NGOs embodied a series of calculated actions from governments and their official aid agencies honing new neo-liberal economic projects and policy agendas. Fisher suggests analyzing "the impact of NGO practices on relations of power among individuals, communities, and the state" (1997: 441). Consequently, anthropologists have looked at power relations in political economy studies (see Blaser, Feit and McRae 2004; Markowitz 2001). While thinking about the complexity and praxis of this concept with Native organizations in urban centres, I envisioned an alternative epistemological framework by juxtaposing theoretical constructs with ethnographic exemplars (Manzano-Munguía 2007, 2009). Native non-governmental organizations (NNGOs), at the grassroots level, are flexible and shifting community entities rather than fixed categories. Thus, Aboriginal people[1] in urban centres view these organizations as non-governmental, cultural learning centres of their traditions and Indigenous knowledge, as well as servicing community entities.

For instance, the NNGO known as Nokee Kwe Occupational Skills and Development Incorporated located in London, Ontario falls within this rationale. this organization describes itself in the following terms:

> Nokee Kwe is Ojibwa for "working woman" and in 1977 through the Native Women's Workshop, a program to serve Native Women in London was created. Nokee Kwe, founded on Aboriginal principles[,] is a community-based and client focused charitable organization; we encourage and support self-determination and personal development through individualized workplace preparation, life skills and vocational training. Incorporated as Nokee Kwe Occupational Skill Development Inc. in 1983 to sponsor a funded employment readiness training program, our organization has always been at the forefront of providing services to unemployed and underemployed Native and Non Native individuals. At Nokee Kwe, we will be known as an organization that is a leader in the provision of holistic and comprehensive services to Aboriginal and Non-Aboriginal individuals, assisting them in making meaningful life choices (Nokee Kwe web site; Manzano-Munguía 2007: 452).

I conducted archival research in 2007-08 at Nokee Kwe and most of the documents described in a limited manner the establishment of this NNGO and the work of its founders. During the second half of the twentieth century there was a major interest from the state (specifically

---

[1] Aboriginal people include Indian, Inuit and Métis as defined by the Constitution Act 1982 s. 35.

55

the Department of the Secretary of State) to support and work in collaboration with Native people, the vast majority females, who migrated from reserves to urban areas such as London. Most of them escaped sexual and physical abuse, oppression and discrimination by the band government on-reserve, and the need for services (see also Maracle 2003; Ekos Research Associates Incorporation and Anishinabek Consultants Inc. 2006; RCAP 1996b: 570-79). By 1977 a group of women voluntarily formed an ad hoc committee that recognized the need to work for the betterment of Native women and their families living in Southwestern Ontario. These individuals were: Joyce Albert from the Chippewas of the Thames, Barbara Antone from the Oneida of the Thames, Carole Aziz representing the Department of the Secretary of State, and Donna Phillips from London. They successfully applied to the Secretary of State for funding to sponsor their Native Women's Gathering, which included guest speakers, seminars and workshops. This initial workshop led to the formation of the Native Women's Workshop, a non-profit organization incorporated on 14 January 1983.

This Native organization had the following objectives: to develop programs and resources unique to Native women that met their socioeconomic needs, to promote better understanding and co-operation between Native and non-Native people, and to support and encourage Native women to participate in the development of their community (Nokee Kwe archives Workshop documents). Since 1977 the Native Women's Workshop organized a series of workshops and gatherings that not only supported Native women's well-being and socio-economic development through Elders' teachings, but it also included the revival of their Native identity. The following examples of gatherings and workshops are illustrative. In April of 1978 the "Native Women Speaking Together" workshop, funded by the Secretary of State, had 100 female participants from Southwestern Ontario who learned and voiced their concerns about their health, nutrition, substance abuse, effective parenting, Native women's rights, and their traditions. By 1979 the Secretary of State sponsored the "Native Youth Gathering" with 150 participants, including elders and youth; the gathering's emphasis was on Native culture, identity and education. In 1980 the same sponsor supported the "Elders' Gathering" and the "Teaching of our Elders" in 1981. Both events emphasized the importance of Elders and the need to preserve their knowledge for future generations.

As early as 1981 there was an employment project that provided contact, support, and liaison from fieldworkers and two facilitators to work with Native women who lived in rural and urban areas and to target their social and economic needs. This project was called "Native Women Working for Tomorrow" and was funded by the local Employment Assistance Program. It sought to develop resource materials and kits with information about Native women's needs and to build the resources for their future. In the same year this NNGO conducted a "Child Care Research Project" funded by Canada Community Development Project; it documented the need for day care within the

56

London Native community. A survey evaluated the feasibility of establishing a Native Day Care Centre. It was not until 1983, however, that "The Four Winds Day Care" was incorporated and housed other projects for children and their mothers.

In May 1982 and April 1983 the program known as "Nokee Kwe Native Women's Employment and Skills Program" established training programs for Native women who, after completion, would be able to obtain meaningful employment. The funds came from the local Employment Assistance Program. In May 1983 Nokee Kwe Occupational Skills Development became incorporated and left the Native Women's Workshop organization. The comments offered by Bryan Loucks, an Anishinaabe leader from Walpole Island, will further illustrate the naissance of this employment Native organization:

> ... One of the natural evolutions that happen[ed] [in London] was that we were able to evolve a women focus within the Native people in the Multicultural centre which very quickly took leadership and direction from women such as Barbara Antone, . . . Colleen Nadjiwon-Johnson, Donna Phillips,. . . so there were a number of them who started to work on women issues. So that they had a joint office to the Native Peoples Resource Centre that was called Native Women Workshop. They started to plan and separate... this is where Nokee Kwe found its way . . . and Nokee Kwe was then officially established (Interview with Bryan Loucks 2007; Manzano-Munguía 2007: 452).

Consequently, Nokee Kwe was indeed founded under the premise that "Native" women's needs were not being addressed through the services provided by social service agencies and government institutions. The founding committee was not solely composed of "concerned Native community members" but it also included a state agent from the Department of the Secretary of State. The state interest in funding Native organizations across Canada followed the call from a broader development in Canadian politics, as Dyck (1983: 198) stated, "the rise of participatory democracy". Indeed this process of "participatory democracy" triggered the funding of Native organizations across Canada during the decade of the 1960 and 70s.

However, giving credit to the Department of State for igniting the process of creating Native organizations during the third quarter of the twentieth century is erroneous. The "political powerlessness" of Aboriginal people, as Dyck (1983: 201) mistakenly argues, needs to be deconstructed (see Miller 2004). Instead the creation of Native non-governmental organizations, like Nokee Kwe, should be seen as a linked project to promote the state and Aboriginal people's interests. This process has been referred in the governmentality literature as the "alignment of interests" (see Miller and Rose 1990). Some of these intersections pertained to employment, training, and economic programs, health programs, educational programs for adults, youth, and children, youth leadership, environmental and development programs. The interests that might not be part of these intersections relate to the incorporation of the traditional teachings within the "official" programs (e.g., Dream Catcher), the use of the Medicine Wheel in the management of the organization, the use of consensus rather than voting for decisions, Elders' involvement in training events, programming and advising for direction in management and traditional practices.

The aforementioned case illustrated what became a pattern, rather than the exception in the establishment of other Natives organizations across Canada. This proliferation was also present in London, Ontario particularly in the last quarter of the twentieth century. For instance, Native the First Nations Housing Co-operative Corporation and the Native Inter-Tribal Housing Cooperative offer housing services. Others give shelter and rehabilitation from addictions services such as, Zhaawananong Women's Shelter, At^Lohsa Native Family Healing Services, the Salvation Army Centre of Hope (which service the non-Aboriginal clientele as well). The N'Amerind Friendship Centre (Life Long Care Program), At^Lohsa Native Family Healing Services, and the Southwest Ontario Aboriginal Health Access Centre offer health services. Nokee Kwe Occupational Skill Development Incorporation and the N'amerind Friendship Centre offer employment and training services. Advocacy and action services are available through the Iroquois and Allied Indians. And post-secondary support services are found at the Indigenous Resource Centre at Western University (formerly known as The University of Western Ontario) and the First Nations Centre at Fanshawe College. Aboriginal people are not only accessing resources from these urban organizations, but they are also socializing and reconstituting their Native identity there, and thus forging a sense of community (see Darnell and Manzano-Munguía 2005: 176-77).

During my fieldwork period (2003-2007) I conducted a number of interviews with a few Aboriginal individuals who, temporarily, resided in London and expressed their views about Native organizations. For instance, Ricardo, from a First Nation community, stated the absence of Native organizations in the area by the 1960s but:

> Now things are different... you have the shelter, housing, the [F]riendship [Centre], even the university has a place for Indians .... I went there [N'Amerind] to check with someone over the rumours that students [pursuing post-secondary education] will have to pay taxes and that is again the government trying to do things without talking [to] us ... the students ....
> I talked and talked and I said what I think: that post-secondary education is a treaty right and the government is attacking our Indian rights and as I said at that time: "they [Indian Affairs] will just affect Indians with status cards [First Nations] and there are just a few of them with scholarships and bursaries ... this means to go back again and remain without university education for Indians. Holy shit ... this is what they [Indian Affairs] want from us to

remain dummies but it's not going to happen". I was told [by the N'Amerind staff] that this was just a proposal and has not yet occurred. Aboriginal leaders, Native organizations [such as N'Amerind, Nokee Kwe, and At^Lohsa] and students are against this and we are putting a lot of pressure [talks, social media, and news releases] to the government (Interview with Paul 2005).

Carol also expressed:

> In Health S.O.A.H.A.C. [Southwest Ontario Aboriginal Health Access Centre] they have traditional healers, ... healing ceremonies, and they are pretty knowledgeable of the culture.... I know that people [referring to the staff and Elders].... I met some of them and they are not with the government they are knowledgeable of our culture. I think, or knowing people in those places and meeting people open up all kind of learning about our traditions, how to care for our people and everything... (Interview with Carol 2005).

Richard also expressed how these organizations help Aboriginal people with government paper work:

> ... people from Indian Affairs [INAC] are there [pointing to the document] and sometimes these Native organizations will help you understand the documents or .... to complete the .... applications. You have to play by their rules and abide to them (Interview with Richard 2007).

These narratives are the storied experiences (Darnell 2004) that exemplify how experiences flow from one individual to another and create a concept. It is this fluidity that gives meaning to my proposition that Aboriginal people identify and define these Native organizations as non-governmental even though the vast majority is government funded. With this in mind, I look at how teaching environmental Indigenous epistemologies illustrates the work achieved at the grassroots level within an NNGO.

Grassroots Teachings at NNGOs

In 2007 I was invited to attend the Native Traditions Workshop facilitated by Elder and Ojibwa teacher Mary Sturgeon at At^lohsa. The workshop included, but was not limited to, teachings on the importance of offering tobacco, the Ojibwe Traditional Values Teachings of the Seven Grandfathers, our Mother Earth, the Strawberry Moon Ceremony, and the importance of making medicine pouches. It was a different kind of learning experience which was not regulated and defined by Western episteme on issues related to how to relate and honour our environment. Approximately fifteen female Aboriginals attended this workshop and we were very enthusiastic. Elder Mary explained to us that each teaching and tradition differed from Nation to Nation but that there are "commonalities... (t)he sameness refers to the basic Truth that interweaves all cultural ways of living" (Elder Mary Sturgeon 2007). One of the teachings included our understanding of Mother Earth, which is related with our mind, spirit, heart, and body... all our relations. It should be the base of any Indigenous environmental course:

> The earth is mother to all creatures.
> On, within, and above.
> We are all related.
> Whatever one does,
> Or what happens to another,
> Touches all (Mary Sturgeon 2007, Native Traditions Workshop at At^lohsa).

Her teaching is concomitant with other women who are also recognized within the community and at Native organizations. For instance, Tammy Fournier, Ojibwe Medicine Woman, whose teachings on Mother Earth emphasized:

> Our bodies are like Grandmother Moon and Aakii (Mother Earth), they never take a day off either, waking or sleeping, unless it's their time to go. I remember an elder teaching me in the early [1990s] that Mother Earth and our greater relatives are responsible for the electricity which keeps our hearts pumping; something to do with a certain vibration that comes in when our spirits enter the womb of our human mothers.... Our elders constantly remind us to get back to our ways of our Mother Earth [to eat on a Mother Earth monodiet, adding single food substances as they were in season] and take care of her so we can take care of ourselves, our families, friends, communities and nations.

Medicine Woman, Wendy Hill recently shared a very important message from her grandfather. He [Grandfather] shared that we must transform our approach to Land Claims to Land Preservation. This way, everybody is included and will support the cause.

So when we celebrate Earth Day on April 22nd and everyday this April (Naabdin Giizis –Snowcrust Moon or Kawa'skattoch Giizis –glittering snow on lake month or Namegine Giizis –Sucker Moon), let us remember how all of our coloured hearts belong to Aakii, Mother Earth, as we walk and talk....

Let us choose carefully [the products we eat and use] and remember to walk softly on our Mother as we are taught, so she is there for us when we need for generations to come (2007: 5).

NNGOs support in an on-going manner the teaching of Indigenous knowledge and traditions. It is always a safe learning environment that connects grassroots knowledge with people's experiences. Native scholars are not the only ones contesting categories and paradigms that

60

are not based from Indigenous epistemologies. Environment Indigenous knowledge that is being offered at universities and colleges is not based on First Nations teachings and traditions. As Stephen Augustine (2005: 2), Hereditary Chief of Sigenitog, noted:

> Oral traditions, what is left, remembered or recorded, can serve as part of the answer. Our peoples have been solving and adapting to problems and situations (environmental catastrophes) for a long time. Knowledge and language explained everything in indigenous contexts. Knowledge, spirit and place connected us to the land. We only need to locate ourselves within that whole and that forms our foundation.

What is needed, as other communities members have noted in this conference, is to place Indigenous paradigms as tools that will help the academia deconstruct their Western constructs into a more reflexively constituted concepts that will reflect the praxis and knowledge of Indigenous people who are "being studied".

Conclusion

This chapter conveyed the idea that Native organizations (NNGOs) are non-governmental from a based on what Aboriginal people articulated while accessing the services and programs offered by these organizations in urban centres across Canada. In other words, alternative epistemologies construct and define what these organizations stand for and how they work from the ground-up.

Moreover, within these organizations Aboriginal people learn about Indigenous knowledge and traditions, such as environmental Indigenous epistemologies. The example elaborated on Mother Earth illustrates the work achieved at the grassroots level in deconstructing Euro-Western epistemologies. However, there are some limitations imposed to the present study. On the one hand, future studies need to explore the ways in which Native non-governmental organizations engage on giving force and revival to Indigenous epistemologies through the words of their Elders and other Indigenous scholars. On the other hand, we need to examine if Native organizations are able to connect with other non-Native institutions such as universities, government organizations, and learning institutes in order to give recognition and acceptance of other models of creating knowledge.

So what theoretical model is necessary to understand this complex situation? I think the Fourth World model (Manuel and Posluns 1974) may be the answer for creating an alternative Indigenous epistemology based on First Nations' principles and needs:

Our Identity as Indian peoples must be enshrined in the fundamental law of Canada. We do not need either the British North America Act or the Indian Act to give us our identity. We need them to tell us what

Canada's attitude to us is likely to be. We cannot talk about a partnership that is not written down on a paper that all parties understand and that is put beyond the easy grasp of governments that change from day to day (Manuel & Posluns 1974:232).

> ... We will need to support many of our own programs.... In one sense, this is nothing new. Indian people have always supported our own institutions and organizations, long before we were made dependent. Throughout this past century of struggle, Indian people have raised vast sums of money to support their leaders. We would never have survived through this past century if we had been entirely dependent on government handouts and lacked our own tradition of giving and sharing (Manuel & Posluns 1974:251).

Only time will tell if the model of the Fourth World could be applied to Indigenous epistemologies. I will end my analysis with this proposition in order to give force and saliency to Indigenous epistemologies forged from the bottom-up in urban and on-Reserve contexts.

◊ ◊ ◊ ◊ ◊ ◊

María Cristina Manzano-Munguía is a professor and researcher in the Sociocultural Anthropology graduate program at the Institute of Social Science and Humanities "Alfosno Vélez Pliego" (ICSyH) at the Benemérita Universidad Autónoma de Puebla (BUAP). She is member of the National Research Council (SNI) of the National System of Science and Technology (CONACYT) Level 1 in Mexico. She has published on issues related to Aboriginal-State relations, Indian policy and legislation, Native non-governmental organizations, Indigenous forced transnationalism, Indigenous diaspora, and Aboriginal leaders in urban centres. Her current research interests include fIndigenous forced transnationalism across borderlands (Mexico, Canada and the United States) and the Transpacific relations between Mexico and China.

Author e-mail: mmanzanomunguia@gmail.com.

References

Achebe, Chinua. 2001. *Home and Exile.* New York: Anchor Books.
Alfred, Taiaiake.
1999. *Peace, Power, Righteousness. An Indigenous Manifesto.* Toronto: Oxford University Press.
2005. *Wasase. Indigenous Pathways of Action and Freedom.* Toronto, ON: Broadview Press.
Augustine, Stephen. 2005. *Termites, beavers, and little red experimental mice.* Unpublished manuscript.

Basso, Keith 1996 *Wisdom sits in places.* New Mexico: University of New Mexico Press.

Blaser, Mario, Harvey A. Feit and Glenn McRae (editors). 2004. In the Way of Development. Indigenous Peoples, Life Projects and Globalization. London: Zed Books Ltd.

Briggs, Charles. 1996. The politics of discursive authority in research on the "invention of tradition." *Cultural Anthropology* 11: 435-69.

Churchill, Ward. *2003. Acts of Rebellion The Ward Churchill Reader.* New York: Routledge, 2003.

Constitution Act. 1982. RSC. Ottawa: Government Services Canada.

Cruikshank, Julie. 1990. *Life lived like a story.* Nebraska: University of Nebraska Press.

Darnell, Regna. 2004 "Qualitative demographics of aboriginal urban-rural migration: the Persistence of Nomadic Habits". In the *Proceedings of the 35th Algonquian Conference.* Edited by Wolfart, H. Pp: 75-89. Winnipeg, Manitoba: University of Manitoba Press.

Darnell, Regna and Maria Cristina Manzano-Munguía. 2005. Nomadic Legacies and Urban Algonquian Residence. In the *Proceedings of the 36th Algonquian Conference.* Edited by Wolfart, H. Pp: 173-186. Winnipeg, Manitoba: University of Manitoba Press.

Deloria, Vine, Jr. 1995 *Red Earth, White Lies. Native Americans and the Myth of Scientific Fact.* Toronto: Scribner.

Dyck, Noel. 1983. Representation and Leadership of a Provincial Indian Association. In *The Politics if Indianness: Case Studies of Native Ethnopolitics in Canada.* Edited by Adrian Tanner. Pp: 197-306. St.John's, Newfoundland: The Institute of Social and Economic Research Memorial University of Newfoundland.

Edwards, Michael and David Hulme (editors). 1996. *Beyond the Magic Bullet: NGO Performance and Accountability in the Post-Cold War World.* West Hartford, CT: Kumarian.

Edwards, Michael and David Hulme. 2002. NGO Performance and Accountability: Introduction and Overview. In *Changing Challenges for NGDO Management.* Edited by Michael Edwards and Alan Fowler. Pp: 187-203. London: Earthscan Publications Ltd.

Escobar, Arturo. 1995. *Encountering Development. The Making and Unmaking of the Third World.* Princeton, New Jersey: Princeton University Press.

Esteva, Gustavo. 1997. Basta! Mexican Indians say 'Enough!' In *The Post-Development Reader.* Edited by Majid Rahnema and Victoria Bawtree. Pp: 302-306. Nova Scotia: Fernwood Publishing Ltd.

Fisher, William. 1997. Doing Good? The Polictics and Antipolitics of NGOS Practices. *Annual Review of Anthropology* 26:439-464.

Foucault, Michel.

1980. *Power/Knowledge: Selected Interviews and Other Writings 1972-1977.* Edited by Colin Gordon. London: The Harverster Press.

1991. Politics and the study of discourse. In *The Foucault Effect. Studies in Governmentality.* Edited by Graham Burchell, Colin Gordon and Peter Miller. Pp:53-72. Chicago: University of Chicago Press.

Gill, Sam D. 1987. *Mother Earth: an American story*. Chicago: University Press.

Haley, Brian and Larry R. Wilcoxon. 1997 Anthropology and the making of Chumash Tradition. *Current Anthropology* (38):761-790.

Linnekin, Jocelyn. 1991. Cultural Invention and the Dilemma of Authenticity. *American Anthropologist* 93: 446-449.

Manuel, George and Michael Posluns. 1974. The Fourth World An Indian Reality. Don Mills, Ontario: Collier-Macmillan Canada Ltd.

Manzano-Munguía, María Cristina.

2007. "Conceptualizing Native Non-Government Organizations in Canada: An ethnographic approach". The International Journal of Interdisciplinary Social Sciences 2 (1): 449-459.

2009. Mediating Aboriginal-State Relations through Native Non-Governmental Organizations and Aboriginal Leaders: An Alternative Model. Unpublished Doctoral Dissertation. The University of Western Ontario, London, Ontario.

Markowitz, Lisa. 2001. Finding the Field: Notes on the Ethnography of NGOs. *Human Organization* (60): 40-46.

Martens, Kerstin. 2002. Mission Impossible? Defining Nongovernmental Organizations. In *Voluntas: International Journal of Voluntary and Nonprofit Organizations* 13(3): 271-285.

Miller, James Rodger. 2004. *Reflections on Native-Newcomer Relations*. Selected Essays. Toronto: University of Toronto Press.

Miller, Peter and Nikolas Rose. 1990. Governing economic life. In *Economy and Society* 19:1-31.

Nokee Kwe web site.: http://nokeekwe.ca/

Nokee Kwe Archives Workshop documents (undated).

Peat, David. 1994. *Lighting the Seventh Fire: The Spiritual Ways, Healing, and Science of the Native American*. New York: Citadel.

Rice, Brian. 2013. "Bridging Academia and Indigenous Environmental Science: Is It Too Late?" In *The Nature of Empires and the Empires of Nature Indigenous Peoples and the Great Lakes Environment*. Edited by Karl Hele. Pp: 67-84. Waterloo, Ontario: Wilfrid Laurier University Press.

Thayer, Millie. 2000. Travelling Feminisms: From Embodied Women to Gendered Citizenship. In *Global Ethnography: Forces, Connections, and Imaginations in a Postmodern World*. Edited by Michael Burawoy et al. Pp: 203-233. California: University of California Press.

◊ ◊ ◊ ◊ ◊ ◊

PART II -- ENVIRONMENTAL INDIGENOUS IMAGERY

Anecdote of Dominion: Industrial Sand Exploitation on Bkejwanong Territory in the Late 19th and Early 20th Century.

Rick Fehr

Dominion

The history of industrial sand extraction on the Walpole Island First Nation (known henceforth as Bkejwanong Territory – where the waters divide) reveals a concerted effort to make inanimate the natural forces that actively create the Indigenous territory. The sand in question is located on Squirrel Island, on the southernmost portion of the St. Clair River delta in present-day southwestern Ontario. In the late 19th and early 20th centuries, Canadian Indian Agents and industrialists literally re-wrote the cosmology of Bkejwanong Territory to justify the exploitation of its sand for short term profit.
Colonization by European settlers and colonial governments has always been met with resistance on Bkewjanong Territory. The Three Fires Council of the Ojibwe, Potawatomi and Odawa peoples of the Anishinaabeg nation that live there often assert that they know the territory, as they have called it home since Creation. Culture and tradition spring from this experience and root the Anishinaabeg to the territory in ways unknown to industrial settler society. Community historian Dean Jacobs contends that when outsiders encountered the territory in ignorance they often paid the price (1). The territory had not been *terra nullius*, nor had it been a mirror image of every other place they had encountered or conquered. An intimate knowledge of the place had been lacking in many of these instances and the respect for Indigenous Knowledge had been almost if not entirely absent.

The lack of meaningful engagement by outsiders underlies the colonial and later industrial history of the area, where social marginalization and ecocide are constant reminders of this disconnect. This lack of engagement and assumption of being has long been the hallmark of imperial and economic dominion across North America, where the headlong rush through the industrial revolution wreaked simultaneous havoc on nature and Indigenous peoples. One such person to note the entirely antagonistic relationship with the land was Wallace Stevens, the early twentieth century American poet who expressed quite poignantly the constant struggle underway,

I placed a jar in Tennessee,
And round it was, upon a hill.
It made the slovenly wilderness
Surround that hill.

The wilderness rose up to it,
And sprawled around, no longer wild.
The jar was round upon the ground
And tall and of a port in air.

It took dominion everywhere.
The jar was grey and bare.
It did not give of bird or bush,
Like nothing else in Tennessee.
      (Stevens, "Anecdote of the Jar,")

Highlighting the constant war against nature through the manmade artifice of a simple jar, Stevens' constant reference is to the monumentalizing impact humanity has on place. The industrial force is lasting because it commodifies the forces of nature, bending, melting and freezing timeless rhythms through production techniques perfected through the blast furnace and assembly line. The jar rises like a tower to the sky, with its base planted deep into the ground, becoming an industrial *axis mundi* that obliterates space. However, this marshalling and control of space through industrialization eventually yields, just as the jar, to the forces of nature (2). Geological time and climate metes out ruination on a scale that ultimately outlasts the industrial ethos of permanence. However, this meant little to politicians and business leaders in late nineteenth and early twentieth century Ontario, where the push for industrial and national development accelerated side by side with the capacity to consume natural resources.

In order for imperial and industrial interests to move onto Bkejwanong Territory and exploit sand resources, two things occurred. Firstly, the Canadian government, through Indian Affairs, had to control access to the resources. The precedent for this had been set in the 1860s and 1870s with the boom of the timber industry. By manipulating which companies had access to the old growth white oak forests on Bkejwanong, Indian Affairs could effectively eliminate American business interests on the territory while handpicking their Canadian favorites (3). Even if the joint Ojibwe and Potawatomi Band Council had wanted to assign timber contracts to American companies with the highest bid, Indian Affairs favored Canadian companies often with lower bids. The second development that allowed government and industrial interests unfettered access to sand resources was the constant adaptation of bureaucratic language to limit resistance. This latter development reveals a fascinating look at the power dynamics of orality and written literacy, and how the latter was skillfully honed to enact imperial and industrial dominion on Bkejwanong Territory.

Cosmology

Few settlers bothered to ask the Anishinaabeg what they knew about the territory. Instead, the government relied on the information sent in by land surveyors, settlers, and the British military. One settler familiar with the Anishinaabeg went one step further than merely asking about the territory, he knew enough to ask its origins. The poet William Leonhardt of Port Lambton, originally from Wyandot Michigan, befriended Chiefs Joe White and Charles Jacobs in the early twentieth century. At some point between 1907 and 1913, Leonhardt interviewed Chief Peterwegeschick, a Walpole Island hereditary chief who lived to be 114 years old. Leonhardt later published an account of his encounters on Bkejwanong Territory in the *Sarnia Canadian-Observer* newspaper in a 1925 article titled "Legends of the St. Clair River" (4). He wrote that Chief Peterwegeschick told him about a great storm in the past that changed the landscape and the flow of the river system. Years later, Charles Jacobs (5) further illuminated this story and its significance to the Anishinaabeg. As a story written in a newspaper, the catastrophic storm becomes a tale stripped of humanity, as it takes on a static representation of a conversation between two people long ago. The newsprint fades, is eventually recorded on microfilm, and then shelved in a cabinet.

Such treatment is also represented through the scientific cosmology of the region that situates Bkejwanong Territory as the sedimentary build-up left over from Wisconsinan glaciation. As the massive wall of ice pushed north up Lake Huron, the St. Clair River formed as the primary drainage basin, eventually making its way to the St. Lawrence River after filling Lakes Erie and Ontario. Such a story, however, is notable for its studious lack of human agency. Humans figure prominently in the Anishinaabeg account of how the St. Clair River took its shape. In the moment of its telling, the story shared by Jacobs reveals just how precariously placed the world is and just how easily it can be turned on its head,

> ...one day there came a great bird. Its wings would be two miles long. It lit in or near the mouth of the river and began to wash itself, ducking and diving and flapping its wings and it got up a great commotion, whirling and diving its extended wings, threshing the waters at a furious rate and making a terrible commotion causing the winds to blow so fiercely that the trees were uprooted, and their wigwams were destroyed. The canoes were lifted in the air and blown far to the southward and later many canoes were found in the treetops along the river Thames. The wind had driven them across the country in its fierce storm, all caused by the great bird and its wing flapping. The front of the

shores was changed and in the commotion the river burst through where it now is on the American side (6).

The force carried by the great bird may have only been apparent to Leonhardt after his own participation in the shipping and timber industry ended because of an injury he received in Duluth. Leonhardt had previously worked on a river tug that carried the old growth oak forests off Bkejwanong Territory (7), and following this, as a mariner on the upper Great Lakes (8). Leonhardt may have appreciated the warning in this story following his own sudden irrelevance to the rise of industrialism on the Great Lakes. After all, in 1911 he wrote with dismay what had transpired on the St. Clair River system,

> I might say that there [are] few places now so [busy] as the River in front of the island [Walpole]. Nearly 80,000,000 tons of freight pass there in 245 days. A ship passes every five minutes, and the Ships are nearly all built of Iron, and run from 500 feet to 600 feet in length, and carrying nearly 14,000 tons of freight in a single cargo... (9)

As he witnessed the storm of progress grow exponentially, Leonhardt may have seen the story both as a warning to the forces of nature on the territory and the potential cost of development in the early twentieth century. He may have also noted the resiliency of the people to begin again at the head of the St. Clair River. The long-term commitment to place in Jacobs' story situates the Anishinaabeg as residing on Bkejwanong since time immemorial. Such a perspective is irreconcilable with the short-term gain industrial capitalism offered the territory. National interests

Just as it was in the case of timber on Indigenous Territories and Reserves, the Canadian government considered sand and gravel a resource that could only be surrendered upon a vote by the Band Council, typically to the highest bidder (10). However, Indian Agents and interested businessmen indicated that a number of people had already been excavating sand from the southern shore of Squirrel Island for years without permission. In 1882, Indian Agent Ebenezer Watson received the first official request to begin excavating. Watson wrote to Indian Affairs, asking how he should proceed, and the fees he should charge,

> 1st, it appears to one that sand may be removed from the Island without injury to every shore from the North, West or South (illegible) in a great supply. The places where sand can be easily obtained and are (illegible) on the West and South of the Island. The sand at the (illegible) part is of (illegible) quality and has been used to some extent in Detroit for the manufacture of glass. 2nd, what I would consider a fair value for the sand would be about 2.00 per barrel – the value of a barge load would of course depend

entirely as to its capacity. For the sand at the South of the Island probably a (illegible) more might be obtained (11).

Having just dealt with a number of timber interests, Watson's primary concern had been how much money could be made from an apparently unlimited resource. Watson had been instructed by Indian Affairs to put the question to the Council, seeking their permission to surrender sand from Squirrel Island. He did so, and the proposal was unanimously rejected. Within a year, however, Watson managed to get the majority of Council to consent to the selling of sand, with certain conditions (12). Watson, however, never stated precisely what these conditions were, only that a man by the name of James Muir would act as overseer and collector of barge and scow fees at 20 Cents per ton. Watson later indicated that only the sand on the lakeshore, and not the riverbank, would be sold.

The Council apparently held Muir in trust, as he had been the Caretaker of the St. Clair Flats Shooting Club on the southern end of Bkejwanong (13). Muir is said to have lived on nearby Harson's Island on the Michigan side, and could thus easily monitor the water traffic. By the end of 1883, Alexander McKelvey took over the position of Indian Agent on Walpole Island. McKelvey apparently knew little or nothing about the deal to sell sand when he took the position, and came to the conclusion rather quickly that more money could be collected. In a letter outlining the matter to Indian Affairs in Ottawa, McKelvey took great care in describing the process of how sand accumulates and how it perpetually regenerates its form,

> With regard to sale of sand off the Island, I think these could be four or five hundred dollars worth sold every year without injury to any one as (illegible) sand is taken off the beach the place fills up again almost immediately with more sand, as it is washed up out of river and is not any portion of the soil of Walpole Island, there is no sand to begat (except on Walpole) nearer than Lake Huron shore about (30) thirty miles so that people wanting sand would be willing to pay a good price for it here (14).

The intersection of scarcity and perpetual regeneration is worth noting here, as McKelvey indicated Bkejwanong Territory is a place of endless capitalist potential. The supply appeared seemingly endless as the currents of the St. Clair River dictate the flow of sand from Lake Huron, as for the demand, McKelvey writes, "I have applications nearly every day from parties wishing to buy sand from the St. Clair side of Walpole Island" (15). From McKelvey's point of view, the potential for profit seemed too good to ignore.

McKelvey also indicated he had been at odds with Muir, who, in his mind had no business surpassing McKelvey's authority by collecting fees. Bear in mind the Council gave Muir the authority to collect the money, and the discontinuity between Indian Agents is well apparent in

71

this letter, sent mere months after McKelvey replaced Watson as Indian Agent.

Another important feature of McKelvey's letter to Ottawa is his investigation into one particular company (which is not named) that had been regularly excavating sand from Bkejwanong,

> On further enquiry since I found that the party wishing the exclusive privilege is engaged in the Manufacture of glass and that the sand they get there is used in the manufacture of glass and is very hard to find and of course very valuable. Please instruct me in this matter and also say what authority Muir has got and from whom obtained (16).

It appears as though the company McKelvey is referring to is from Michigan, possibly Detroit, where a glass manufactory had been in operation. This would be in keeping with McKelvey being at odds with Muir, as he indicated he would rather see the excavating be open to competition rather than granted to an exclusive contract. McKelvey later wrote that he would do his best to prohibit Americans from getting access to the sand, as Indian Affairs was only interesting in allowing Canadian companies access to the site (17). In 1894, the Government expressed concern that this endless resource that offered so much prosperity was going to waste because it was being sold to Americans. Hayter Reed, the Deputy Superintendent General of Indian Affairs said he would rather see the sand used to develop industry along the Canadian border and interior,

> I certainly would recommend that all sales to the Americans be stopped, unless we are firmly assured that there is much more sand than the Wallaceburg manufactory may require, and if other Canadian parties from a distance desire to get any of this sand, that the Wallaceburg manufactory still have priority, we fixing the price ourselves for the sand (18).

Whether or not the Americans actually paid for the sand, or if the revenue made it from Muir to the Council is beside the point because this illustrates Government coercion by setting limits on who could do business on Bkejwanong. McKelvey maligned Muir when he stated the caretaker moved to the American side (19) (Harson's Island) and the amount of money given to Indian Affairs only amounted to $26.00 (20). The distrust of Americans is consistent by government officials when dealing with Bkejwanong Territory. For instance Ebenezer Watson referred to Anishinaabeg who sold timber to Americans as "plotting Indians" (21), and later accused Americans of interfering, as they wanted to do business on the territory (22).

There is, however, quite a double standard when it came to Indian Affairs dealing with American business interests in Canada. One notable example was the illegal removal of 1,129 trees from the Dokis

Reserve in Northern Ontario by a Michigan logging company. Although community members were enraged when they learned about the apparent mistake, the government allowed the company to tow the logs back to Michigan without penalty (23). In this case, historian James Angus notes how Indian Affairs actually admonished Chief Michel Dokis for not protecting his own timber and for the angry tone of his letters (24).

A space made void

By late 1894 glass manufacturing began at the Sydenham Glass Company in Wallaceburg, Ontario. While later tests indicated the sand found in much of the region could not produce a high quality glass (25), there had still been great interest in acquiring it for such a purpose, particularly on the south shore of Squirrel Island. A request for exclusive rights to the south shore of Squirrel Island had been made by company officials to the Minister of the Interior in late 1894 (26). Within one week, Ebenezer Watson traveled to Wallaceburg from Sarnia to see the viability of this proposal. He replied to Ottawa that such an exclusive contract could be of great benefit. During this time, Watson also met with McKelvey to develop a rental and fee plan, as well as a strategy to keep American interests out of the area (27). In his letter to Ottawa, Watson indicated the company had plans to hire "no less than 300 Indians" (28), and also that if other Canadian companies were to know the price being offered by the Sydenham Glass Company, competition for a premium price might ensue (29).

While officials in Indian Affairs informed the company that the Band Council would have to vote to surrender the sand, they also indicated that this would in all likelihood occur,

> The Department is disposed... to grant a lease to your Company for a term of ten years at a rental of $150.00 per annum on the understanding that the Department may sell to others in Canada and for purposes other than for glass works, and also that the lease may be renewable for another term of ten years on payment of such increased rental as may then be agreed upon (30).

Superintendent General of Indian Affairs Hayter Reed may have underestimated the Council, as the vote to relinquish the south end of Squirrel Island was rejected when McKelvey put the motion forward. Once again, however, Reed indicated this should not concern the glass factory,

> ...further negotiations have been rendered futile, at any rate for the present, in consequence of the Indians having emphatically refused to lease it. This, however, will probably not prevent your Company from getting what sand you may require (31).

Reed went straight to the point in a letter he sent to McKelvey the following day, "I beg to inform you that you should submit the matter to them (Indians) again, as soon as you consider the time favourable for doing so" (32).

Within a few months, in May of 1895, the St. Clair Flats Shooting Club objected to the Wallaceburg Glass Factory being granted exclusive rights to Squirrel Island sand (33). The Shooting Club may have been motivated by their sudden exclusion in the sand business. Regardless of their motivation, Indian Affairs outright dismissed the objection.

The Anishinaabeg had been in a pressure situation mainly because Indian Affairs had already stated unequivocally that the Sydenham Glass Company should have the southern end of Squirrel Island. Such decisions reveal the Canadian government's underhanded approach when dealing with Bkejwanong Territory. By going outside of the Council and determining who should and should not have access to resources, the government stood in direct opposition to the terms of the 1790 McKee Treaty which reaffirmed Anishinaabeg autonomy over the territory. By the twentieth century, the treaty was flipped end over end, and through the Indian Act of Parliament (not one single Indigenous person in Canada agreed to this colonial legislation) the government placed itself in the position of leadership, giving it the power to determine matters such as sand rights.

In 1898, David Alexander (D.A.) Gordon, president of the Sydenham Glass Company (and later the Dominion Sugar Company of Wallace-burg) sought permission to obtain sand on Squirrel Island. He made a very subtle proposal as if to measure the response, interestingly not to Indian Affairs, but to Clifford Sifton, Minister of the Interior,

> We would like to have permission to get a few loads of sand, from the head of Walpole Island, for use in our Glass Works. We might state that this would in no way effect the property, as it is taken from the Flats, where it is washed up from the River. Our Company got permission three years ago from the former administration for sand for this purpose. ... As to our statement that it will be no injury to any one, whatever, we would refer you to the Indian Agent Mr. McKelvie (sic), or to Mr. C.B. Jackson, Pres'd (president) of the Reform Association, who is thoroughly acquainted with the location, also the statement, we have made. We might ad(d), that we will not require any more than three or four small loads, per year. (34)

Again, the Government stated they had been bound to the Indian Act, and no such permission can be granted unless first surrendered by the Band Council (35).

Following this, Gordon wrote a letter that offers a fascinating insight on how language was actively shaped to enact a very particular reality. The desire and refining of language is quite apparent, when Gordon makes another attempt to acquire the sand, not for the purposes of glass manufacturing, but for industrial agriculture. Again, he addressed the letter to Sifton, and not Indian Affairs (original letter underlined),

We presume you are aware of the fact that we are to begin the erection of a Beet Sugar factory at this point within the next thirty days. We would like to get permission to get sand from the head of Walpole Island. <u>Understand this sand is washed up out of the river and not a part of the island and no way interferes, as the vacant place made by loading a barge is filled up again in a short time</u>. In the past there has been some objection to this on the part of the Indians, although it is no less to them whatever. We would not object to paying a small fee of say, three or four dollars per barge load for the privilege (36).

The point made by Gordon is felt at three significant levels. Firstly, Gordon connected the extraction of sand to the development of industrial agriculture. This leaves open the opportunity for Indian Affairs to achieve its now decades old mandate of civilizing Indian peoples through agriculture. Secondly, he disconnected the Anishinaabeg from the territory with a surprisingly dismissive attitude. The dismissal of their concern can only stem from an idea that the Anishinaabeg can have no concern for the sand in question because they would not utilize it in the most profitable way, such as Gordon intended. Finally, the most important point is also remarkable for its subtlety, and some time must be spent here in consideration of his underlined sentence.

Gordon noted that the sand in question is washed up out of the river and therefore not a part of the Island. This is of fundamental importance because Indian Affairs had to this point been stating that only the resources (such as trees) that actually form a part of Bkejwanong Territory must be surrendered. If Gordon could convince Indian Affairs that the sand was not actually a part of Squirrel Island, then the surrender would be unnecessary in the eyes of the government. Gordon carefully crafted his letter, not only severing the fundamental role sand serves in its glacial span building the river delta, he also reasserted that such a process is self-perpetuating, offering (as McKelvey did) potentially endless prosperity. Gordon stated, "as the vacant place made by loading a barge is filled up again almost immediately." Such an assertion, immediately following his belief that the sand is entirely severed from the territory, could only be agreed on by likeminded bureaucrats and industrialists. Gordon might have been right, assuming such a vacuum exists.

The discourse used by Gordon demonstrates a long line of Western thinking that strips agency from place. The process of objectifying place had been entrenched in Cartesian thinking, and this was only enshrined through property laws that emphasized the physical process of "improvement" to transform land into individual property. Gordon,

75

acting as a CEO of an emerging Canadian industrial town, was an agent of the broader colonial process that crafted, through writing specifically, a process by which territories like Bkejwanong were to become the severed fragments of a much bigger ecological process.

As sediment is washed down the St. Clair River, Bkejwanong Territory is given form. As a process enacted by Wisconsinan glaciation, which saw the constant grinding and carrying of rock, this process has been thousands of years in the making, or as the Anishinaabeg might say, since Creation. This is part of the long term commitment the Anishinaabeg have with the territory. There is little short term gain with this knowledge. The breaking of this connection is revealed through the severing of one element from another to further short term gain through industrialism and possessive individualism. Men like Gordon enacted this severance and possession by stating that the sand does not form any part of the territory as it is transported via the river, and of the Anishinaabeg protests, "it is no less to them whatever."

This insidious perception is contrary to the belief that the territory is an animate force rather than a lifeless entity to be stripped apart piece by piece. One often hears how the continent floats on the back of a turtle. Territory, in this way of thinking, is a living entity. A further example of this understanding is that weather and climate, the forces that birth the territory through time, is also alive (37). The story of the great bird provides incredible insight into this way of thinking of the world, as it speaks of a highly integrated river system that connects the flow of water and the continual birth of territory beginning upriver on Lake Huron and downriver to the Thames (38).

The idea that sand exists as a separate entity from Bkejwanong (and is subsequently of 'no concern to the Indians') appealed to Indian Affairs. This line of thinking is worked through considerably by the department and Gordon in their pursuit of Squirrel Island. For instance, J.D. McLean of Indian Affairs stated that if indeed the sand is on the shore, then it falls under the jurisdiction of Indian Affairs, as it does form a part of the Island and the Band Council would have to vote on the matter. Curiously, however, McLean follows this line with an echo of Gordon's belief, "If, however, the sand applied for does not form a portion of Walpole Island, it is not under the control of this Department and permission for its removal could not therefore, be given" (39). In other words, if reality is as Gordon dictated, then McLean suggested no surrender would be required, as Gordon would be the rightful owner.

In an apparent power struggle between Indian Agent Alexander McKelvey and D.A. Gordon, McKelvey admonished Indian Affairs for suggesting the sand was not under the control of the government. McKelvey stated that if the government followed Gordon's line of thinking, then Indian Affairs stood to lose a lot of money,

Now I did not quite expect to hear that the Department had no control at all over this sand as it certainly is on the shore of the Island where it accumulates and it is impossible to take it away without trespassing on the shore it would seem as if parties taking sand without consent of the Department could be ordered off and as the Sugar Beet Company must have sand in large quantities to erect the Buildings they will require and are willing to pay for the privilege of taking it without making too much enquiry as to the ownership which is admitted to be sufficiently ('found' or 'moved') by the Payment of $4.00 for each Barge or scow load already taken and which is herewith enclosed, "3 barge loads at $4.00 each - $12.00" which was handed to me today without asking by "Mr. Gordon" the President of the Sugar Beet Co. himself and Mr. Gordon is willing to sign an agreement with the Department to pay $4.00 per scow load such as they have been for what sand they will require for completion of the extensive Brick buildings the propose to erect (40).

McKelvey continued to state that an agreement had been reached between the Council and D.A. Gordon to extract sand. However, he made a very troubling statement that appears to conceal the wording of the agreement. Of the agreement, McKelvey states, "the enclosed copy of Resolution is taken out of the secty's (secretary's) book and the composition is a little rank, but it was getting dark when he wrote it and darker when I copied it and no lights available" (41).

A resolution that had been written in the dark, and then copied in the dark can only result in questions about what else was left in the dark. The fact that this statement is left unchallenged only speaks to the banal colonial legacy of the written word on the territory, as it immediately raises questions as to what precisely happened in the Council meetings and in the community at the time. McKelvey indicates two things, firstly, that the Potawatomi were against the motion to grant excavating rights to Gordon, and also that McKelvey used his power as Indian Agent to defeat a motion that would put the question to a general council that would have led to more community discussion and debate (42).

In response to the resolution, Indian Affairs clarified its position by making an explicit distinction between surface and subsurface resources,

The sand though liable to drift does so long as it remains upon the reserve, form part thereof. If it is to be gotten from the bed of the St. Clair River the case is very different because the bed of the river is the property of the Crown, but even in that case while there is no power to convey the sand, there is power to grant a right of access over the Indian reserve (43).

While government and industry officials crafted language to best suit their desires, frustration at the community level reached a boiling point.

It is important to bear in mind that a near constant campaign of outside interests had been on Bkejwanong for close to a century. Each time new interests appeared on Walpole, the profit flowed in a steady outward stream benefiting many people outside the community (44). This harsh economic reality is one shared by most Indigenous communities across Canada. The perception of this marginalization by non-Native Canadian society is almost always lacking in depth, resulting in the stereotypes of stagnant economic, political and cultural values of reserve life. The overbearing assimilationist history of the Indian Act is rarely considered a contributing cause to the disparities on reserves, as government policies are often cloaked with good intentions of advancement, progress, and social welfare.

There had been, however, a near constant resistance to government and industry attempts to get the community to surrender the territory. Alexander McKelvey had been well aware of this and could only express outrage that people were willing to stand up to him. In one letter, McKelvey went out of his way to identify the people he saw as problems, and suggested further action might be necessary to silence them. In the letter, he connected the unrest to the vote he cast at the Council meeting that prevented a general Council from determining whether or not to go ahead with a contract for D.A. Gordon. McKelvey indicated that any further decisions on the sand contract should be made by Indian Affairs alone because more discussion on the matter would only, "give the fire Brand element another relight of which they are badly in need at present" (45).

In a move that can best be described as divide and conquer, McKelvey indicates how he broke resistance to his rule on Bkejwanong Territory by aligning key votes to side with Gordon. Such a move, he suggested, left one of the Chiefs in opposition with little support, as it, "left the redoubtable Joe White (who is the Head and front of all opposition to Progress) standing alone, the rest having joint together in a body and it would seem as if they intended to remain that way" (46). Further to this, McKelvey pointed the finger at Ojibwe Methodist Missionary William Elias, whom he held a particular disdain for (47). In the conclusion to his letter, McKelvey indicated that Indian Affairs had best keep their eyes on both White and Elias,

> These two (Joe White and Elias) constantly make fire brand spectacles and frighten and deter the Indians from acting as they would if left to themselves so that at this time if it could be avoided it be better not to bring anything that would cause a split among the Council or the Rank and file to come (48).

There is a flawed assumption by McKelvey that the Anishinaabeg would be behaving as they would on their own if men like Chief Joe White and Minister William Elias were not meddling in the affairs of their community. Such an assumption removed McKelvey and Indian Affairs from the constant coercion they inflicted on the territory for the complete

78

liquidation of the hereditary chief structure, the old growth forest, and the very sand that creates the land. In the years following the treatment of the Anishinaabeg by McKelvey, Reverend Elias wrote of the late nineteenth and early twentieth centuries as a period of constant fraud on the part of Indian Agents, land speculators and the neighboring Canadian and American white population. During this period, Elias acted as recording secretary to the Chief, making him a daily thorn in the side of men like McKelvey, when he witnessed their constant underhanded activities (49).

The great disconnect imported onto Bkewjanong Territory from Indian Agents and late nineteenth century industrialists continually severed the process of sand birthing the soil just as it had severed the function of fallen oaks feeding the forest floor. Agent McKelvey exemplifies this disconnect on a couple of levels. With McKelvey's help, Gordon successfully won a contract to extract sand from the Band Council in 1901. The terms of this contract were never expressed to Indian Affairs, as McKelvey stated 'the light was dimming when the resolution was recorded and almost entirely dark when copied.' Indian Affairs promptly wrote back, asking for clarification, "I have to ask that you will answer the question asked by the Department in letter addressed to you on the 7th Instant, whether it is proposed to take the sand from the Island above high water mark or from the bed of the St. Clair River" (50). Indian Affairs received no reply, as McKelvey died in late 1901.

This disconnect no doubt left Gordon the impression that he could go ahead with his contract, despite the many questions left unanswered about the legitimacy of the agreement, as well as the terms and monitoring. The sand in question had been used for cement mixing to build a Sugar Beet factory in Wallaceburg, as well as to support the soil needed to grow the crop on a large scale. Until this point, the Anishinaabeg had been successful farmers on Walpole Island, supplementing hunting and fishing with home grown produce that could either be sold in markets or kept for personal consumption. Industrial sugar beet production, however, further eroded this independence as it forced many people off the Territory to work for wage labour (51).

As capacity for the production of a sugar beet industry in Wallaceburg grew, Gordon continued extracting sand from Squirrel Island. In 1903, Walpole Indian Agent J.B. McDougall expressed concerns about Gordon, writing to Indian Affairs,

> Will you please inform me what arrangements were made about Mr. D.A. Gordon Manager of the Wallaceburg Sugar Beet Co. taking sand of the reserve according to the secretary's books he was to pay $4.00 per Scow load. Mr. Gordon informs me that he understood from late Agent Mr. McKelvey that he was to get the sand free but is not sure on the matter… (52)

The disconnect between agents McKelvey and McDougall had been well exploited by Gordon in the year following McKelvey's departure. McDougall wrote to Ottawa that it appeared much of the sand taken had come from the beaches of Squirrel Island, breaking Gordon's promise to magically take only the particles of sand that were carried downstream on the St. Clair River (53).

It Took Dominion Everywhere

Although men like Alexander McKelvey and D.A. Gordon appear, are present for some time, and then disappear into history, they set a very clear course for the imperial and industrial dominion in Canadian. Perhaps by deliberate or subconscious recognition of this exercise, the sugar processing plant in Wallaceburg had been named "Dominion Sugar Company Limited." The Sydenham Glass Company would later take on this name when it merged with the "Diamond Glass Company" in Montreal, forming the "Dominion Glass Company." For a number of decades the company produced mason jars with the Dominion logo.

The poet Wallace Stevens used such a jar as the inspiration for "Anecdote of the Jar" (54). In his poem, the jar transcends its literalism and stands as a monument to the constant war industrial man enacts on nature. The jar became both a literal and metaphoric representation of how dominion rises up, initially to subdue the land, eventually to be itself reduced to minutia in the face of a much bigger world. The sand that made the jar is not excluded from this exercise in dominion. The animating forces that transform sand into soil are interrupted, as they are now transformed into the transparent and fragile form of the jar.

The process that allowed this to occur ground to a standstill in Wallaceburg as the Glass factory closed its doors permanently in 1999, leaving approximately five hundred residents without work. Yet the efforts to realize a lasting industrial sovereignty on the land did occur, requiring a very deliberate shaping of the English language. This effort required that the territory be described as a set of independent parts that have very little connection if any at all. The exchanges between the "Sydenham Glass Company" and later the "Dominion Sugar Company" reveal the metamorphosis of the language to match the desire for resources. The reason company officials and Indian Agents took such great care to write their desire was because of the great resistance by the Anishinaabeg to surrender their territory. By using a very carefully crafted discourse, the story of Bkejwanong Territory became a story of disintegrated parts. No longer part of an integrated whole, the very particles of sand, the rock matter crushed by thousands of years of glacial action that fused with organic matter (i.e., decaying oak) could be justifiably exploited, giving new meaning to the phrase divide and conquer.

Long Term Commitment And Return

While industrialists and nationalists of the late nineteenth and early twentieth century could only foresee a positive future building on the foundation of outdated pasts, other people see only warning signs for a future that fed on the past like a voracious monster. For these people, the past had not been a failure for the future to repair. Neither had the past been a static fixture enshrined on paper or stone as an inanimate monument. Rather, the past had been those moments that returned with cyclical regularity providing the necessary foundation for the community and nation to exist. In communities that resisted colonization, this foundation is often known as tradition, and this is the basis for culture. In many indigenous communities, tradition forms the basis for the continuation of culture, which not surprisingly, can only be sustained as long as the territory is sustained. As Vine Deloria Jr. noted, removing the people from the territory removes the people from their cultural foundations (55).

A society that builds itself on the mass consumption of the territory and marginalization of people is not free of this past. Indeed, the cyclical regularity will return even to those who view it as quaint and outdated, turning moot even the loftiest vision of industrial, national and now global utopia. The immediately local past will return begging the question, 'what foundation will it have?' Will it have the surety of an old growth forest or sand wash out as its basis? Or it will have the promise of a new Call Centre or a Wal-Mart as its foundation? Men like Charles Jacobs may have known the story of great bird as a warning for what happens when a world is turned upside down. He may have also seen in it the promise traditional knowledge holds in maintaining the territory, the culture and the Anishinaabeg way of life.

Another man who may have appreciated Jacobs' sentiment was Walter Benjamin, a persecuted German Jewish scholar who died while trying to escape to Spain during the Second World War. Benjamin may have seen the dangers of rushing headlong into an industrial future where all of civilization is free of the past. He knew well that any document of civilization was also a document of barbarism (56). The past itself returned with frightening regularity to the civilization that focuses solely on achieving a future utopia or paradise because the past, like nature, is flawed. Whether it had been past oppressions or the denial of past oppressions, such pasts pile up. On reflecting on the work of a contemporary artist, Paul Klee, in which an angel is flying, Benjamin also spoke of a world turned upside down in a manner frighteningly similar to Charles Jacobs,

> His eyes are staring, his mouth is open, his wings are spread. This is how one pictures the angel of history. His face is turned toward the past. Where we perceive a chain of events, he sees one single catastrophe which keeps piling wreckage upon wreckage and hurls it in front of his feet. The angel would like to stay, awaken

the dead, and make whole what has been smashed. But a storm is blowing from paradise; it has got caught in his wings with such violence that the angel can no longer close them. This storm irresistibly propels him into the future to which his back is turned, while the pile of debris before him grows skyward. This storm is what we call progress (57).

Such a progression has held Bkejwanong in its industrial grip for the past century, where tradition is continually considered an outdated path to a better, more profitable, industrial future. Such notions, however, are often kept in check on the territory, where tradition actively informs community resistance and collective action to the continual threat of spills from Chemical Valley upriver in Sarnia. The constant threat of spills weigh on the Anishinaabeg as a chronic worry, not just over the potential of future spills, but for the possibility of persistent organic pollutants that rest undisturbed on the river and lake bed.

The massive dredge works of the 20th century offered similar promise as navigation channels were broadened and deepened to allow post Second World War ocean freighters access to the upper Great Lakes. The digging of sand and stirring of sediment offer a frightening relevance to past oppressions that return with regularity, and according to Benjamin, pile ever higher. There is no space void of presence in the history of stirring up sand on Bkejwanong Territory, as something always fills that void.

The intent of industrialists and Indian Agents to carve a paradise on the Ontario mainland came at a great expense to Bkejwanong Territory and the Anishinaabeg. In spite of the decades of environmental degradation, political, and economic marginalization, the territory, just as the Anishinaabeg who call it home, continue to exist. Neither has met colonial expectations to disappear into an antiquated past. Rather, both continue to exist while utopias of progress continually fail. As each promise fades within decades, however, the foundations of traditional knowledge on Bkejwanong reaffirm the Anishinaabeg knowledge that once progress has run its course, they will still be there.

◊ ◊ ◊ ◊ ◊ ◊

Rick Fehr is the Acting Director of the First Nations Studies Program at Western University, in London Ontario. Originally from Wallaceburg Ontario, Rick's research focuses on the historical ecology of Southwestern Ontario, with a particular emphasis on the perception of Anishinaabeg and settler societies, cross cultural community relations, and environmental change.

Notes

(1) Dean Jacobs, "'We Have but our hearts and the traditions of our old men': Understanding the Traditions and History of Bkejwanong." in Gin Das Winan: Documenting Aboriginal History in Ontario, ed. David T, McNab and S. Dale Standen, (Toronto: Champlain Society. 1996.), p-3.

(2) Robert Pogue Harrison's research on memorialization and the altering of landscapes as the desire for immortality in his book Dominion of the Dead, (Chicago: University of Chicago Press).

(3) David T. McNab, "'An Insuperable Objection': The Treaty of January 30, 1883, The Department of Indian Affairs and the Extension of the 1883 Timber Lease on Walpole, St. Anne and Squirrel Islands in Lake St. Clair and the Bkejwanong Reserve, 1883-1888." (Draft Historical Report, Nin.Da.Waab.Jig, 2002).

(4) William Leonhardt. "Legends of the St. Clair River," Sarnia Canadian-Observer (July 18, 1925). Trans. Carrie Kewayosh, Nin.Da.Waab.Jig Heritage Centre.

(5) It should be noted here that Charles Jacobs was the grandfather to community activist, researcher, and former Chief Dean Jacobs, referred to in the introduction of this study. (D. Jacobs, pers. comm..)

(6) Ibid.

(7) Gurd to Gray. 29 January 1931. Norman S. Gurd Papers, Lambton Room.

(8) Articles of Agreement between the State of Minnesota and William Leonhardt, undated, Lambton Room.

(9) Leonhardt to Greenwood, 2 February 1911. William Leonhardt papers, Lambton Room.

(10) David T. McNab, "'An Insuperable Objection': The Treaty of January 30, 1883, The Department of Indian Affairs and the Extension of the 1883 Timber Lease on Walpole, St. Anne and Squirrel Islands in Lake St. Clair and the Bkejwanong Reserve, 1883-1888." (Draft Historical Report, Nin.Da.Waab.Jig, 2002).

(11) Ebenezer Watson, Sarnia Indian Agent to Indian Affairs, 22 July 1882, LAC RG 10 Vol. 6975, File 471/20-3-7-46, pt.1., reel #C 15,861.

(12) Ebenezer Watson, Sarnia Indian Agent to Indian Affairs, 20 June 1883, LAC RG 10 Vol. 6975, File 471/20-3-7-46, pt.1., reel #C 15,861.

(13) The St. Clair Flats Shooting Club had recently leased the wetlands from the Band Council.

(14) Alexander McKelvey, Walpole Island Indian Agent to Indian Affairs, 24 November 1883, LAC RG 10 Vol. 6975, File 471/20-3-7-46, pt.1., reel #C 15,861.

(15) Ibid.

(16) Ibid.

(17) Alexander McKelvey, Walpole Island Indian Agent to Indian Affairs, 6 December 1894, LAC RG 10 Vol. 6975, File 471/20-3-7-46, pt.1., reel #C 15,861.

(18)   Hayter Reed, Deputy Superintendent General of Indian Affairs to T.M. Daly, Indian Affairs, 7 November 1894, LAC RG 10 Vol. 6975, File 471/20-3-7-46, pt.1., reel #C 15,861.

(19)   Alexander McKelvey, Walpole Island Indian Agent to Indian Affairs, 31 May 1894, LAC RG 10 Vol. 6975, File 471/20-3-7-46, pt.1., reel #C 15,861.

(20)   Alexander McKelvey, Walpole Island Indian Agent to Indian Affairs, 6 December 1894, LAC RG 10 Vol. 6975, File 471/20-3-7-46, pt.1., reel #C 15,861.

(21)   Ebenezer Watson, Sarnia Indian Agent to Indian Affairs, 29 June 1880, LAC, RG 10 Vol. 2,063, file 10,072, reel #C 11,148, in David T. McNab, "'Their Pound of Flesh': Racism, The Department of Indian Affairs and the Taking of Timber from Walpole, St. Anne and Squirrel Islands in Lake St. Clair and the Bkejwanong Reserve, 1878 – 1888," (Draft Historical Report, Nin.Da.Waab.Jig, 2007).

(22)   Ibid.

(23)   James T. Angus, "How the Dokis Indians Protected Their Timber," in Ontario History, Vol. LXXXI, No.3, September 1989, p-192.

(24)   Ibid.

(25)   After further tests on regional deposits revealed poor quality sand for glass production, the Glass factory began importing most if not all of its sand for production, in Alan and Frank Mann's Settlment on the Sydenham: The Story of Wallaceburg. (Wallaceburg: Mann Historical Files. 1984), p-11.

(26)   A.G. Laird, Sydenham Glass Company to T.M. Daly, Minister of the Interior, 14 November 1894, LAC RG 10 Vol. 6975, File 471/20-3-7-46, pt.1., reel #C 15,861.

(27)   Ebenezer Watson, Sarnia Indian Agent to Indian Affairs, 20 November 1894, LAC RG 10 Vol. 6975, File 471/20-3-7-46, pt.1., reel #C 15,861.

(28)   Ibid.

(29)   Ibid.

(30)   Indian Affairs, Ottawa to A.G. Laird, Sydenham Glass Company, 4 December 1894, LAC RG 10 Vol. 6975, File 471/20-3-7-46, pt.1., reel #C 15,861.

(31)   Hayter Reed, Superintendent General of Indian Affairs, to A.G. Laird of Sydenham Glass Company, 16 January 1895, LAC RG 10 Vol. 6975, File 471/20-3-7-46, pt.1., reel #C 15,861.

(32)   Hayter Reed, Superintendent General of Indian Affairs to Alexander McKelvey, Walpole Island Indian Agent, 17 January 1895, LAC RG 10 Vol. 6975, File 471/20-3-7-46, pt.1., reel #C 15,861.

(33)   Alexander McKelvey, Walpole Island Indian Agent to Indian Affairs, Ottawa, 15 May 1895, LAC RG 10 Vol. 6975, File 471/20-3-7-46, pt.1., reel #C 15,861.

(34)   D.A. Gordon, Sydenham Glass Company to Clifford Sifton, Minister of the Interior, 29 October 1898, LAC RG 10 Vol. 6975, File 471/20-3-7-46, pt.1., reel #C 15,861.

(35)   J.D. McLean, Indian Affairs, Ottawa to D.A. Gordon, Sydenham Glass Company, 2 November 1898, LAC RG 10 Vol. 6975, File 471/20-3-7-46, pt.1., reel #C 15,861.

(36) D.A. Gordon, Sydenham Glass Company to Clifford Sifton, Minister of the Interior, 19 July 1901, LAC RG 10 Vol. 6975, File 471/20-3-7-46, pt.1., reel #C 15,861.

(37)   Ojibwa scholar James Dumont speaks of myth as having a fundamental importance to the Anishinaabe view of history, which follows what he describes as a three-hundred-and-sixty-degree vision, able to use mythic events as guides to live a better life. Whereas Western conceptions of time follow a linear model of progression, in which the past is inherently flawed, and everything civilization works toward is paradise or utopia. See "Journey to Daylight-Land: Through Ojibwa Eyes," in Laurentian Review, (1976), p-14.

(38) This movement may speak to Anthropologist Tim Ingold's assertion that "Beings do not exist at locations, they occur along paths." This sense of movement connects a particular culture with their territory in a way that acknowledges the biological, aquatic, terrestrial, aerial and celestial world as always being flux, in a sense, living. See "Rethinking the Animate, re-animating Thought," in Ethnos, 71:1, 01 March 2006.

(39)   J.D. McLean, Indian Affairs, Ottawa to D.A. Gordon, the Wallaceburg Sugar Company, 24 July 1901, LAC RG 10 Vol. 6975, File 471/20-3-7-46, pt.1., reel #C 15,861.

(40)   Alexander McKelvey, Walpole Island Indian Agent to Indian Affairs, Ottawa, 24 October 1901, LAC RG 10 Vol. 6975, File 471/20-3-7-46, pt.1., reel #C 15,861.

(41) Ibid.

(42) Ibid.

(43)   J.D. McLean, Indian Affairs, Ottawa, to Alexander McKelvey, Walpole Island Indian Agent, 7 November 1901, LAC RG 10 Vol. 6975, File 471/20-3-7-46, pt.1., reel #C 15,861.

(44) In a 1931 economic assessment of Walpole Island, Economist Bert Hudgins referred to the community as being home to "1,000 backward Indian people." Hudgins, like many people with little or no understanding of colonization, or as participants and supporters of colonialism, could not look past the immediate effects of economic marginalization. Such a shallow assessment could only result in casting blame on those being victimized by systemic and institutionalized racism. "Human Occupance of the St. Clair River Delta," Economic Geography. Vol. 11, No. 1. (Jan., 1931), p-54.

(45)   Alexander McKelvey, Walpole Island Indian Agent to Indian Affairs, Ottawa, 12 November 1901, LAC RG 10 Vol. 6975, File 471/20-3-7-46, pt.1., reel #C 15,861.

(46) Ibid.

(47) Ibid.

(48) Ibid.

(49) David T. McNab, "'those freebooters would shoot me like a dog': American Terrorists and Homeland Security in the Journals of Ezhaaswe (William A. Elias (1856-1929))", Lines Drawn upon the Water", Aboriginal People and the International Boundary through

the Great Lakes Watershed, Karl S. Hele (ed), Waterloo: WLU Press, 2007.

(50)   J.D. McLean, Indian Affairs, Ottawa, to Alexander McKelvey, Walpole Island Indian Agent, 18 November 1901, LAC RG 10 Vol. 6975, File 471/20-3-7-46, pt.1., reel #C 15,861.

(51)   Dean M. Jacobs (Ed.), Minishinhyeng Anishinaabe-Aki: Walpole Island, The Soul of Indian Territory, (Nin.Da.Waab.Jig: 1987), p-57.

(52)   J.B. McDougall, Walpole Island Indian Agent, to Indian Affairs, Ottawa, 21 May 1903, LAC RG 10 Vol. 6975, File 471/20-3-7-46, pt.1., reel #C 15,861.

(53)   J.B. McDougall, Walpole Island Indian Agent, to Indian Affairs, Ottawa, 28 May 1903, LAC RG 10 Vol. 6975, File 471/20-3-7-46, pt.1., reel #C 15,861.

(54)   Roy Harvey Pearce suggested Wallace Stevens based his poem on the jar, after traveling through Tennessee in the spring of 1918, in "'Anecdote of the Jar'": An Iconological Note," The Wallace Stevens Journal 1:2 (Summer 1977), 65, http://www.usm.maine.edu/~jkuenz/391/jar.htm.

(55)   Vine Deloria Jr. For This Land: Writings on America in Religion, (New York: Routledge, 1999), p-244.

(56)   Walter Benjamin, "Theses on the Philosophy of History", in Illuminations, ed. Hannah Arendt, trans. Harry Zohn, (New York: Schocken Books, 1973), p-256.

(57) Benjamin, p-257.

Works Cited

Angus, James T. "How the Dokis Indians Protected Their Timber." Ontario History. Vol. LXXXI, No.3. (September 1989).

Benjamin, Walter. Illuminations. Edited by Hannah Arendt. Translated by Harry Zohn, New York: Schocken Books, 1973.

Deloria, Vine Jr. For This Land: Writings on Religion in America. New York: Routledge, 1999.

Dumont, James. "Journey to Daylight-Land: Through Ojibwa Eyes." Laurentian Review. (1976).

Gurd Norman S., Papers. Lambton Room.

Harisson, Robert P. Dominion of the Dead. Chicago: University of Chicago Press. 2005.

Hudgins, Bert. "Human Occupance of the St. Clair River Delta," Economic Geography. Vol. 11, No. 1. (Jan., 1931).

Ingold, Tim. "Rethinking the Animate, re-animating Thought," Ethnos, 71:1, (01 March 2006).

Jacobs, Dean M. ed. Minishinhyeng Anishinaabe-Aki: Walpole Island, The Soul of Indian Territory. Walpole Island First Nation: Nin.Da.Waab.Jig, 1987.

—. "'We Have but our hearts and the traditions of our old men': Understanding the Traditions and History of Bkejwanong." In Gin Das Winan: Documenting Aboriginal History in Ontario, ed. David T, McNab and S. Dale Standen, Toronto: Champlain Society. 1996.

Leonhardt, William., Papers. Lambton Room.

Lytwyn, Victor. ed. "Walpole Island First Nation Surrenders for Timber on Walpole Island." Draft Historical Report, Walpole Island First Nation: Nin.Da.Waab.Jig, 2004.

Mann, Alan. Frank Mann. Settlement on the Sydenham: The Story of Wallaceburg. Wallaceburg: Mann Historical Files. 1984.

McNab, David T. "'An Insuperable Objection': The Treaty of January 30, 1883, The Department of Indian Affairs and the Extension of the 1883 Timber Lease on Walpole, St. Anne and Squirrel Islands in Lake St. Clair and the Bkejwanong Reserve, 1883-1888." Draft Historical Report, Nin.Da.Waab.Jig, 2002.

—. "'Their Pound of Flesh': Racism, The Department of Indian Affairs and the Taking of Timber from Walpole, St. Anne and Squirrel Islands in Lake St. Clair and the Bkejwanong Reserve, 1878 – 1888," (Draft Historical Report, Nin.Da.Waab.Jig, 2007).

—. "'those freebooters would shoot me like a dog': American Terrorists and Homeland Security in the Journals of Ezhaaswe (William A. Elias (1856-1929))", Lines Drawn upon the Water", Aboriginal People and the International Boundary through the Great Lakes Watershed, Karl S. Hele (ed), Waterloo: WLU Press, 2007.

National Archives of Canada. 1882 – 1949 Record Group 10 Vol. 6975, File 471/20-3-7-46, pt.1., microfilm reel #C 15,861.

Pearce, Roy H. "'Anecdote of the Jar'": An Iconological Note," The Wallace Stevens Journal 1:2. (Summer 1977)   .
http://www.usm.maine.edu/~jkuenz/391/jar.htm.

◊ ◊ ◊ ◊ ◊ ◊

Weather or Not?: Weather and the Environment in the Indigenous Thought and the Written Word of Ezhaaswe (William A. Elias -- c. 1848-1929)

David T. McNab

Introduction-- Mindscape, Nature and the Weather

Indigenous knowledge comes from the Land. Indigenous people view their Lands and Waters, indeed all of Nature as the conjoining of Mindscape and Landscape. This paper explores the meaning and significance of one aspect of these basic principles of Indigenous knowledge by an examination of the weather and the environment in the writings of Ezhaaswe (William A. Elias). Elias was a significant figure in late nineteenth and early twentieth century First Nations' history in Ontario. The finding of his twenty-five Journals (in the Fall of 2003) which span the period from 1885 to 1928 offer an unusual, if not a unique, opportunity to reflect on this theme from an Indigenous perspective. (1)

Weather or not? Weather is an integral part of Nature. It is ubiquitous and an everyday occurrence. Human beings know that they cannot control the weather; yet they often ignore this fact. It is often assumed away; yet it is significant. The sky world-air, in the four sacred elements of earth, water, air and fire-and its spirit beings in it, help us to understand the weather on an everyday basis. This understanding of the weather is critical to our everyday activities and Indigenous people and to all human beings. Weather or not is an essential component of Nature and mindscape-and to our understanding of Indigenous knowledge.

What is Indigenous knowledge? Indigenous knowledge is all about experiential learning. We must first learn who we are before we first out where we are going. The Compact Oxford English Dictionary defines "Nature" as "the physical world, including plants, animals, the landscape, and natural phenomena, as opposed to humans or human creations". (2) For Indigenous people, their concept of Nature includes human beings as well as the physical and the spirit worlds. Perhaps, George Blondin, the Dené Elder said it best when he observed that the proper relationship between the Dené and the rest of creation seems to be governed more by the spiritual rather than by the laws of man. And indeed, "with regard to medicine power, it is attached to mother earth and all the animals, birds, fish, the air, the weather [emphasis added], and so on." When I say everything was based on medicine power, it was just that. That's the way the aboriginal people of the north governed themselves. ... To them [the Dené, for he only speaks out of his own experience] the land represents a creation of the Creator, that is why they have a lot of spiritual culture. That is why some elders pray to the sun, because it is a creation of the creator. That is why some elders carry a drum at all times because it is used to pray with. ... They would say that the creation of the land by the creator represents a mother feeding her children, so our motherland is feeding us. We should thank the creator for that favour. Some elders would thank the creator for other benefits, and so on. They had a lot of spiritual and cultural attachments to the land. ... They thanked the creator for everything they got. ... In time the land became part of their minds." (3) Using Indigenous knowledge, Indigenous people can understand the sky world and the weather.

Nature, including the weather, is landscape and mindscape conjoined. To understand it on an everyday basis, we must understand the spirit beings of the sky world and their Names. We must also follow the Names in the first instance. Each name has a story which is one of healing and balance within and without mindscape and landscape. Ezhaaswe is one such name. This chapter takes a seasonal approach from the Journals of Elias

WHO WAS EZHAASWE (WILLIAM A. ELIAS?)

Born and raised at Bkejwanong (the Place where the waters divide), also known as Walpole Island, Elias was a grand nephew of the hereditary Chief of the Bkejwanong First Nations (Chief Peterwegeshick (In Between Dawn) (c.1798-c.1926)) in present-day southwestern Ontario. Walpole Island was the Third Stopping place in Anishinabe history. As such, it was the capital of Anishinabe Territory which stretched through the watershed of the Great Lakes and well beyond. Educated by his adopted mother, and at the Mount Elgin Residential School, Elias was one of the first Indigenous people who attended Victoria College, Cobourg (now Victoria University in the University of Toronto). He worked as a medicine person, teacher, and Methodist missionary on both sides of the international border between Canada and the United States between 1876 and 1929.

Below is his description of his life story which he wrote in his Journal on Sunday, December 2nd, 1923, after preaching at a missionary service at Parry Island:

> The class meeting was well attended and enjoyed the testimonies given to the honor of God through our Lord Jesus Christ. Our dinner at James Walker's home well enjoyed: it was prepared with skilled hands: seldom excelled with the neatness for she has learned the art of cooking in the Boarding Houses. While many of our women has not the training at home will be trained in this art by working outside. With the exception of my wife, who was trained this art at home, her mother being the first Indian Lady who was educated Indian Boarding Institution, at Aldervill

[Alderville]- Also her mother being brought up in the Methodist minister's home. Likewise become the wife of Chief H.H. Madwayosh, Saugeen Reservation.

There my wife became the daughter of an Indian Chief: we made our acquaintance to each other while attending the Mount Elgin Industrial Institution at Muncey, Ont. Caradoc. Co. Middlesex, Ont. And we were married in the month of August 22, 1876, in January 1877 engaged to teach school at Cape Croker, Co,. Bruce Ontario for 15 months. Taught school at Saugeen Reservation 3 mos. April, May, and June 1878. In July came to Parry Island as Native Assistant Missionary for 5 years. 1883 Thence to Christian Island 4 years as Missionary became a probationer for the Methodist Ministry. In 1887 Went to Victoria College at Cobourg Ont. In 1889 was ordained as Minister of the gospel Went to Walpole Island Co Kent Ont.

In 1899, went into evangelical work both in Canada and in the State of Michigan United States lived in the town of Sarnia Ont. In 1904 was invited to be engaged in the Missionary Work in connection with the Michigan Conference Methodist Episcopal Church of United States for 3 years. Under the Traverse City District. Petowsky, Charlevoix, and Kewadin Missions along the shores of Grand Traverse Bay. In 1907 was invited to return to Canada, wintered in the Saugeen Reservation, In 1908 I entered into teaching the Indian School at Shawanaga Reservation till 1911. I resigned the school.

I rested and located 200 acres of Crown Land in the township of Shawanaga Parry Sound District Ontario, in lots 10, con. 5th and 6th. Built a house 24 X 28 dimension, and some out buildings.

Some times engaged selling Indian medicines which I studied since I was old enough to learn the herbs and roots under my grandmother teaching me and for forty years among the Indians I studied the art of being an Indian Doctor [since 1871], which no other man ever learned, then I became a assistant Missionary in the month of July 1920 for three years was under the superintendent 1923 in September, I began to take the superintendency a Mission Parry Island and North shore: God gave the success in this Ministry.

Here I am preaching the gospel in Parry Island: this Church I undertake to build in the year of 1883.

Now God has appointed me to minister in this Church in this later years to begin the work over again. I see some great wonderful results in the hands of God, since, assuming the responsibility on this charge; thanks be unto the Father, unto the Son, and unto the Holy Spirit for the success to gather the souls unto the fold of Christ the Savior of the World. .... (6)

Elias' Ojibwa name in English-Ezhaaswe-means "never gone there" or "the longest way around." (7) His English name comes from a variation of the name of the Hebrew prophet, Elijah. Elijah was a "troubler" who went to Places and did things that no one had ever gone before and certainly always took the longest way around any issue in his own life. (8) An Odawa, likely of the Bear Clan, his father was Medweskug (or Jonas Elias) who had come to Walpole Island from Grand Traverse Bay in present-day Michigan in the late early nineteenth century. Elias was also the grandnephew of the hereditary Chief of the Bkejwanong First Nations Chief Peterwegeshick (In Between Dawn) (c.1817-c.1926)) at the Walpole Island Reserve in present-day southwestern Ontario. Chief Peterwegeschick posed for the following family photo in 1923 when he was 106 years old. (See image, next page)

His only uncle was Ash-qua-geezhig (Esquageeshig, James Elgin) (c.1831-c.1910), also a prominent Islander who was appointed as Secretary and Interpreter for the Walpole Island Council on August 25th, 1882.(10) His younger brother Waldron Elias was also a teacher, interpreter, Methodist missionary and Secretary to the Council at the Saugeen Reserve for many years. (11) A teacher, interpreter and a Wesleyan Methodist missionary, Elias was educated at Victoria College, Cobourg (which subsequently moved to Toronto), University of Toronto, where he was educated as a Methodist minister. His adopted daughter, Mildred G. Elias (1917-1982), married Emerson Sands (1912-1991) at Walpole Island and they had twelve children.

Elias married Eleanor Anne Madwayosh, daughter of Chief Madwayosh from the Saugeen Reserve, in Saugeen Township on August 22, 1876. (12) They met when both were students at the Mount Elgin Institute, a residential school, (13) and were married thereafter. They had four daughters, Dorothea Florence (1884?), who perhaps died in childbirth, Lizzie (1885-) and Beatrice (1891-) and his adopted daughter Mildred G. Elias (Sands) (1917-1982).

There is a wonderful story about his relationship with his wife in his Journal of 1885. In August 1885, while residing at the Christian Island Reserve, William asked Eleanor whether he could go to Parry Sound for two weeks. At first he recorded that she did not reply to him. When he asked again he got an earful

This was, he said, the first harsh word that she had ever spoken to him since they had been married. He did not put down the swear word or words, likely in the English language, she had used. He confessed that he was at fault and that he hoped that their perfect union in the eyes of God would be restored. The next day, he wrote that they had reconciled.

On August 25th, 1885, he wrote that the local Ojibwa midwives, Mrs. George Monague and the "Widow Ka de ge gwan" had come to their place and that all was ready for the birth of his second child, Elizabeth, aka Lizzie, who was born at 9 am the next morning. (14) I am not sure what the moral of this lesson was for Elias, although it certainly appears that he had learned it the hard way.

Chief Peterwegeschick, and family, 1923

His career included primary stops working as a teacher and a missionary at the Parry Island mission which included Cape Croker (1878-1887), Henvey Inlet, French River and Grumbling Point (Point Grondine), (July, 1876-1884), Christian Island (1884-1885), Victoria College, Cobourg (1889-1890), Walpole Island (1888-1898, 19114-1918?), Mount Pleasant, Michigan (1899-1903), Petowsky (1903-08), Parry Sound, Shawanaga (1908-1914 and 1918-1929). He passed away in July, 1929 at Walpole Island. Elias also was educated in the traditional way as a medicine person sometime between 1871 and 1918. There are no diaries for the war years and, since he was likely too old to serve in the Canadian armed forces (being about 65 in 1914).

Elias was also a "troubler" in a political sense since he was the one of the first Indigenous persons to request enfranchisement under Duncan Campbell Scott's (1862-1947), who was an Indigenous person himself, revised Indian Act of 1921. He raised issues of integration and modernism by the very actions of his life. The Department of Indian Affairs, after he became enfranchised, took monies from the Walpole Island trust fund accounts and paid him his share and also gave him his lot on the Reserve without first making a Treaty, thereby alienating part of the Reserve. This remains a black hole in the unceded Reserve to this day. (15)

Weather or Not in the Journals of Ezhaaswe

Above all, however, these Journals contain a plethora of detail about these First Nation communities. Elias had a keen eye for detail and his almost daily entries give us an insider's portrait of these communities on such topics as politics, the landscape, the weather and above all, the names-both English and Ojibwa-of the community members. The entries are not humdrum meaningless observations. He was a natural story-teller. They describe the people and the land and the stories which came from the land. Since he knew English well, Elias acted as the recording secretary for the Chief and Council and he often clashed with the Indian Agents who consistently manipulated the written records of what was sent to Ottawa. Sometimes they contain the only written record of what happened during these meetings.

The Journals also provide commentary on the various spiritual practices-Christian or otherwise-of community members. Although primarily written in English, there are some of Elias's sermons written in Ojibwa as well as some of his drawings of the places in which he resided such as at Bay Mills when he first visited that place in 1903. Elias was fluent in Ojibwa and preached his sermons in his own language. The Journals contain portraits of the individuals in the communities in which Elias resided. For example, this portrait is of his grand uncle, of the hereditary Chief "Peterwekeshig" at Walpole Island, who was one of the best sources for both the oral and the written history of the community in the nineteenth century. His Journal entry of Tuesday, October 20th, 1891, is particularly striking especially since the former chief was then about ninety years years old. He starts with the weather:

> The storm is a good sized one [.] on [On] returning home I called on grand uncle Petwekeshig who was at home. He was glad to see me once more in his old fashioned shanty [.] a [A] wooden chimney at the one end of the house, a bright fire was before him, a big wooden pipe in his left hand and a piece of sliffer (sliver) in his right hand reaching down to the fire apparently to the interest of lighting his pipe. When I commended his piece of workmanship on that rustic chimney of his a bright happy smile lit his sallowed face. To [To] describe his furniture would not be much. But [But] would readily be understood by those who have visited the poor Indian home with a careful eye [.] on [On] the right hand side of the shanty two logs laid cross-wise on which some planks are resting almost reaching the whole height of that home, constituting a bed on which five or six blankets were lying strewn in every shape to suit the careless living [.] some [Some] cooking utensils were carelessly laid on a place near the fire, left there apparently in readiness for their use- On the left hand corner near the door a board was fastly nailed diagonally, so into that enclosure, three or four different kinds of apples, which holds about five or six bushels, were stored, ready for their consumption. a [A] square little box was pointed to me for a seat on which I gladly rested to begin a good old chat. This aged friend was one time a great man of the island-who was head chief of the place for a long time-and was the wealthiest Indian of the place. But my dear reader what brought him into this most dismal little home? it [It] was, I will answer the question through that demon drink of alcohol, which dragged this poor old soul to such sad circumstances. (16)

Now, while not denying the impact of alcoholism, it is a bit too much to make such moral judgements when the person is more than ninety years old and about someone who went on to live about one hundred and sixteen years. Elias did have his biased Wesleyan Methodist blinders on even when he was in the presence of greatness.

Right from the beginning of his Journals in 1885, the weather is part and parcel of Elias' mind:

> Friday Sept 18th After morning prayers Mr. Elias went out trying to get some women to pick berries, could not get any all were very busy- Mrs. Frederick Copigog brought some berries which Mrs. Elias bought. In the after noon Mr. Hyde and Mr. Jackson came to Mr. Elias, after the money which was deposited the previous day. Hyde and Jack- son started off for Owen Sound on the previous after noon [afternoon]. ["U", stroked out] But they had to turn back on account the threatening and stormy cloud, before they got around to a sheltery spot. The sudden squall overtook them which driven them ashore. the craft was wrecked- but the cargo ["l",

stroked out] was saved consisting 80 fish kegs and fish corks 1500
Tuesday Sept 22nd Elias studied all day – very stormy day-
Wednesday Sept 23rd Mr. Elias worked pretty hard at his studies-
still windy day- no person dared to sail because of heavy wind[.]
(4)

Indigenous people pay respect to the weather and Nature. When they
read the signs in the sky world, they take the proper precautions and do
not travel.

The weather was also linked to health and healing, as every Canadian
knows. Adverse weather conditions especially in the transition seasons,
can affect the health of anyone. Elias found out for himself early in
October 1885:

Saturday Oct 3d Mr. Elias and his party arrived at Beausoleil
Island during the forenoon, they put up into Miss Elizabeth
Simon's new summer cottage- Mr. Elias & Assance left their
families there while they were gone to Midland with Joseph N. On-
wahtin, and Mr. Elias went from there and back to
Penetanguishene for his mail. he [He] paid one dollar $1.00 for a
rig- they got back very late at night about twelve oclock where
they returned to Beausoleil Island. Mr. Elias was very cold- Sunday
Oct 4th Mr. Elias preached in the morning to a small but attentive
congregation which was 12 persons of rejoicing for most of them
were made happy. Mr. Elias was not very well in the after noon
[afternoon] resulting from the cold he got the previous night-The
consequence was the evening service omitted [second "m", stroked
out]. The day was very cold and a wet one- (5)

The weather remained cold and windy until October 6th. On that
Tuesday, Elias went hunting which was an annual and seasonal event
for the Anishinaabeg when the weather was good. He must have felt
healthy with the improved weather. However, he lacked either the skill
or the experience in this traditional activity: "Tuesday Oct 6th Mr. Elias
after the morning worship went out for shooting partridges, he saw one
partridge sitting on the log, he made a careful aim at it, but when he
fired he thought his eyes were closed consequently missed the aim
which when he opened the eyes the bird was siting [sitting], not much
frightened by the report of the hunter's gun and while he was yet
loading it the bird flew away. That reminded him he was no hunter, for
his profession is to shoot the sinful hearts with the Gospel gun [.] (6) So
thereafter, Elias hunted souls with the "gospel gun", while calling on
others in the community who were better hunters. Later that fall, on
Monday Nov 16th, 1885, he wrote in his Journal: "Mr Elias soon after the
morning prayers went to assist the men who were engaged in
slaughtering a stag. They could not secure him in a good place for the
slaughter after the pursuit about an hour an half they at last shot the
beast while running along the shore-" (7)

One of the ways in which weather is determined by Indigenous knowledge was reading the signs in the sky world. One of the best ways was the direction and presence of the wind and the clouds. The sky leaves tracks in the context of the weather. In his Journal in the middle of November 1885, Elias noted these signs of Nature:

> It was very heavy wind in consequence Mr. Elias ["and', stroked out] could not start for Penatang. …. Tuesday Nov 17th Mr. Elias with John Lake and many others started for the Penatang they got to the town at six oclock p.m. Mr. Elias was engaged to tea with A.C.Osborne and stopped over night [overnight] with Rev. S. Sing, breakfast and dinner with them. Rain all day, on the following [day] …. Thursday Nov 19th Started off for home it was cold sailing, almost freezing the par- ty arrived home in the evening at 5.30 PM prayermeeting [prayer meeting] was conducted by Mr. Elias – (8)

In the winter, Elias showed the Indigenous respect for Nature and also thanks to the Creator by the gift of the knowledge given to them by the Creator. On Monday Dec 14th [1885] he wrote that he had "worked very little during that day- in the way of studying, the day was very stormy, some men intended of going to Penatang but could not venture out on this storm." (9)

Sometimes it pays to stay home and out of harm's way. Likewise, if one is away from home, one should stay put. He recorded, on Monday Jan 11th, 1886, that he went with the Chief of Christian Island "in a small Canoe but they were obliged to retreat because the ice so thick as to render impossible for any one to go forward. They went to the sand beach, where a forlorn Indian was camping. Mr. Elias sent out the Indian to the French settlement for provision. he [He] preached to the poor Indian." On Tuesday Jan 12th he noted that "early in the morning soon after breakfast started off for the Island they were almost frozen out while crossing the channel. They got to the light House point, with the help of Mr. John Hoar [the lighthouse keeper], by throwing them a roop [added above] [rope] on the ice with an attached axe which was slid on the ice- then tying the bow of Canoe, with the roop [rope] and were drawn to the shore with ease- They surprised the people when they got to village in ["a", stroked out] such a stormy day." (10) The next day it had been safe to travel.

In the Spring, after the frozen grip of winter had been broken, it was time to the maple sugar bush with the warm sunny days and cold nights. On Wednesday, March 25th, 1886, he wrote that he "attended to the business of the Band the whole day in writing. The prayermeeting [prayer meeting] was not held because the people moved away to the sugar bush-" Even the work of the Lord bowed before sugaring time. On "Tuesday April 6th, 1886, he observed he "studied and read in the papers, and visiting in the after noon [afternoon] to the sick Mrs. Lake and to Miss Jackson with Mrs. Elias and the children- James G. King came to the Mission House brought taffy [snow taffy made from maple sap] for Mr. Elias and took lessons from Mrs. Elias-" (11) On Thursday April 15th, the whole family-indeed it was a community activity-again started "off with Mr. Precour, for the sugar bush" and they called on "Mrs. Precour and Mr. Elias went off alone to visit the rest of camp: he visited Hawk, Jno. [John] Monague, Noah Assance, George Copigog, Lewis King, and David L. King; they retired home very late in the night."

The same sugaring happened again on Saturday April 17th, when he and his wife and the First Nations schoolteacher, "Miss Jackson" and with "all the little girls started off for the sugar camps: [.] They have had very good times; they returned home after visiting five camps, according to the previous engagement with Charlie King met them with a horse and rig and conveyed them home safe and sound [.]"(12) Weather was of such significance that it guided all Indigenous seasonal community activities.

Individual and community well-being and health were guided by the medicine wheel, as the circle of health. The basis of this model is "circles within circles" with the spiritual being balanced with the "corporal" as an integral and intertwined system of intricate relationships to enable good health and to maintain it. (13) The weather was part and parcel of this approach to Nature and to the health and healing of Indigenous people.

This holistic model was understood and acted upon by Elias and his family. On 1st March 1887, a Tuesday, he noted the following, "A mild weather.":

Got up early this morning, and went to work with his books. he [he] finds it an interesting study on the St. John's Commentary (international) [.] he [He] was also reading in Sam Jones' [1847-1906] Select Sermons (14). he [He] admires the plain narrative discourses. The day is cloudy the wind [added above] being from south. Rev [.] George Clark was expected on Christian Island during the day [added above] but did not appear- The band of Hope met in the school House. We had many visitors the children had a good time, in seeing many the visitors. Mrs. Noah Assance visited Mrs Elias During the after noon [afternoon] Mr. Elias called upon Mr. Enoch Monague who was very ill. he [He] seems to improve little. The children had a good time in looking at the magic sceneries, there were some aged people among the children [last three words added above] to amuse themselves- It is a great treat to them all. he [he] wrote one letter for Mr. Elias. 2nd March 1887 Mr. Elias got up early to [added above] take up his studies. he [He] was reading in the 15th chapter the Proverbs of Solomon [.] he [He] was out early to see the choppers in the woods. he [He] wrote one letter to Mrs. Jas. [James] Marsden] for Mrs. Elias. The day was clear, bright, calm, and thawing weather. he [He] studied in the after noon [afternoon]. In the study of Proverbs he was greatly edified. he retired at 11 oclock p.m. visited at J.W. Monague [name added above]- 3rd March 1887 Mr. Elias rise up at 4 a.m. he worked hard- Studied in the Proverbs of Solomon- he [He] wasout airing himself, while the air was still fresh, and vigorous [.] he [He] worked hard with his studies during the fore noon. Chief Noah Assance called on Mr. Elias about noon who kindly asked the kindness of Mr. Elias to go with him; to have an interview with Mr. Belyea's Clerk about the payment for his son, who had not yet received anything for his work. The Clerk measured 68 cords on the beach, which Wellington Assance had drawn out from the bush. Mr. Elias studied all in the after noon [afternoon]. Mr. Elias was out visiting to several families during the evening. A prayermeeting [prayer meeting] was conducted by Mr. Elias- Mrs. Waubnance and Mr. Solomon Mark called at the Mission House after the prayermeeting [prayer meeting]. The meeting was a good one, deep impressing. May God increase the influence of the Gospel- Mr. Elias retired at 10.30 p.m. good night reader- (15)

In many other parts of his Journal, Elias observes Indigenous principles of knowledge about weather or not, For example, on "Friday.- Nov. 11, 1910", he wrote that it was a

Snowing Morning once more not milder that the storm had only just begun and according to the version of the old man James Pawis that the winter had settled down for good: because there were no snow during the time that the leaves were yet attached to the tops and branches. This is the old Indian signification that a long winter was coming and the snowing time would not cease till a plenty of snow have fallen on the ground. then the wintry weather may slack for some time again. Last night we had a very good prayer-meeting and had a good old-time in the prayer service: about fourteen persons attended the prayermeeting. a good attendance. (16)

It is also noteworthy how Elias' Methodist beliefs were subsumed by his Indigenous knowledge about Nature and, in particular, the weather. It is a salutary lesson in the borders of spiritual ideas and Indigenous knowledge.

Retrospect

With such a plethora of references to the weather, Elias' Journals encapsulate how very significant is Indigenous knowledge about the weather then and now. This example from Elias' Journals is not unusual. Such Indigenous knowledge is still understood and practiced by First Nations today in Canada and the United States. Let us remember and leave the subject of weather or not with the answer being: the weather and Indigenous knowledge can be answered in the affirmative with a resounding yes. While never claiming to be a poet, weather or not was embodied in his Journals on March 26th, 1925 in poetic form:

An enrapt spring
The spring cometh out of sun's rays.
Sooner desolveth the snow by-ways:
The birds do come with joy insight.
Crows made their plaintive growling sigh;

The children can turn to rapture,
O'er the return of joyful 'stir:
Their voices are mingled streamlets,
As they ripple through furro'ed grass.

The rocky bluffs, with snow daubing,
Mingled with fur scrub contrasting,
Creates a scene, incomparable:
No artist painter can compare. (17)

◊ ◊ ◊ ◊ ◊ ◊

David T. McNab is a Metis historian and Associate Professor of Indigenous Thought and Canadian Studies at York University. He received his PhD from the University of Lancaster, England, for his doctoral dissertation on Herman Merivale (1806-1974) and the British Empire in 1978. His research interests include Indigenous Thought, history and literature, land and treaty rights, British imperial history, Canadian Studies, and Ontario history. He has written widely on these topics having written 12 books and over 90 other publications. McNab also serves as an advisor on land and treaty rights and governance issues for a number of First Nations and other Indigenous organizations in Ontario and Newfoundlan

Notes

1. David T. McNab, "Landscape and Mindscape conjoined: the Empire of Nature and the Nature of Empire in William A. Elias' (1856-1929) Journals", Karl S. Hele (ed), The Nature of Empires and the Empires of Nature, Waterloo: WLU Press, 2013, 221-238.
2. John M. MacKenzie, The Empire of Nature, Hunting, Conservation and British Imperialism, Manchester: Manchester University Press, 1988, "Introduction", ix; Empires of Nature and the Nature of Empires, Imperialism, Scotland and the Environment, East Linton: Tuckwell Press, 1997, 1-30; 70-86.
3. MacKenzie, Empire of Nature. See also my chapters on the history of the Bkejwanong Territory in my Circles of Time: Aboriginal Land

Rights and Resistance in Ontario, Wilfrid Laurier University Press, 1999, 147-85; (Edited for Nin.Da.Waab.Jig.), Earth, Water, Air and Fire: Studies in Canadian Ethnohistory, Wilfrid Laurier University Press, 1998, 35-64.

4. I am grateful for this information on Elias' name which was provided to me by the linguistic/cultural experts at a meeting at Nin.Da.Waab.Jig., the Walpole Island Heritage Centre, Jennie Greenbird, Elizabeth Isaac, Elaine Jacobs and Reta Sands, on April 26, 2005.

5. Elias's Journals came to me in 2003 through my community-based research at Shawanaga First Nation and by the First Nations' oral traditions that are embedded in their family histories. They remain the property of the First Nation. They were given by his daughter, Mrs. George Sharkey, to her friend, Lucy Adelaide Clark, who taught at the Shawanaga School at the end of the Second World War. Her friend's daughter returned them to the Shawanaga First Nation in the summer of 2003. These twenty-five Journals cover various years for the time period from 1884 to 1928 and consist of more than four thousand pages of his journal entries. Some of them bear the marks of living in the bush for many years having porcupine teeth marks on the margins. They cover the time period beginning when Elias was at Victoria College in Cobourg in the mid to late 1880s. They provide a fascinating glimpse of what an Aboriginal person thought about college life and his training as a Methodist minister in the 1880s. They also provide information about the individuals who were then teaching at the College.

6. Elias, Journal #11, 1921-1923.

7. I would like to thank Elder and former Chief Donald Keeshig of Cape Croker for this information which he told me in a conversation with him on August 9th, 2005 at Keeshigonong, the Place of the Sky, at Cape Croker.

8. See II Kings in the Old Testament.

9. Walpole Island First Nation, Nin.Da.Waab.Jig. Files, Historical Photos Binder, c. 1890-1950. I would like to thank the Heritage Centre for kindly allowing me to use this historical photo.

10. Nin.Da.Waab.Jig. Files, Binder on "Charles Jacobs Family Tree", Reference No. 1672, Ebenezer Watson, Indian Superintendent, Sarnia, to Sir John A. Macdonald, Prime Minister and Superintendent General of Indian Affairs, dated August 25th, 1882.

11. Elias, Journals, #8, 1921-1922.

12. Provincial Archives of Ontario, Ontario Marriage Index, Microfilm 19, Registration #001369, Saugeen Township, August 22nd, 1876-on-line April 4th, 2006.

13. Elizabeth Graham (compiler), The Mush Hole, Life at Two Indian Residential Schools, Waterloo, Ontario, Heffle Publishing, 1997. The original name of this school was "The Wesleyan Ojibway Industrial School, Mount Elgin" which was named after the Governor General in 1849-Lord Elgin.

14. Elias, Journals, #1, #2, 1885-1887.

15. Elias also seems to have played a significant and pivotal role in the Methodist Church in Ontario and nationally and helped to bring the Church into its union as the United Church of Canada at its key meeting in Sundridge, Ontario in 1928. To date, nothing has been written about Elias perhaps because he was an Aboriginal person and was thus seen not to be a part of the written history of Canada. Other than his recently discovered journals, left behind only a brief Reminiscence of his life which is in the United Church Archives in Toronto. He is not referred to in any of the standard studies of the history of Methodism in Canada such as in William Westfall's Two Worlds, The Protestant Culture of Nineteenth-Century Ontario, Kingston and Montreal: McGill-Queen's University Press, 1989; Neil Semple, The Lord's Dominion, The History of Canadian Methodism, Kingston and Montreal: McGill-Queen's University Press, 1996). Nor is there any reference to him, much less any separate biography, in the most recently published volume of the Dictionary of Canadian Biography in which he would have appeared since he passed on in 1929. Semple in his official history of the Methodist Church states incorrectly that Aboriginal people disappeared as ministers of the Methodist Church in the 1860's, and thereafter. Such was clearly not the case.

16. Elias, Journals, "Pocket Journal Cobourg 1887". It should be noted that, in spite of the title of this Journal, it does contain entries for other years.

17. McNab, "Borders of Water and Fire: Islands as Sacred Places and as Meeting Grounds," Jill Oakes, Rick Riewe, et.al. (ed), Aboriginal Cultural Landscapes, Winnipeg: Aboriginal Issues Press, 2004, 39-44.

18. McNab, "'The land was to remain ours'": The St. Anne Island Treaty of 1796 and Aboriginal Title and Rights in the Twenty-first Century", Native American Speakers of the Eastern Woodlands: Selected Speeches and Critical Analyses, Barbara Alice Mann (ed.), New York: Greenwood Press, 2001, 229-50.

19. McNab, Circles of Time, 203-8.

20. McNab, "Conjoining Mindscape and Landscape: the Borders of Knowledge in Indigenous Thought and the Written Word of Ezhaaswe (William A. Elias (1848-1929)", paper presented at the Austrian Association for American Studies Conference, University of Vienna, Vienna, Austria, November 16th, 2006.

21. McNab, (co-editor, with Bruce W. Hodgins and Ute Lischke), Blockades and Resistance: Studies in Actions of Peace and the Temagami Blockades of 1988-89, Waterloo: WLU Press, 2003.

22. McNab, "Borders of Water and Fire," 44-5. See for example the following reference to Americans fishing: Vankoughnet wrote to his counterpart, Major John Tilton, then the federal Deputy Minister of Fisheries, on July 8th, 1885 regarding the marshes and fishing in Lake St. Clair, as follows: "On the occasion of an interview which I had recently with Mr. C.H., Gooderham Esq., and Mr. Bright, of Toronto , who, with others, have a Shooting lease from the Dept. for part of Walpole Island & its marshes, these gentlemen informed me that American fishermen cast their nets near the northern mouth of

102

the streams running through Walpole Island. They do not violate the law exactly by throwing their nets across the streams, but they have them sufficiently far out on each side of the mouth of the streams to impede effectively the passage of the fish up the streams. These gentlemen stated that the streams are ["therefore in consequence", stroked out] consequently almost completely depleted of fish & that the Indians are suffering as a consequence. I feel convinced that I have only to bring this matter under your notice to cause you to have the proper remedy applied." There was no reply from the Deputy Minister of Fisheries to this letter. See NAC, RG 10, Volume 2118, File 22,610 Part 1, (Microfilm Reel # C-11,162).
23. Louise Erdrich, The Last Report on the Miracles at Little No Horse.
24. Elias, Journals, May 26, 1888-December 3, 1913.
25. Walpole Island First Nation, Nin.Da.Waab.Jig., Files., Dean M. Jacobs, Research Worker, "Land Claims Research Paper Walpole Island Reserve, Association of Iroquois and Allied Indians", undated, 1976. 156-62.

Works Cited

Erdrich, Louise, The Last Report on the Miracles at Little No Horse, New York: Harper Collins Publishers, 2001.

Ezhaaswe, (Elias, William A.), Elias Journals, Microfilm, Shawanaga First Resource Centre.

Graham, Elizabeth, (compiler), The Mush Hole, Life at Two Indian Residential Schools, Waterloo, Ontario, Heffle Publishing, 1997.

MacKenzie, John M., The Empire of Nature, Hunting, Conservation and British Imperialism, Manchester: Manchester University Press, 1988.

Empires of Nature and the Nature of Empires, Imperialism, Scotland and the Environment, East Linton: Tuckwell Press, 1997.

McNab, David T., (co-editor, with Bruce W. Hodgins and Ute Lischke), Blockades and Resistance: Studies in Actions of Peace and the Temagami Blockades of 1988-89, Waterloo: WLU Press, 2003.

"Borders of Water and Fire: Islands as Sacred Places and as Meeting Grounds," Jill Oakes, Rick Riewe, et.al. (ed), Aboriginal Cultural Landscapes, Winnipeg: Aboriginal Issues Press, 2004, 39-44.

_____ Circles of Time: Aboriginal Land Rights and Resistance in Ontario, Wilfrid Laurier University Press, 1999.

_____ "Conjoining Mindscape and Landscape: the Borders of Knowledge in Indigenous Thought and the Written Word of Ezhaaswe (William A. Elias (1856-1929)", paper presented at the Austrian Association for American Studies Conference, University of Vienna, Vienna, Austria, November 16th, 2006.

_____ McNab conversation with the linguistic/cultural experts at a meeting at Nin.Da.Waab.Jig., the Walpole Island Heritage Centre, Jennie Greenbird, Elizabeth Isaac, Elaine Jacobs and Reta Sands, on April 26, 2005.

_____ McNab conversation with Elder and former Chief Donald Keeshig of Cape Croker on August 9th, 2005 at Keeshigonong, the Place of the Sky, at Cape Croker.

_____ (Edited for Nin.Da.Waab.Jig.), Earth, Water, Air and Fire: Studies in Canadian Ethnohistory, Wilfrid Laurier University Press, 1998.

_____ "Landscape and Mindscape conjoined: the Empire of Nature and the Nature of Empire in William A. Elias' (1856-1929) Journals", Karl S. Hele (ed), The Nature of Empires and the Empires of Nature, Waterloo: WLU Press, 2013, 221-238 .

_____ "'The land was to remain ours'": The St. Anne Island Treaty of 1796 and Aboriginal Title and Rights in the Twenty-first Century", Native American Speakers of the Eastern Woodlands: Selected Speeches and Critical Analyses, Barbara Alice Mann (ed), New York: Greenwood Press, 2001, 229-50.

National Archives and Library of Canada, (NAC), RG 10, Volume 2118, File 22,610 Part 1, (Microfilm Reel # C-11,162).

Provincial Archives of Ontario, Ontario Marriage Index.

Semple, Neil, The Lord's Dominion, The History of Canadian Methodism, Kingston and Montreal: McGill-Queen's University Press, 1996.

Walpole Island First Nation, Nin.Da.Waab.Jig., Files.

Westfall, William, Two Worlds, The Protestant Culture of Nineteenth-Century Ontario, Kingston and Montreal: McGill-Queen's University Press, 1989.

◊◊◊◊◊◊

Part III -- Traditional Knowledge and Western Science

First Nations, Traditional Ecological Knowledge and the State of the Great Lakes Ecosystem:

Deborah McGregor

Introduction

It has been fourteen years since significant First Nations participation was first sought as part of the State of the Lakes Ecosystem Conference (SOLEC) in 2000 in Hamilton, Ontario. Since that time there have been in terms of how TEK is considered under the SOLEC process, yet, meaningful First Nations participation remains elusive. This chapter provides a summary of First Nations participation in SOLEC over the past fourteen years and discusses successes, challenges and recommendations made by First Nations participants to improve First Nation engagement in the process.

These observations focus primarily on areas for improvement vis-a-vis Indigenous involvement in SOLEC. The idea of "co-existence" as a solution to current shortcomings is then presented. Finally, a list of recommendations intended to bring about partnerships with based on principles of co-existence between Environment Canada and First Nations in the Great Lakes ecosystem is offered

Initially, a brief history of the SOLEC process is offered. This is followed by discussions of the nature of TEK and the barriers which currently exist in applying it to environmental management initiatives. Next is a summary of observations made of the SOLEC process by First Nations participants who attended SOLEC in 2000, 2002, 2004, 2006 and 2008; including key findings from a 2004 critical assessment report on SOLEC, First Nations participation and TEK. These observations focus primarily on areas for improvement vis-a-vis Indigenous involvement in SOLEC. The idea of "co-existence" as a solution to current shortcomings is then presented. Finally, a list of recommendations intended to bring about a partnership based on principles of co-existence between Environment Canada and First Nations in the Great Lakes ecosystem is offered.

A Brief History of SOLEC

The discussion below focuses on what SOLEC currently achieves and aims to achieve, with a view to broadening that scope to include First Nations and TEK. Unless otherwise stated, information on the history and achievements of SOLEC is taken from Environment Canada - Ontario Region Web pages (Environment Canada 2013a)

The SOLEC process is a direct result of the Canada/US Great Lakes Water Quality Agreement (GLWQA), first signed in 1972 and updated in 1978 and amended in 2012. This agreement committed both countries to controlling pollution in the lakes and reducing the amount of new pollution entering the system via industrial and community wastewater. Specifically, the agreement's aim is to "provide a vital framework for binational consultation and cooperative action to restore, protect and enhance the water quality of the Great Lakes to promote the ecological health of the Great Lakes Basin" (Environment Canada 2013b). As part of the implementation of these goals, the "1987 Protocol" was signed in order to establish Remedial Action Plans (RAPs) and Lakewide Management Plans (LaMPs). RAPs are developed to address identified Areas of Concern on an ecosystem basis and involving the local community. RAPs deal with "nearshore" waters and include lands along the shore while LaMPs focus on the reduction of critical pollutants in the open waters of the Great Lakes. The International Joint Commission (IJC), originally set up to resolve disputes over water use between Canada and the US as part of the 1909 *Boundary Waters Treaty*, is now responsible for overseeing and evaluating the progress of both countries towards meeting the goals of the GLWQA.

The SOLEC process was thus established as a way of monitoring such progress from a biochemical and biophysical standpoint. Hosted jointly by the United States Environmental Protection Agency (USEPA) and Environment Canada (EC), each conference brings together representatives from government as well as the private sector and non-profit organizations whose work and decisions affect the Great Lakes. These representatives then exchange "information on the ecological condition of the Great Lakes and surrounding lands" (Environment Canada 2013b).

A "State of the Great Lakes" report is produced in the year following each conference and provides an ecological update for the entire Great Lakes Basin. The status of ecological conditions, including human health, is the key focus of SOLEC and the State of the Great Lakes reports; other conferences and reporting methods are used to monitor and evaluate the Great Lakes programs aimed at improving these conditions.

Although the SOLEC process represents an important monitoring and reporting mechanism for the Great Lakes Ecosystem, Indigenous peoples have also been assessing the quality of Great Lakes utilizing their own knowledge. For thousands of years, First Nations have lived in the Great Lakes area and have utilized their own knowledge to maintain a sustainable relationship with the ecosystem upon which they rely (McGregor 2008, Mandamin 2012). Over the past two centuries, colonial forces have undermined the ability of Aboriginal peoples to manage and take care of their environment, including the Great Lakes. Exclusion has characterized Indigenous involvement in Great Lakes initiatives in recent years. SOLEC represents a unique opportunity for the inclusion of

Indigenous peoples and their knowledge in better understanding the status of the Great Lakes.

SOLEC and TEK

Missing from the earlier (prior to 2000) SOLECs was the input of those who have the closest ties to, are most directly affected by, and have the longest-standing knowledge of, the Great Lakes ecosystem and the ecological conditions within it. In Canada, there are 63 First Nations situated within the Great Lakes Basin, few of whom had had any dealings or involvement with the SOLEC process prior to 2000. Environment Canada and the other SOLEC 2000 organizers recognized that not only was this an injustice to First Nations, but that non-Native scientists and decision-makers involved in SOLEC were missing out on the potentially invaluable contribution of those who collectively held thousands of years of knowledge and understanding of the Great Lakes ecosystem. This knowledge, referred to here as "Traditional Ecological Knowledge", or TEK, has allowed Indigenous peoples to live, prosper from, and contribute to the Great Lakes ecosystem for countless generations, and could provide valuable insight as to how current society might reestablish more harmonious ways of relating to the lands and waters of the area (McGregor 2009).

Environment Canada's approach to establishing a partnership between TEK and western science in the work of SOLEC was originally one of integration or incorporation of TEK into the existing process. As the discussion below indicates, however, the disparate natures of TEK and western science make this model a challenge to implement. Instead, as the result of feedback and advice from First Nation participants in SOLEC, alternate models for applying TEK to Great Lakes issues are proposed.

Background to TEK

The Semantics of TEK

The field of Traditional Ecological Knowledge (TEK) and its potential use in resource and environmental management has emerged relatively recently in Canada. In spite of rapid development and burgeoning areas of research, the state of TEK research and application remains largely unsatisfactory from an Indigenous perspective (AFN 1995, McGregor 2010). This is due primarily to the fact that TEK, from its definition to its utilization, has been for the most part controlled by interests external to the Indigenous communities from which it originates (Whyte 2013). TEK has therefore not yet realized its potential in Canadian environmental management regimes, although there are a few noteworthy exceptions (see Lickers 1997a, Ellis 2005, McGregor 2009, O'Flaherty et al. 2008).

One major criticism of the TEK field as it stands is the use of the term "TEK" itself. The term originates from western academia, rather than from Aboriginal communities themselves. Many First Nations people object to the use of the term TEK to describe their knowledge systems. This is in part because the term TEK as it is used tends to connote a false homogeneity of knowledge across the diverse nations and cultures of Aboriginal people. As well, each of the words "traditional," "ecological," and "knowledge" limits this form of understanding in many significant ways. For example, "traditional" implies that the knowledge is static and confined to information gained in the past (Houde 2007).

In reality, this form of knowledge is continually evolving and expanding to incorporate new information as part of adapting and responding to current challenges. "Ecological" (sometimes "environmental" is used) limits TEK to a field of study defined by western science. TEK, from an Aboriginal viewpoint, is a holistic form of understanding, encompassing all areas of human existence. As will be discussed further below, specific components such as "ecology" cannot appropriately be separated out. Even the use of "knowledge" as a descriptor for this form of understanding is problematic, as Aboriginal people tend to describe TEK as more of a "way of life" than something which can be concisely described or written down (LaDuke 1997) . This will be discussed further below.

The search for alternate terms for TEK is difficult, however, given the holistic nature of this form of understanding. Any term applied to it tends to limit it in some way or another. Nevertheless, various alternatives have been proposed. Among these are "Traditional Knowledge", "Ethno-Science" and "Indigenous Knowledge" (Grenier 1998, Wolfe et al. 1992, Nakashima, D, et al. 2012). For the purposes of the SOLEC 2000 gathering, the term "Naturalized Knowledge Systems" (NKS) was used, as described by Henry Lickers (1997b). In subsequent SOLEC conferences, traditional knowledge or Aboriginal knowledge have also been utilized. The term is thus dynamic and First Nations are starting to utilize their own terminology to describe ecological processes.

For the moment, TEK continues to be the most widely used and recognized term in discussions on the subject. For that reason, it will also be the term used in this chapter. Perhaps a more all-encompassing term will come to replace TEK in the future.

What is TEK?

As reflected in the debate over the title itself, there is considerable controversy in the field of TEK as to exactly what is referred to when one uses the term or its alternatives. Not surprisingly, Aboriginal and non-Aboriginal people hold contrasting views on what the concept actually entails. Academics and western-trained researchers generally view TEK as a "body of knowledge," with a strong bias towards labeling it as a product or commodity (see e.g. Berkes 1993 and 1999, Johnson 1992, Nakashima 1993). The following quotes indicate this western academic view of TEK as a noun, something whose boundaries can be readily delineated and which can be packaged for general consumption. According to Berkes (1999, 8), TEK is:

...a cumulative body of knowledge, practice and belief, evolving by adaptive processes and handed down through generations by cultural transmission, about the relationship of living things (including humans) with one another and with their environment.

According to Nakashima (1993, 99), TEK is simply, "the knowledge of Native people about their natural environment."

From an Aboriginal viewpoint, TEK is conceptualized as both more than and different from western definitions. Aboriginal understandings of TEK tend to focus on relationships between knowledge, people, and all of Creation (the "natural" world as well as the spiritual). TEK is viewed as the process (a verb) of participating fully and responsibly in such relationships, rather than specifically the knowledge gained from such experiences. For Aboriginal people, TEK is not just about understanding relationships, it is the relationship with Creation. TEK is something one does (McGregor 2004).

Equally fundamental from an Aboriginal perspective is that TEK is inseparable from the people who hold it (McGregor 2005, Roberts 1996). As stated by Roberts (1996, 115), "Capturing a single aspect of traditional knowledge is difficult. Traditional knowledge is holistic and cannot be separated out from the people. It cannot be compartmentalized like western scientific knowledge."

This means that, at its most fundamental level, one cannot ever really "acquire" or "learn" TEK without having undergone the experiences originally involved in doing so. This being the case, the only way for TEK to be utilized in environmental management is to involve the people, the TEK holders. This is a process which has not yet received sufficient attention. The field to date has focused more on gathering and documenting, using social science methods, those aspects of the knowledge base considered to be of value to external non-Native interests. These "TEK" fragments, where they are used at all, are frequently applied with minimal if any Aboriginal involvement. From an Aboriginal view, such misappropriation of TEK is disrespectful and potentially dangerous (Lickers in Lukey 1995). Once separated from its original holders, TEK loses much of its original value and meaning. Moreover, there are no guarantees that the controls that once came with the knowledge to keep it safe as well as useful will still be applied.

Concepts of TEK are gradually changing as more Aboriginal people gain a voice in the environmental arena. For example, it can be seen internationally at least that TEK, in addition to referring to knowledge, has also come to include (in conceptual terms if not in practice) the innovation, creation, and transmission of TEK (Mason et al. 2012, Kimmerer, R. 2012).

Barriers to TEK Use: Hurdles to be Overcome by SOLEC

The divergence of western from Aboriginal views on TEK has had a huge impact on how TEK is "gathered", "documented" and then "applied" in resource and environmental management. "Accepted" tools for working with TEK are derived from the western scientific tradition, especially in terms of its acquisition. This has lead to a host of other problems, including the issue of intellectual property rights (see Anderson 2010). Many barriers thus exist to the effective use of TEK (see Houde 2007, Menzies 2006. Shackeroff et al. 2007,). Three important problems of relevance to the SOLEC process are noted briefly below:

1. Aboriginal peoples are not accorded sufficient meaningful participation in studies and other work which should, and in some cases does, attempt to use TEK. As TEK is not separable from the people, the meaningful involvement of the people is necessary in order to utilize TEK in environmental work.
2. Aboriginal people and their knowledge are viewed as objects suitable for study rather than as people for working with. It is time to begin building positive long-term relationships with Aboriginal people rather than simply studying them and their knowledge at the mercy of project-by-project funding.
3. Aboriginal people have little control over how the knowledge they share will be used. Such knowledge can be (and has been) used against its original holders at a later date or otherwise misused. Again, meaningful involvement of Aboriginal people is required for TEK to be implemented effectively.

In general terms, it is important to realize that Environment Canada and the US EPA (the US lead for SOLEC) are western science-based departments whose work is directed by western scientific paradigms. Adherence solely to this framework is a significant barrier to the use of TEK in SOLEC initiatives. Being science-based, SOLEC is biased towards bio-physical and bio-chemical information. In more recent years, however, SOLEC has broadened its focus to include wider views of the Great Lakes ecosystem. This understanding is reflected in its development of "societal indicators" of ecosystem health. This broadening of focus represents a significant opportunity for Aboriginal people in expanding the concept of ecosystem health. Aboriginal people have a holistic understanding of the environment and ecosystems. One of the main strengths of their knowledge systems lies in a balanced approach that automatically includes societal aspects as part of the ecology of relating to Creation. This balanced approach, taken for granted for millennia by Aboriginal people, is just beginning to be recognized and explored by the western scientific community.

The barriers confronted by TEK on the interface with western-derived environmental management pose challenges for SOLEC in its attempts to involve Aboriginal people. However, there are also many opportunities for the meaningful participation of Aboriginal people and their knowledge. Certainly there is widespread interest in TEK in the environmental and resource management fields, including ecological restoration, wildlife management, environmental assessment, forest management and watershed planning and management (Cheveau, M. et al. 2008, Martinez 2013). Learning from the experience of others, SOLEC made use of one such opportunity through its inclusion of an Aboriginal agenda in the year 2000 conference.

SOLEC 2000

SOLEC 2000, held in October of that year in Hamilton, Ontario, was the first of the SOLEC gatherings to formally include Indigenous participation in its agenda. This was achieved through the involvement of an Elder and six First Nation environmental professionals throughout the conference, as well as specific workshop presentations by First Nations representatives and a First Nations-only discussion session. The goal of Indigenous in SOLEC was, and continues to be, to develop a process which facilitates the utilization of TEK in SOLEC initiatives. As will be discussed further in this chapter, this goal necessitates the establishment and maintenance of positive, long-term and mutually beneficial working relationships between Aboriginal peoples and the SOLEC organizers. While this chapter focuses on First Nations and Environment Canada (EC), it is intended that the relationship-building strategies discussed here will be shared with and hopefully used by representatives from other Great Lakes jurisdictions on both sides of the Canada/US border.

The role of the First Nations participants who attended SOLEC 2000 was to make observations, participate in the SOLEC process and then assess whether (and if so, how), TEK might be meaningfully considered in that process. A significant feature of SOLEC 2000 was the presence of an Elder, who opened and closed the proceedings with the *Thanksgiving Address* and led a field trip to Six Nations of the Grand River for interested participants to learn more about local First Nations environmental initiatives. In addition to these activities, a TEK workshop was held at SOLEC and was widely popular. The purpose of the TEK workshop was to raise awareness of what TEK is and to demonstrate the use of TEK in environmental projects around the Great Lakes. The TEK workshop provided an opportunity for conference participants to learn about TEK from a First Nations perspective.

As a result of these activities, key issues were raised by First Nations delegates, presenters and the Elder at SOLEC 2000. These are summarized by topic below:

Lack of Indigenous Representation

Indigenous representation at SOLEC was seen to be lacking in the following ways:

1. given that there are 63 First Nations in the Great Lakes Basin, the handful of First Nations people who attended SOLEC 2000 is not representative of Aboriginal concerns.
2. those First Nations people who were present were not necessarily TEK holders.
3. the range of First Nations interests represented was minimal in comparison with the range of non-Indigenous interests represented.

Lack of Respect for Aboriginal Viewpoints

Participants noted that although there was a First Nations presence at the conference, workshop facilitators, presenters and researchers frequently did not appreciate insights offered by First Nation participants. In some cases commentary offered by First Nations delegates was met with hostility. The First Nation participants agreed that little can be accomplished until a greater respect is afforded TEK and Indigenous input.

Limitations of the Indicator Selection Process

While participants stated that while the indicator selection process had been well done insofar as it went, it was nonetheless limited due to the following:
1. exclusion of Indigenous input into developing the indicator set.
2. lack of consideration of atmospheric sources of Great Lakes contamination.
3. focus on end-point monitoring instead of on source monitoring and control, which raises such issues as end-point safety standards (e.g., levels of contamination in fish considered "safe" for human consumption are based on non-Aboriginal populations with much lower rates of fish consumption than their Aboriginal counterparts).
4. focus on monitoring delays the need to exercise political will to act on pollution sources.

SOLEC: A Process Already Underway

First Nations participants observed little room for Indigenous ownership of any significant aspect of SOLEC. TEK is being approached as an "add-on", to be "incorporated" or "integrated" into the existing western scientific framework.

SOLEC: Potential Benefits to First Nations

All First Nations participants shared the view that the SOLEC process has the potential to benefit First Nations, depending on how it is undertaken. First Nations could benefit from increased capacity to carry out western scientific studies, if only there were an equal respect for Aboriginal knowledge on the part of non-Aboriginal researchers.

SOLEC 2002

SOLEC 2002 was held in Cleveland, Ohio, and featured a TEK workshop. First Nations/Tribal presence was not as significant as at the previous conference and this concern was noted by some delegates. The purpose of the TEK workshop was to demonstrate how First Nations are utilizing TEK in assessing and monitoring the Great Lakes environment. A presenter from Bkejwanong Territory shared examples of partnerships between his community and the scientific establishment. Such projects include an ecosystem recovery project with the Royal Ontario Museum and a project to ensure a safe haven for mussels. An Elder from the Anishinabek/Ontario Fisheries Resource Centre (A/OFRC) also participated in the workshop to share examples of how A/OFRC utilized TEK in its work.

One such example discussed the declining populations of walleye the Elder's community of Binjitiwaabik Zaagning First Nation (BZFN). The people of BZFN noticed the overall population of walleye declining, the fish were getting smaller (it took more fish to fill up a box), and there were fewer females. In BZFN the community imposed its own closure of the fishery and waited two years for the Ontario Ministry of Natural Resources (OMNR) to do the same. The First Nation thus noticed the decline first and took measures to ensure recovery of the species.

Another example shared by the Elder illustrates how TEK indicators contrast with those of western science. OMNR based its assessment of whitefish on juveniles in their testing programs. The people of BZFN did not have confidence in that method because they know juveniles and adults are different- they migrate differently and at different times of the year. BZFN used its own traditional knowledge instead to assess the state of whitefish. In conjunction with BZFN, A/OFRC mapped the differences in whitefish stocks and habitats. This led to a new assessment, combining TEK and western science to get a more accurate determination of the health of the lake whitefish.

Key issues raised by First Nations people at SOLEC 2002 included discussion of the need to:

    1. Recognize the value of local knowledge. Science is not the only source of knowledge in resource management. Local people often

notice changes first, especially if they rely on the environment for survival.

2. Improve the set of indicators. There are too few TEK-based indicators (i.e., indicators based on long-term observation).

3. Ensure that if science is used, it must be accessible to all; it is too frequently full of jargon and not readily understandable by lay people.

5. Recognize that relationship-building is a critical aspect of collaboration, and allow for the time it takes to achieve positive results.

6. Understand that the federal government's duty to consult with First Nations peoples on issues that impact their lands and lives (rights) applies to the SOLEC process as well.

SOLEC 2004

SOLEC 2004 was held in Toronto, Ontario. A different approach to Indigenous involvement than the previous 2 conferences was taken in 2004. Instead of highlighting the presence of Indigenous participation through a separate workshops, First Nation representatives were expected to attend as delegates. The First Nation delegates were expected to raise their issues as part of the regular workshops.

Four years had passed since the first formal inclusion of First Nation participation in the conference, and the Toronto conference was considered an opportunity to determine whether progress had been made in including TEK in SOLEC processes. An assessment was conducted that included a review of SOLEC materials and Aboriginal participation at the conference. Key findings included the following:

1. Western science is privileged over Traditional knowledge in the SOLEC process. TEK is still regarded as "unscientific" and thus there is resistance to the idea of utilizing TEK alongside western science.

2. The bias toward western science creates barriers to the inclusion of Aboriginal perspectives and knowledge in SOLEC processes (e.g., the development of indicators), and to the mutual sharing of perspectives to gain further insights into the state of the ecosystem.

3. Although there are some partnerships with Indigenous communities (First Nations and Tribes) in Great Lakes ecosystem initiatives, First Nations and Tribes in general are still largely ignored.

4. Although a traditional opening and closing for the conference provided an excellent opportunity to introduce TEK to the conference, there was little in terms of actual conference content (e.g., workshops) in which participants could engage further. The opening offered context for TEK by explaining philosophical/spiritual bases of TEK. Perhaps a workshop could then have been conducted to demonstrate how TEK and western

science can serve as complementary knowledge systems in assessing the Great Lakes.
7.   None of the SOLEC workshops were designed specifically to address TEK. Indigenous delegates were expected to participate in the workshops, but workshop facilitators were at a loss as to what to do with the TEK that was shared by First Nation and tribal delegates.

In summary, there is an increasing recognition of the need to accept TEK as a valuable source of information. However, scientists, policy makers, decision makers and researchers often do not know what to do with the knowledge shared by Aboriginal people. This is understandable in many cases, as it is very difficult if not impossible to simply make TEK "fit" into western scientific rubrics such as the one within which SOLEC is framed.

Despite these challenges and the shortcomings of the approach taken at SOLEC 2004, in which Indigenous participants were expected to participate as equal "delegates", participants felt that SOLEC still offers a potentially important venue for the sharing of TEK. On the research front, it was felt that Universities could perhaps take a leadership role in establishing collaboration between SOLEC and Indigenous peoples, and in facilitating the effective and respectful inclusion of TEK.
SOLEC 2006

This conference, held in Milwaukee, WI, was the fourth SOLEC in which Aboriginal people were formally involved. This SOLEC included a TEK Indicators workshop focusing on developing indicators of ecosystem health. This session recognized some of the work Aboriginal people are undertaking regarding the use of TEK in environmental initiatives and in utilizing indicators to understand changes in the Great Lakes ecosystem. The workshop also assisted participants in better understanding how Aboriginal people utilize TEK to address environmental challenges through the use of tradition-based indicators.

The workshop featured two key presentations. First was the Haudenosaunee Environmental Protection Process (HEPP), in which indicators are being developed for assessing ecosystem health based on Haudenosaunee worldview, traditions and values. The second presentation discussed a TEK and Source Water Protection (SWP) project involving the Chiefs of Ontario and Ontario First Nations representatives. This project's focus was on traditional perspectives of water and how to appropriately consider TEK in SWP work at the community and watershed levels.

The HEPP presentation described a radically different process from any that had been shared at previous SOLECs. Rather than working from western-based systems of environmental resource management, HEPP starts with Haudenosaunee traditions. Traditional teachings such as the Creation story, the Thanksgiving Address, the Two Row Wampum, the

Silver Covenant Chain, the Great Law and the Code of Handsome Lake are used to form the basis for the development of ecosystem health indicators for the Haudenosaunee people. A cornerstone of the HEPP process is that people must respect the natural world and exercise their responsibilities given to them by the Creator to ensure sustainable relationships with all of Creation. A sustainable relationship in this context implies balance and harmony with the natural world.

The TEK-SWP presentation discussed how the Chiefs of Ontario, in collaboration with Environment Canada, had embarked on a project to highlight First Nations' traditional views on taking care of water, and to determine how this knowledge can appropriately be considered in SWP plans at the community and watershed levels. The project was organized into four workshops which brought together Elders and knowledge holders from the main First Nations cultural groups in Ontario: Haudenosaunee (Iroquois), Anishinaabe (Ojibway and Oji-Cree) and Mushkegowuk (James Bay Cree). These workshops were held in the respective regions of each group. Workshop participants consisted primarily of Elders, with band councillors, environmental technicians and academics also attending. Each group was asked to discuss selected topics such as traditional teachings on respecting water, current relationships to water, sharing of traditional knowledge, and use of that knowledge in SWP at the community and watershed levels.

Overall, participants in the workshops stressed the need for TEK to inform an integral part of decisions regarding water. Primary topics of discussion included: water as a living entity; the interconnection between water and all life; impacts of industry; treaty rights and obligations; meaningful involvement in decision-making; and community education. Similar to the HEPP presentation, Elders who participated in TEK-SWP project stressed the requirement for people to accept their responsibility for taking care of water.

Key insights gained from this workshop include:

1. The Two Row Wampum offers an important paradigm for external relations. In this process, indicators developed from both the western scientific and traditional knowledge worldviews would come to together in the spirit of equality. The Two Row Wampum is a core conceptual framework for how people from very different cultures can work together in a harmonious way.
2. Treaty rights must be recognized and respected. The groups emphasized that negotiations about water must be held on a nation-to-nation basis. The Elders noted that such a basis for a relationship already exists.
3. Any plans or developments affecting water must include consulting First Nations and providing adequate resources. Furthermore, Elders should be involved in these discussions, and they expressed a great desire to be included.

4. Elders and participants stated that TEK should be shared judiciously. Most participants shared the view that ATK should be shared with non-First Nations society since dissemination could lead to greater understanding of and sympathy for First Nations worldviews.

4. Non-Aboriginals who seek TEK must be willing to respect and accept that knowledge.

SOLEC 2008

Indigenous presence at SOLEC 2008 held Niagara Fall, ON waned considerably, although an opening and closing to acknowledge the territory of Indigenous peoples was observed. The theme of SOLEC 2008 was "Nearshore" focused on the nearshore lands and waters of the Great Lakes, where biodiversity and human impact is the greatest. The highlight of SOLEC 2008 for Indigenous and non-Indigenous participants alike was a presentation by Grandmother Josephine Mandamin. Grandmother Mandamin has lead the Great Lakes Mother Earth walk around each of the Great Lakes since 2003. It was recognized by SOLEC organizers, that she, more so than anyone else knows the state of the Great Lakes nearshore. She was best able to describe the state of the water and land close to the shores of the lakes. Mandamin described her journey of thousands of kilometers and support she received from Indigenous and non-Indigenous alike to protect the waters (Mandamin 2012). The presentation was on the most popular at SOLEC 2008 and demonstrates the continued keen interest in TEK.

SOLEC 2011

SOLEC 2011 was held in Erie, Pennsylvania and did not include any formal inclusion of Indigenous peoples. The theme of the conference was "Linking Lands To the Lakes". It is disappointing that, interest and inclusion of Indigenous peoples formally into SOLEC has waned over the years.

Summary

Overall, in the fourteen years since, the first SOLEC in which Indigenous involvement was given consideration, there remains an interest to better understand Indigenous peoples and their knowledge, values and perspectives in Great Lake governance. However, the models currently being applied to achieve better Indigenous representation in SOLEC are generally inappropriate. Integrating or assimilating TEK into western scientific paradigms or frameworks is not an effective way to respectfully consider TEK in SOLEC as I have shown in this chapter. At this point in time, there is little (if any) TEK being considered in SOLEC processes. Although there have been efforts in the past (SOLEC 2000, 2002 and 2004), Indigenous representation since has been sporadic, an afterthought, rather than regarded as an integral part of the reporting progress on the state of the Great Lakes. Efforts have not been consistent or sustainable over time as shown by the minimal representation of Indigenous peoples from 2006 to 2011. Indigenous representation has been dependent on the leadership of key individuals in EC and USEPA and once they moved on or retired, interest waned. Indigenous participation has not been institutionalized in the SOLEC process, and thus, there is a lack of commitment from a organizational point of view.

Indigenous peoples, however, are utilizing TEK in their own environmental work in the Great Lakes ecosystem, seemingly in parallel to the efforts of western institutions.

Without the support to have sustainable working relationships, the knowledge gaps will continued and greater and more mutually beneficial knowledge sharing will continue to elude SOLEC and other Great Lake initiatives. Indigenous peoples have indicated they are willing to share TEK and work with external agencies, but will only do so in a climate of respect and equality (Lavalley 2006) This means that not only are Indigenous peoples willing to share TEK when appropriate, but it is reasonable to expect non-Indigenous people to share science in an appropriate manner in an effort to resolve environmental challenges. Relationships must be mutually beneficial, or again, as noted earlier, the interactions are not sustainable. The next section offers a model of cooperation and mutual sharing that is based on a Nation to Nation treaty-the Two Row Wampum.

CO-EXISTENCE: A Model for a New First Nations/Environment Canada Relationship

Although it is hoped that SOLEC organizers continue to seek Indigenous involvement and participation in SOLEC activities, there is much work to be done to meet the goals originally set out in 2000. Over the past 14 years, and over six SOLEC conferences, numerous insights into the difficulties associated with trying to incorporate an entirely different worldview in the form of TEK into an existing non-Aboriginal framework have become obvious. In recognition of this, Elders and other participants have offered suggestions and recommendations for addressing the challenges.

Indigenous representatives who have participated in SOLEC over the years agree that First Nations support the goal of long-term sustainability of the Great Lakes Ecosystem. They, after all, rely upon a healthy Great Lakes ecosystem as a direct source of food and other resources. The problem is, as was stated earlier in the paper, that the current process has been created without Indigenous input and therefore leaves little room for Indigenous viewpoints which challenge the current system. As also noted earlier, Indigenous people are already engaged in community work similar to that of SOLEC. Rather than trying to integrate or "force-fit" TEK into an existing process not designed to accommodate TEK in the first place, a "parallel" process is offered as a viable alternative. What is proposed, therefore, is that a "co-existence" model replace current efforts to "incorporate" or "integrate" Indigenous knowledge systems into a non-Aboriginal initiative.

Far from being a new idea, co-existence is a concept that has its roots in the way that numerous First Nations had originally hoped to work with the "newcomers" when they first arrived on this continent. Depicted in the Two-Row Wampum belt of the Haudenosaunee, the concept provides a framework for how Aboriginal and non-Aboriginal peoples can retain their integrity through undertaking their own processes according to their own worldviews. At the same time, the two sides are to share information and work in partnership on issues of common concern. This is a long-term, mutually beneficial relationship, where each side respects the other's worldview and its right to live accordingly (Ransom, R. & K. Ettenger, 2001)

The Two-Row Wampum belt is supplemented by a later belt, known as the Friendship Treaty belt. The two belts go together, describing different aspects of the relationship. The Friendship Treaty belt depicts two figures holding hands, with the idea being that Aboriginal and non-Aboriginal people are linked together, and that it is their responsibility to each other to never let go of each other, to always assist one another as they travel through life together. Each people is to retain its own identity while being strengthened through the support of the other.

TEK and SOLEC: Final Recommendations

Based on findings from the four SOLEC conferences, including input from Indigenous participants and concepts associated with the co-existence model, it is recommended that:

1. an equitable, long-term and mutually beneficial partnership be established between the parties of SOLEC (USEPA and Environment Canada) and Indigenous peoples in the Great Lakes Basin and that this form the basis for discussion regarding TEK. Such relationships will facilitate the sharing of information, including scientific knowledge and TEK, among the involved parties.
2. First Nations capacity-building for the purpose of contributing meaningfully to this partnership be supported by parties to SOLEC. This will ensure that the best results possible are achieved in all areas and will help to "level the playing field" in terms of information availability. Such support must ensure that communities have the resources they need to conduct any necessary follow-up activities following specific projects.
3. The unique status of First Nations in establishing and maintaining environmental partnerships be recognized by all parties. Any such partnerships must be negotiated on a Nation-to-Nation basis, accounting for the fact that First Nations continue to hold Aboriginal and Treaty rights.

4. A Cultural Sensitivity Training Program be established for any staff who can be expected to come into contact with Indigenous peoples as part of their official duties. This training should be organized in partnership with First Nations and be delivered by Indigenous peoples. Financial resources should be set aside by the respective governments for this training.

5. existing First Nations projects on the health of the Great Lakes ecosystem be continued and built upon so that the wealth of information arrived at through such undertakings is not lost.

6. The SOLEC parties take steps to officially recognize TEK as a valid source of knowledge on a par with western science.

7. An Indigenous focus be included in SOLEC web sites and reports. As part of establishing and maintaining partnerships, SOLEC Web pages should contain links to documents and other Web sites (e.g. EAGLE Project, Indigenous Environmental Network, Bkejwanong.com, etc.) which provide Indigenous perspectives on Great Lakes issues and describe First Nations undertakings in this area.

8. A representative group of Indigenous people be included from the outset of any Great Lakes initiative and that such representation is gender balanced. TEK is often gendered knowledge; it is important to ensure that women are adequately represented.

9. Community control be maintained over projects involving community TEK. If the people are to be expected to share their knowledge, they must be assured of having a meaningful say in how that knowledge is used. In order to guarantee this to the fullest extent possible, community members must be involved in all project stages, and must have a thorough understanding of all aspects of the project as it unfolds.

10. SOLEC conferences include projects that involve working with Indigenous peoples. Furthermore, that SOLEC delegates identify which First Nations/Native American communities they are working with and how they are working with them. This process will assist in gaining a better understanding of collaborations between Indigenous and non-Indigenous peoples in the Great Lakes Ecosystem, rather than relying on one workshop at the conference to provide such insights.

11. Indigenous peoples must be included in the SOLEC Organizing Committee and have an equal role in setting the agenda. Insights and networks of contacts achieved through such representation will assist in raising the profile of SOLEC in Indigenous communities and encourage more meaningful participation.

12. An Indigenous caucus form an integral part of an SOLEC conference. This caucus will assist Indigenous peoples attending SOLEC with networking and developing strategies for how they will address indicators at the conference. Furthermore, that this caucus have the opportunity to address the plenary regarding its findings.

122

13. All SOLEC meetings should be opened by the host First Nation. This act demonstrates respect and recognition of the presence of Aboriginal people in the Great Lakes ecosystem

Many of the recommendations shared by Indigenous participants in the SOLEC process over the past fourteen years are consistent with the *United Nations Declaration on the Rights of Indigenous Peoples* and should form the basis of mutually beneficial relationships and equitable sharing of traditional and scientific knowledge.

Conclusion

Despite the declining efforts by SOLEC organizations to include Indigenous peoples, there remain hopeful signs of progress on perhaps at a more meaningful levels. The recent amendments to the Great Lakes Water Quality Agreement (2012), makes specific mention of Indigenous peoples. The Protocol to amend the GLWQA states in the preamble

"Recognizing that , while the Parties are responsible for decision-making under this Agreement, the involvement and participation of State and Provincial Governments, *Tribal Governments, First Nations and Métis*, Municipal Governments, watershed management agencies, local public agencies, and the Public are essential to achieve the objectives of this Agreement (Environment Canada 2013c, para 10). (Emphasis mine).

The above commitments recognize the importance of Indigenous peoples in achieving the goals of the GLWQA which include reporting on the Great Lakes Ecosystem every three years (Environment Canada 2013c). Furthermore, in relation to TEK, the GLWAA states as part of principles and approaches in Article 2, section 4 (l) states:

Science-based management-implementing management decisions, policies and programs that are based on best available science, research and knowledge, as well as *traditional ecological knowledge*, when available (emphasis mine).

The amended GLWQA calls for cooperation and consultation with Tribal governments, First Nations and Métis to achieve its goals. SOLEC is part of the reporting process to the governments and others on the GLWQA. In the years to come, it is hoped that the governments of the United States and Canada will come to draw upon the considerable work already achieved through the five previous SOLEC conferences to address the goal of the current GLWQA to "protect the Great Lakes" a vision shared by all.

◊ ◊ ◊ ◊ ◊ ◊

Deb McGregor is Anishinaabe from Whitefish River First Nation. She has been an educator and trainer at both the university and community levels for over twenty years. She has also been involved in curriculum development, research and teaching for many years. Her focus is on Indigenous knowledge in relation to the environment. Currently, Dr. McGregor is an Associate Professor at the University of Toronto, in Geography. She has taught various courses on Indigenous Knowledge and environmental issues and is engaged in a number of research projects involving Indigenous knowledge in relations to environmental governance .

References

Anderson, J. 2010. Indigenous/Traditional Knowledge & Intellectual Property. Centre for the Study of the Public Domain. Issue Paper. Duke University School of Law. North Carolina, USA.

Assembly of First Nations. 1995. The Feasibility of Representing Traditional Indigenous Knowledge in Cartographic, Pictorial or Textual Forms. National Aboriginal Forestry Association and National Atlas Information Service, Ottawa, ON. 39 pp.

Berkes, F. 1999. Sacred Ecology: Traditional Ecological Knowledge and Resource Management. Taylor and Francis, Philadelphia, PA. 209 pp.

Berkes, F. 1993. Traditional Ecological Knowledge in Perspective. In: Inglis, J. (ed.). 1993. Traditional Ecological Knowledge: Concepts and Cases. International Program on Traditional Ecological Knowledge and International Development Research Centre, Ottawa, ON. pp.1-9.

Cheveau, M., Imbeau, L., Drapeau, P. & Belanger, L. 2008. Current Status and future directions of traditional ecological knowledge in forest management: a review. The Forestry Chronicle. 84(2): 231-243.

Ellis, S. 2005. Meaningful Consideration? A Review of Traditional Knowledge in Environmental Decision Making. Arctic, Vol. 58, No. 1, pp. 66-77

Environment Canada. 2013a. State of the Great Lakes Reporting. http://www.ec.gc.ca/grandslacs-greatlakes/default.asp?lang= En&n=70FFEFDF-1

Environment Canada. 2013b. A Renewed Commitment to Action: the 2012 Great Lakes Water Quality Agreement. http://www.ec.gc.ca/grandslacs-greatlakes/default.asp?lang= En&n=B274CBC1-1

Environment Canada. 2013c. Great Lakes Water Quality Agreement. http://www.ec.gc.ca/grandslacs-greatlakes/default.asp?lang= En&n=A1C62826-1

Grenier, L. 1998. Working with Indigenous Knowledge: A Guide for Re-searchers. International Development Research Centre, Ottawa, ON. 115 pp.

Houde, N. 2007. The Six Faces of Traditional Ecological Knowledge: Challenges and Opportunities for Canadian Co-Management Arrangements. Ecology and Society 12 (2): 34.

Johnson, M. (ed.).1992. Lore: Capturing Traditional Environmental Knowledge. Dene Cultural Institute and the International Development Research Centre, Ottawa, ON. 190 pp.

Kimmerer, R. 2012. Searching for Synergy: Integrating traditional and scientific ecological knowledge in environmental science education. J.Environmental Sudies Sci.

LaDuke, W. 1997. Voices from White Earth: Gaa-waabaabiganikaag", In H. Hannum (ed), People, Land and Community: Collected E.F. Schumacher Society Lectures. New Haven, CT: Yale University Press, p 22-37.

Lavalley, G. 2006. Aboriginal Traditional Knowledge and Source Water Protection: First Nations' Views on Taking Care of Water. Chiefs of Ontario, Toronto, ON. 65 pp.

Lickers, F. 1997a. Perspectives I: Statement to the Chiefs of Ontario Working Group on Nationhood and Sustainability. In: Chiefs of Ontario Working Group on Nationhood and Sustainability. Nationhood and Sustainability: Framework Document. Adopted by Resolution 97/20, Special All Ontario Chiefs Conference, Thunder Bay, Ontario, October 16, 1997. Chiefs of Ontario, Toronto, ON. pp. 29-35.

Lickers, F. 1997b. Can't See the Forest for the Trees: A Native American's Perspective. In: Baker, N. (ed.). Biodiversity: Toward Operational Definitions. The 1995 Plum Creek Lectures. School of Forestry, The University of Montana - Missoula. pp.39-53.

Lukey, J. 1995. Native and Non-Native Perspectives on Aboriginal Traditional Environmental Knowledge. [unpublished major paper]. Faculty of Environmental Studies, York University, Toronto, ON. 69 pp.

Mandamin, J. 2012. N'guh izhi chigay, nibi onji: I will do it for the water". In: Anishinaabewin Niizh: Culture Movements, Critical Moments. Corbiere, A., McGregor, D., Migwans, C. (eds). Ojibwe Cultural Foundation, McChigeeng, Ontario. pp.13-22.

Martinez, D. 2013. The Complementarily of Indigenous Kincentric Ecology and Western Science in Ecocultural Restoration and Ecosystem-Based Adaptation and Climate Disruption. In: Simmons, E. (ed) Indigenous Earth: Praxis and Transformation. Theytus Books. Penticton, BC. p. 390-416.

Mason et. al. 2012. Listening and learning from traditional knowledge and western science: a dialogue on contemporary challenges of forest health and wildfire. Journal of Forestry. 111(4): 197-193.

McGregor, D. 2012. Traditional Knowledge: Considerations for Protecting Water in Ontario. Special Issue on Water and Indigenous Peoples. The International Indigenous Policy Journal. 3 (3). http://www.iipj.org/.

McGregor, 2010. The Earth Keepers Solid Waste Management Planning Program: a Collaborative Approach to Utilizing Aboriginal Traditional Knowledge and Western Science in Ontario. The

International Journal of Canadian Studies. Les représentations des Premières nations et des Métis/Representations of First Nations and Métis (2010.1). No. 41. p. 69-98.

McGregor. D. 2009. Linking Traditional Knowledge and Environmental Practice in Canada. Journal of Canadian Studies 43(3):69-100.

McGregor, D. 2008. Linking Traditional Ecological Knowledge and Western Science: Aboriginal Perspectives on SOLEC. Canadian Studies 28(1):139-158.

McGregor, D. 2005. Traditional Ecological Knowledge: An Anishinabe-Kwe Perspective. Atlantis Women's Studies Journal 29(2):103-109.

McGregor, D. 2004. Traditional Knowledge and Sustainable Development: Towards Co-existence. In The Way of Development (eds) Mario Blaser, Harvey Feit, Glenn McRae, Zed Books, p. 72-91.

Menzies, C. (Ed.). 2006. Traditional Ecological Knowledge and Natural Resource Management. University of Nebraska Press. Lincoln

Nakashima, D. 1993. Astute Observers on the Sea Ice Edge: Inuit Knowledge as a Basis for Arctic Co-Management. In: Inglis, J. (ed.). 1993. Traditional Ecological Knowledge: Concepts and Cases. International Program on Traditional Ecological Knowledge and International Development Research Centre, Ottawa, ON. pp. 99-110.

Natashima, D., Galloway McLean, K., Thulstrup, H.D., Ramos Castillo, A. & Rubis, J.T . 2012. Weathering Uncertainty: Traditional Knowledge for Climate Change Assessment and Adaptation. Paris, UNESCO, and Darwin United Nations University.

O'Flaherty, M., Davidson-Hunt, I & Manseau, M. 2008. Indigenous Knowledge and Values in Planning for Sustainable Forestry: Pikangikum First Nation and Whitefeather Forest Initiative. Ecology and Society 13 (1): 6.

Ransom, R. and K. Ettenger. 2001. Polishing the Kaswentha': A Haudenosaunee View of Environmental Cooperation. Environmental Science and Policy. 4: 219-228.

Roberts, K. 1996. Circumpolar Aboriginal People and Co-Management Practice: Current Issues in Co-Management and Environmental Assessment. [conference proceedings]. Arctic Institute of North America and Joint Secretariat -Inuvialuit Renewable Resources Committees. Arctic Institute of North America, University of Calgary, AB. 172 pp.

Whyte, K. 2013. On the role of traditional ecological knowledge as a collaborative concept: a philosophical study. Ecological Processes 2013, 2:7.

Shackeroff, J. & Campbell, L. 2007. Traditional Ecological Knowledge in Conservation Research: Problems and Prospects for Constructive Engagement. Conservation and Society, Vol. 5 (3), p 343-360.

Wolfe, J., Bechard, C., Cizek, P., and D. Cole. 1992. Indigenous and Western Knowledge and Resource Management Systems. University School of Rural Planning and Development, University of Guelph, ON. 40 pp.

Listening to the Trees: Traditional Knowledge and Industrial Society in the American Northwoods

Aimée Cree Dunn

Introduction

According to anthropologist John Bodley, the Industrial Revolution in England "launched the developing Western nations on an explosive growth in population and consumption called 'progress,' which led to an unprecedented assault on the world's indigenous peoples and their resources." (1)   European corporations, running low on "natural resources" after having fully exploited their own rural regions, sought resource-rich lands abroad over which they could gain political and/or economic control in order to extract those resources. Their most resistant obstacle was neither distance nor expense but rather the Indigenous peoples who called those resource-rich lands home. In attempting to gain access to the coveted resources, Western corporations and their governments were apparently willing to stop at nothing: forced removals, taxations, "human rights" missions, and even ethnocide, genocide, and, after control of the resources was secured, eventual ecocide.

Frighteningly enough, these multinational corporate horrors continue in various parts of the world today – for example, the open pit mines of Papua New Guinea, the Amazonian oil wars, the massive hydro-electric projects built throughout Cree territory in Canada, and, until recently, the deadly battles between Shell Oil and the Ogoni in Nigeria's Niger Delta. Within the United States itself, much of this continues as well.

Although many people are aware of the above, few know the details behind the industrial invasion of the northern Great Lakes area. As a land once replete with vibrant forests, rich veins of minerals, and abundantly healthy waters, American industrial society was quick to place the Northwoods in its sights and to proceed, methodically, to open it up for industrial exploitation. The tales of how this happened are told by various state-sponsored marks of interest, corporate museums, and other similar entities, and have become part of the political mythology that makes up American history. In relating the advent of corporate mining and logging in the northern Great Lakes areas, these tales are often full of the warm fuzzies, painting an image not of intent robber-barons out to make a buck off the Anishinaabeg homeland, but of resourceful and stalwart immigrants forging homes out of a howlingly forsaken northern wilderness after having "discovered" the area's rich "natural resources."

Contrary to these popular versions, however, the story of the Northwoods begins well before industrial society forced its way onto this land, and the arrival of industrialism, instead of the boon it is made out to be in this mythology, actually brought about the near-destruction of the people who had made this land home for generations, and so undermined the health of the land as to alter the Northwoods to this day. Government institutions, corporate agendas, and social engin-eering worked together to colonize the North for its resources and undermine the subsistence lifestyle (2) enjoyed by both the Native and non-Native rural residents who lived here.

The treaties made with the Anishinaabeg were one of the earliest manifestations of this resource colonization; they helped clear the land by removing the Anishinaabeg to small areas of reserved lands in the 1800s. This was followed by a brief but resolute attempt to relocate the Anishinaabeg in 1850 to west of the Mississippi. Later other policies (elitist, urban-biased, and frequently based on eugenicist attitudes) were used to favor a profit-based economy over subsistence economics. These policies included the emergence of game laws and rural zoning that made it difficult for both Native and non-Native northerners to continue their self-reliant lifestyle.

Today, most of us who live in the north country survive as wage-earners or for-profit farmers. Made dependent on the volatile money-based economy in this way, northern residents have a difficult time remaining on the land and often are forced to forsake the rural for more lucrative urban areas offering a greater number of jobs. As more people are economically forced to remove themselves from the land, fewer people learn traditional land-based knowledge as the years pass by, and fewer people are left to defend the North from more industrial invasions. Like the treaties, this economics-based forced removal opens up the land for resource colonization. While it may surprise some outsiders, due to this colonization, the North is no longer the pristine wilderness many like to believe it is. And the more polluted the area becomes, the more difficult it is to maintain subsistence activities.

It does not have to be this way, however.

As a collection of knowledge that comes from intergenerational residency in the Northwoods, traditional land-based knowledge offers proven guidelines for how to interact with the community of the land. Further, inherent in this body of knowledge is the responsibility to look after the land, to be what Michigan organic farmer, Maynard Kaufman, calls "the eyes on the land." Thus not only do rural people, Native and non-Native alike, have a cultural and spiritual right to live on the land, they also have the responsibility to protect the land from that element of human society that threatens it. Rural residents are the ones who, through their very proximity, can listen to the trees, the waters, the animals, the land. From this listening comes vital questions about industrial society: What do the increasing number of dead trees lining our northern roads tell us? How do we stop the PCB-contamination of our animal relatives, the mecury poisoning of the fish? Who speaks for the deformed, three-legged frogs? How is this industrial contamination impacting the human community?

We need to listen to what the land is telling us. In turn, those who are not of the land need to listen to us. Will enough people listen in time to make the necessary changes? Only time will tell.

Traditional Knowledge

When the land is inhabited by people living a responsible subsistence lifestyle, it tends to stay ecologically healthy. Like much of America, the Northwoods was ecologically whole prior to European arrival. For example, Henry Schoolcraft, on an 1820 expedition with Governor Lewis Cass into northern Michigan and the Upper Peninsula, frequently remarks in his journal on the abundant richness of the northern land. Along the shores of "Saganaw Bay," some distance north of European settlement at that time, Schoolcraft comments on "the riches of the soil, and the natural beauty of the country" and on how the Ojibwe and Odawa of that area "have long enjoyed the advantages of an easy subsistence from the fine hunting grounds . . . and the abundance of fish." (3) Near present-day Oscoda, Michigan, at the "river aux Sables," Schoolcraft writes of abundant sturgeon in the river. (4) The Sault Sainte Marie area is described as a "dense forest of elm, sugar maple, ash, and pine." (5) In part this abundance was possible because of the Anishinaabeg ability to live within the land's carrying capacity – this largely came from lifestyles that were based on traditional land-based knowledge. Today this is often referred to as traditional ecological knowledge (TEK). After European contact, non-Natives in the North came to live a subsistence lifestyle both in the Northwoods and elsewhere on the American continents; some of these Euro-Americans also learned to maintain a healthy land based on traditional land-based knowledge, which, for the sake of discussion, I will refer to as traditional rural knowledge (TRK) (although this is a bit of a misnomer as the Native societies discussed in this essay are rural as well). Both TEK and TRK offer philosophies that vastly differ from the economic theories that run the world today.

Perhaps because traditional rural knowledge has a much shorter span of existence on this continent, it may be a less easily identified body of knowledge than traditional ecological knowledge. TRK strongly exists nevertheless. Further, when we discuss the TEK of the northern Great Lakes area, we can generally discuss it in terms of the traditional Anishinaabeg cultural worldview. When we discuss the TRK of the same region, however, it is more difficult to discuss it within one cultural paradigm. Without a well-established and cohesive cultural base, TRK can seem fragmented and vague at times, yet there are certain general rural cultural attitudes that are common enough to the non-Native rural experience to form the basis of TRK. Generally speaking, TRK is based on the following principles:

1. the right to live on healthy land
2. the right to be self-reliant
3. the right of families to land that is of a sufficient size to provide physical, emotional, mental, and spiritual sustenance for one's family as well as the right to hunt, fish, and gather on land not already claimed by other families (i.e. lands belonging to corporations, absentee landlords, and the state)
4. the obligation to be a responsible caretaker within one's own human community and within the community of the land
5. honoring time-tested methods of accomplishing various activities (e.g. canning, farming, hunting)
6. the right to freedom from extensive governmental interference with all of the above.

With land a person can provide for the needs of one's family and can survive even when the larger society is having difficulty. Further, for many TRK-people, taking away their land is like taking away their soul.

TEK, of course, also has this strong connection to the land as its basis. TEK creates a human relationship with the land that comes from providing for one's family and community from the land following TEK guidelines. The primary principles guiding one's participation in this relationship are respect, reciprocity, and generosity both within one's human community and within the community of the land. That is, the TEK relationship asks its participants to provide for their family and community in a manner that

1. looks out for all one's relations: if someone cannot procure sustenance on their own, provide it for them; if an animal or plant is no longer abundant in numbers, leave it alone
2. honors the plant and animal whose life is taken in order that you and yours may continue to live
3. respects the right of plants and animals to live their lives in a good and healthy environment
4. honors the future by protecting the earth today
5. shares unstintingly without resentment and gives back when something is taken
6. recognizes the spiritual and cultural right of all to participate in the community of the land

The late activist-scholar-philosopher, John Mohawk, calls this the "subsistence paradigm." For him, this paradigm is not about economics

130

at all. Instead, he says, "[i]t's a cultural, spiritual, social exchange that's intended to go on for generations . . . it's the most moral relationship with nature that humans have ever devised." (6)

When a society is based on the subsistence paradigm, emphasis is placed on a healthy land. When a society is based on an industrial economy, however, whether capitalist, communist or socialist, emphasis is placed on extracting resources. As Mohawk writes,

> Let's say you have three people who approach a tree. One's a socialist materialist, one's a capitalist materialist and one's a traditional native person. The capitalist materialist will explain to you that he has to cut the tree down because this is in the best interest, not only of himself but also of society; that it is a kind of destiny; that by cutting the tree down, he will rationally distribute the materials from the tree and he'll do the most good for the people. A socialist person approaching the tree will also tell you to cut the tree down, because after cutting the tree down you can distribute it equally to everybody and it's going to do the most good for the world that way. But a native person looking at the tree will say that the tree, in its unharmed, original form, has a value that's far greater than anything the others are proposing. . . . The materialist argument boils down to who can make the best argument about the best, fastest and most efficient use of the world's resources. . . . If we think that way, then we're just caught in the socialist versus capitalist paradigm. But we want to have a different kind of discussion; we want to talk about "subsistence." (7)

The problem in the north country is that this materialist paradigm invaded and colonized the Northwoods. As part of this invasion, it deliberately gutted the North's subsistence-based societies in the name of profit and so-called industrial progress. This had a two-fold effect on the subsistence cultures, an effect that is found nearly everywhere on the planet where industrial society seeks to extract resources from rural/Indigenous lands:

1. it makes self-sufficiency difficult, if not impossible, through economic pressures, environmental destruction, and the incorporation of the formerly self-sufficient people into the industrial economy as wage-workers, and

2. a feedback loop develops where the formerly self-sufficient people become less self- sufficient with their increasing dependency on wage-work – the more wage-work, the less self-sufficiency. The less time devoted to the subsistence activities of a self-reliant lifestyle, the less opportunities there are to maintain and/or learn traditional land-based knowledge. As a result, over the years, and particularly over the generations, people begin to lose TEK/TRK and, in the process, lose the knowledge and the values they need to combat the further industrialization of the land.

Anthropologist John Bodley writes, "small-scale cultures [like rural/Indigenous societies] represent a rejection of the materialistic values of the global [industrial] culture. Yet, individuals can be made to reject their traditional values if outside interests create the necessary conditions for this rejection." (8)   Thus, handily for industrialism, through its resource colonization industrial society not only undermines those cultures that stand in opposition to it but also absorbs and transforms the members of those cultures, converting them into more fodder for the industrial machine and its accompanying economy of over-consumption.   The "industrialization process," Bodley writes, "disempowered millions, driving formerly self-sufficient rural peoples to a precarious and dependent existence in the cities." (9)

How, then, did this "industrialization process" unfold in the Northwoods?

Industrial Policies Shaping the American Northwoods

Not long after the Northwoods came under the domain of the United States, it came under American plans for industrial expansion. While Europeans had economically invaded the North well before this through the fur trade, the industrial invasion did not begin in full force until the early part of the nineteenth century. The fur trade subtly hooked many Native people into European economics and made them consumers of European trade goods. It could be argued that this began the initial breakdown of the economic self-sufficiency found in traditional subsistence lifestyles. However, trade in the Americas had been ongoing for millennia, and most Native societies, unless preyed upon by a particularly nefarious trader, adapted, in general, to the influx of European goods without disrupting the overall pattern and essence of their traditional subsistence lifestyles. This changed, however, when the American government and corporations developed a keen interest in the "resource-rich" Northwoods.

Treaties & Removal

From the early 1800s, it was obvious that the United States was greatly interested in the minerals found on Anishinaabeg land. For example, in 1819/1820, Governor Lewis Cass of Michigan Territory made an expedition to the Upper Peninsula. One of his primary goals was to assess the mineral wealth of the region. To do this, Cass took along a mineralogist, Henry Schoolcraft. (10) On this expedition, as written in his journal, Schoolcraft found indications of a great deal of the "natural resources" they sought: iron ore near Marquette, copper along the Ontonagon River, seemingly endless forests – everything they had hoped for.

The two primary goals of the treaties urged on the Anishinaabeg by the United States were first to gain access to the minerals on Anishinaabeg land and later for the U.S. to gain the land itself. For example, the treaty made between the U.S. and the Ojibwe in 1826 only grants the U.S. "the right to search for, and carry away, any metals or minerals from any part of their country." (11) This access was "not to affect the title of the land, nor the existing jurisdiction over it." (12) As early as 1828, however, the Green Bay treaty "allowed [the U.S.] access to lead mines in Illinois and Wisconsin" and relinquished Native jurisdiction over those mines. (13) By the 1842 treaty signing, historian Mark Keller writes, "[t]he stated policy was to buy title to the land, then remove the tribes. . . . Discovery of iron ore and copper in the Keweenaw Peninsula created a desire to obtain these lands . . . Timber and mining interests were eager to establish claims." (14) Aside from ceding land to the U.S., the 1842 treaty paved the way for the legal means of completely removing the Anishinaabeg from the resource-rich Northwoods. The 1842 treaty states, "The Indians residing on the Mineral District, shall be subject to removal therefrom at the pleasure of the United States."(15)

In 1850, the United States found it to its "pleasure" to issue a removal order, calling for the removal of the Ojibwe to lands west of the Mississippi River. This removal resulted in the tragic 1850 Sandy Lake Death March. As Keller writes, "When the government learned the Chippewa refused to leave their ceded lands, it closed the Indian Agency at LaPointe[, Wisconsin], and stopped making annuity payments there. A new site for an agency, Sandy Lake in Minnesota on the Mississippi, was chosen." (16) Anyone who wished to obtain their annuity payment was required to travel to the Mississippi agency at Sandy Lake; those who did not would not receive the annuity payment. (17) In this way, the U.S. government hoped to induce the Anishinaabeg of the Upper Peninsula and northern Wisconsin to move to these lands west of the Mississippi River leaving their traditional land open to industrial exploitation. Over 400 people died as a result of this policy. (18)

The attempted removal was unsuccessful, however. After the tragedy of Sandy Lake, a delegation of Anishinaabeg leaders went to Washington in 1852 to meet with President Fillmore, gathering petition signatures from Natives and non-Natives alike along the way, particularly from small businessmen who appreciated the influx of money provided by the annuity payments. (19) They explained that "[n]one had understood the agreement to give up their lands, and all understood they would never be asked to leave their lands as long as they kept the peace." (20) After consideration, President Fillmore canceled the 1850 removal order and agreed that annuity payments would be made at LaPointe in the future.

The Anishinaabeg managed to resist complete removal from the land they had lived on for generations. The treaties of 1837, 1842, and 1854, however, removed the Anishinaabeg from much of their traditional land in the Northwoods, confining their land claims to small reserved areas. Some, such as the people around the Sault Sainte Marie area, were not even left with reservation lands. Victims of the government's attempts to make the Anishinaabeg into Euro-American-style farmers, the Anishinaabeg around the Sault were apportioned individual allotments instead of a contiguous area of land recognized as a reservation. (21) Most of the Anishinaabeg bands eventually would lose even more land during the allotment era.

Game Laws

When the Anishinaabeg ceded the vast majority of their traditional lands in the 1800s and settled on reservations, confinement to a massively decreased land-base could have quickly destroyed the traditional subsistence lifestyle this society had developed over centuries in the north. However, many of the Anishinaabeg treaty signers reserved their people's rights to provide for their family and community by hunting, fishing, and gathering on the ceded territories. These "treaty rights" were (and continue to be) essential to the maintenance of the Anishinaabeg culture, TEK, and often an individual's physical survival.

By the early 1900s, however, the Michigan, Wisconsin, and Minnesota state governments stopped recognizing the Anishinaabeg subsistence rights and began arresting and fining those who violated the newly developed state game laws. "Then came the laws to control the fishing, the hunting, the trapping, even on the reservation lands," writes Anishinaabe storyteller Ignatia Broker of the turn of the twentieth century. (22) She goes on to say, "The Ojibway, however, continued to net fish and hunt deer as they had always done . . . [They] still laid nets for the fish and pulled them in early in the morning. But they had to clean, salt, and dry their catch inside their house instead of in the outdoor ovens, so the man who enforced the laws against using nets would not know."(23)

Other Anishinaabeg authors tell of similar predicaments. Jim Northrup writes of three "Shinnobs" from Minnesota near the turn of the twenty-first century discussing their treaty rights, at the time still considered illegal by the state of Minesota:

"They said we'd get arrested if we go spearing off the rez," said Tuna Charlie.
"Who is going to arrest us for using our treaty rights?" asked Luke.
"Either the rez game wardens or those from the state," answered Sonny Sky.(24)

Later, Northrup highlights the situation with humor:

"The daylight was used up as they drove down the backroads. They doubled back a few times to make sure they weren't being followed. It sure is hard to sneak around with a canoe on top of the car, Luke thought."(25)

While parallels are rarely drawn between the two groups, non-Native ruralites of the Northwoods underwent an experience with game laws

134

similar to the Anishinaabeg experience. From the arrival of the first French voyageurs in the Northwoods several centuries ago, most non-Natives who moved to the northern Great Lakes area came to depend on hunting and fishing as their primary means of providing for their sustenance needs. Hunting and fishing, often along with subsistence farming, made the non-Native northerner an independent, self-reliant person, the kind governments found difficult to control, something often lamented in frontier situations.

Quite a few of these non-Native northerners, particularly the French, intermarried with the Anishinaabeg. These mixed-blood ("metís" if of French descent) families were important to Native communities. This is frequently noted in the transcripts of Indian communiqués during the treaty negotiations. Concerns that "our mixed-blood brothers" would be fairly dealt with in treaty deals were often expressed. Unfortunately, the U.S. did not treat with the mixed-bloods or consider them truly Indian, so many mixed-blood families, despite the work of their Native friends and families, were left to fend for themselves. One way they were able to do this was through continuing their subsistence lifestyle of living from the land.

Mixed-bloods and non-Native settlers often chose subsistence lifestyles as hunters, fishers, trappers, gatherers, and/or farmers. These activities directly provided food for themselves and their families. Some combined this with selling meat, fur and harvested plants in order not to make a profit but to make enough to provide for the cash needs of one's family. Consequently, when the northern states developed game laws in the early 1900s, these mixed-bloods and non-Native settlers faced a predicament similar to the Anishinaabeg: if they could not hunt and fish as needed, how were they to provide for themselves?

In such circumstances, the rural residents of the north, across ethnic boundaries, often suffered extreme economic hardship. As a result, many had to seek wage-work in order to buy the food they could have previously provided for themselves. Conveniently enough for the industries invading the North, many of these northerners turned to wage-work in the mining or timber industries as a means to providing for themselves and their families. Some tried their hand at for-profit farming, often failing miserably on cutover lands with poor soil and a short growing season that could not produce an adequate cash income. Others left for more lucrative urban areas.

The tragedy of these game laws is that, while they were derived from laudable preservation-oriented values emerging from the non-Native conservation movement, the enactment of these laws was a means to promoting yet another industry, the recreation/tourism industry, at the expense of the northern subsistence lifestyle. This meant that those who were in the lower economic classes and who, through their very way of life, had an intimate knowledge and connection to the land were crudely sacrificed for the sake of the interests of outsiders from the upper economic classes who made the land a hobby rather than a lifestyle.

Much of these game laws came on the books as a result of the then-popular idea that tourism should win out over subsistence activities because there was money to be had in tourism. As one prominent social engineer wrote, "These forests will 'pay' even if not a stick of timber is sold from them."(26) Further, he said, "[p]eople are more and more willing to pay taxes to maintain land for the sole purpose of affording pleasure and re-creation of mind and body so sorely needed in a modern high tension civilization."(27) "Every acre," writes historian James Kates, "would yield some sort of benefit, whether in the form of timber, tourist dollars, or simply a breath of pine-scented air."(28) Thus, the recreation industry would contribute to the economic growth of the nation while subsistence hunting and fishing would do nothing to further the economic goals of the United States.

As the size of the nation's urban population increased, so too did the recreation industry. Non-rural people sought solace, strength, and an enjoyable excursion in rural-wilderness areas like the Northwoods. As Kates writes, "In tune with the forest-recreation movement, planners eventually would recognize the value of facilitating a sort of playacting in the forest – with camping, hiking, and other pursuits serving to refresh vacationing urbanites and to provide a touchstone to [a] bygone frontier experience."(29) Business interests and sportsmen in particular grew concerned about the health of game populations. In order to preserve these populations, not for the animals' sake but for the recreation industry's sake, regulations and the bureaucracy to enforce these regulations came into being. "Management, it seemed, could make the animal kingdom continuously productive," writes Kates.(30

As the conservation movement gained power in the early 1900s, residents of the Northwoods who violated the new game laws were repeatedly arrested by the Department of Conservation (later the Department of Natural Resources). Their equipment was often confiscated. Their harvest taken away. Fines and possible jail time were given as punishment. Sometimes, these northerners were set against each other, neighbor against neighbor. For example, the Bay Mills Indian Community faced armed white vigilante groups as well as DNR game wardens on the shores of Lake Superior as they exercised their longtime netting tradition.(31)

In the decades to come, and after a very hard struggle, the Anishinaabeg had their subsistence treaty rights re-recognized. Treaty rights were finally affirmed in the 1970s for several Ojibwe and Odawa tribes in Michigan. In Wisconsin, the 1983 Voigt decision upheld Ojibwe off-reservation subsistence rights as reserved in the treaties. It wasn't until 1999 that the Mille Lacs decision was handed down affirming Ojibwe treaty rights on the ceded territories in Minnesota.

136

The recognition of Ojibwe treaty rights to hunt, fish, and gather on ceded territory has helped in the revitalization of Ojibwe identity and culture including the increased interest in understanding traditional Ojibwe ecological knowledge. While the hunting and fishing on ceded territory persevered even in the decades it was illegal, it was an expensive and sometimes even dangerous proposition if an Ojibwe person was caught by the DNR or a vigilante. Legal recognition of these reserved rights has helped many low-income Ojibwe families provide for their families and communities.(32)

Mixed-bloods and non-Natives from low-income families, who could be greatly helped by subsistence rights, have yet to have their right to make a subsistence living from the land recognized.(33) As a result, some northern families today are forced into poaching in order to feed their families. They continue to face the economic hardship of breaking the law to provide for one's family but do not, usually, face danger (although game wardens have been known to draw guns on their quarry). The largest obstacle these people face is an increasingly urbanizing world that does not understand, much less have sympathy for, the low-income need for subsistence rights.

Rural Zoning

The treaties of the 1800s worked for the United States to gain access to and essentially clear the land for the mining and timber industries, and, in the process, undermined the traditional subsistence lifestyle of the Anishinaabeg. The game laws at the turn of the twentieth century were designed to further the goals of the recreation industry, and, in the process, undermined the subsistence lifestyles of Native, mixed-blood, and non-Native northerners alike. The rural zoning movement in the early 1900s was yet another assault on northern subsistence rights designed by urban university experts. Again these experts sought to promote and protect profitable industries like the timber, agribusiness, and recreation industries and were deliberately intent on eradicating the northerner's subsistence lifestyle, particularly subsistence farming.

While rural zoning was meant primarily to cut down on municipal costs, its priorities included removing people from those areas the social engineers had designated for timber, agribusiness, and recreational use. For example, in 1936, George Wehrwein, one of the social engineers who had great influence with his colleagues and thus on the shaping of the Northwoods, wrote that the relocation of those families ("nonconforming users" he called them) "living in the [newly established] restricted districts, i.e., the forestry and recreation zones" of Wisconsin "is even more urgent than the resettlement" of "isolated settlers" residing outside of the restricted zones.(34) In 1919, P.S. Lovejoy, another urban university expert who was highly influential in shaping the Northwoods, wrote that land-use policies needed to be formulated and should be based on dividing the land into either farmland or lands for the forest industry.(35) Two questions would determine the designations of land, he said: "1. Is it being profitably farmed now? 2. Is it a reasonable presumption that it will be profitably farmed within the period required for a forest rotation on the site?"(36) "It does not pay to work land which it does not pay to work," he wrote,(37) dismissing the north's versatile subsistence lifestyles. However, it was not enough for Lovejoy simply to farm profitably. He states, "the maximum economic development can only come with the development of all the land. . . . No island of farms, however rich, if surrounded by barrens or pauper ranches can ever be so prosperous as the farm area surrounded by well managed forest."(38) In other words, all of the land was to be used as a means to generating profit.

Further, according to other influential land-planners Richard Ely and Edward W. Morehouse in 1924, "[S]elf-sufficing agriculture is a relic of the past that can be found only in out-of-the-way corners of America."(39) This was precisely what they wanted to see happen. "A crop which will not pay for itself with a fair profit is not worth putting into the ground, and the soil should be put to some other use which will pay for itself," Ely and Morehouse wrote.(40)

According to Kates, in 1939 the Reader's Digest printed an article praising Wisconsin's rural zoning laws: "They declared that the existence of submarginal farms [i.e. ones that weren't oriented toward making a profit] had led to countless social 'evils,' including wasted effort and welfare dependence . . . zoning had allowed communities to 'control the land use for the greatest common good.'"(41)

Thus farmers who were unable to turn a profit were either required or strongly encouraged to leave their farms. The fact that farming may have been a way of life, a means of providing one's subsistence without reliance on a cash economy, did not matter. Wehrwein writes, "In spite of the arguments which can be brought to support the self-sufficing and peasant type of agriculture, I believe the goal we should set for American agriculture is the typical farm of the corn belt."(42) He more specifically describes this vision of his when he writes,

> The nation was on the path to the proper balance between the city and the country during the middle 1920's when the area in farms and then number of people on farms were decreasing rapidly. The trend was toward concentration of agriculture on the better lands, and with greater mechanization, a higher income per man. Had the trend   continued instead of the 'flight to the land' after 1929, the goal of reducing the farm plant to 3½ to 4 million farmers might eventually have been reached.(43)

This attitude perfectly reflected the goals of twentieth century rural planning policies, goals that continue even into today. These policies deliberately facilitated people's removal from wilder areas and actively encouraged migrations to the towns or urban areas. As Wehrwein

138

wrote, "Zoning without relocation is a job half done."(44) Further, he said,

> Instead of looking upon the city as the enemy of agriculture, I believe that the best form of farm relief would be a vigorous urban and industrial civilization and believe that the goal of a land policy should be the stimulation of industry, commerce and export trade . .. This would mean not only a market for the products of the farm but also a place for the surplus youth of the rural areas ....What should worry us is not that farm children move to town but that they are inadequately prepared for a place of responsibility in the city.(45)

In other words, urban-based social engineers like Wehrwein felt that people should be encouraged to forsake the land for the urban world. This is a perfect example of ethnocentrism, although few may recognize it as such because contemporary American society still tends to view traditional rural culture as somehow backward and needing to move forward into "modern times."

Wehrwein also writes that the purpose of rural zoning was "a means of preventing scattered settlement" and "[o]nly with the more or less complete relocation of isolated settlers will the cost of government be reduced."(46) Wehrwein placed the government's ability to balance a budget over the spiritual, cultural, and physical sustenance needs of the "isolated settler." Keeping down "the attendant costs for schools, roads, and other public services" became his priority,(47) disregarding the fact that the "isolated settlers" may have preferred to keep their isolation rather than receive such amenities as maintained roads and schooling. However, these isolated residences were a problem for Wehrwein and other social engineers for reasons other than pecuniary ones. To fully understand the social engineering of the time, we need to look at the engineers' attitudes toward ruralites.

Anti-Rural Attitudes Among the Social Engineers

Issues of control and blatant anti-rural bias played a large role in the minds of regional planners of the 1920s and 1930s. Denigration of the rural/wild was common among these urban experts. Lovejoy wrote in 1919 that "[t]he mossback point of view is a very potent force in the politics of most of our states and especially in the more backward ones."(48) According to Kates, Wehrwein simply felt that "living in the woods was fundamentally illogical."(49) He also worried that isolated settlers would be "tempted by their isolation to violate game laws"(50) thus flaunting governmental control and interfering with the goals of the recreation industry. Further, in tones reminiscent of British author Joseph Conrad, according to Kates, Wehrwein also feared that "without neighbors to watch over them, people in the forest might revert to a sort of savagery, bereft of any standards of morality or cleanliness."(51)

These attitudes are directly related to the European perception of Native Americans as savages. Rather than being bloodthirsty and cruel, however, as the standard definition of "savage" was perceived, those who lived in rural areas were seen as backward and in need of "proper" (i.e. urban) education or as outright "undesirables" who were believed to have no place in modern American society. Such attitudes applied to all cash-poor people, regardless of ethnicity, who lived in the woods and could ill-afford to profligately participate in the money-based economy. From these anti-rural attitudes grew policies that attempted to shape the Northwoods into a profitable contributor to the nation's industrial economy.

Recreation consumers themselves also carried negative stereotypes of ruralites, and these recreationists often worked to promote favorable conditions for sportsmen over the needs of the low-income subsistence hunters and fishers who lived in the north and whose homeland these sportsmen recreated in. In the early 1900s, the Izaak Walton League was one of the most powerful organizations promoting the recreation industry. The League's mission was to perpetuate, through regulations and game re-stocking programs, "the conditions under which fish and game lived, and thus to increase the sporting opportunities for anglers and hunters."(52) The intent of these Waltonians, as they were called, was to "promote the sort of outdoor experiences that had defined the American character in the nineteenth century."(53) That is, game regulation was intended to provide sportsmen with a simulated frontier experience. It would act as a proving ground for manhood, a source of romantic adventure found in battling the challenges of a (planned) wilderness.

This sort of ideology, however, had serious consequences for those who, living in the wild North, hunted and fished in order to survive. There was no room for these folks in the new sportsmen's order of things. As Kates writes, sportsmen "sought to transform the calculus of fish and game, away from the animals' subsistence value as meat and in favor of the sporting experience inherent in the take of wild creatures."(54) The restrictions placed on hunting and fishing came from sportsmen "who embraced the English model of gentlemanly conduct afield."(55) Subsistence hunting and fishing were not refined enough for these "gentlemen" as subsistence activities were seen as common and thus vulgar, lowly pursuits. This can be seen in a cartoon, distributed in 1927 by the Izaak Walton League. Kates describes this image:

> It showed a group of Waltonian men, respectable in appearance, standing with the ghost of Izaak Walton at the edge of a forest. Arrayed against them was a rabble of thuggish-looking characters whose labels included "Bad Sportsmanship," "Poacher," and "Game Hog." Tellingly, the Waltonians were excluding the undesirables by building a brick wall around the woods. (56)

140

Subsistence hunting and fishing ("poaching") was somehow ungentlemanly, beneath contempt, but sportshunting and fishing (that is, killing for fun, not out of necessity) was laudable provided one "restocked" the "game" when one was through.

Contempt for low-income rural culture such as that found with the Waltonians and the anti-rural attitudes of Wehrwein and Lovejoy takes on a sinister and dangerous twist when one examines their writings closer. The frightening truth emerges that these urban-based experts actually harbored a rather nasty view of the people whose lives they would so profoundly impact. Relocating settlers out of the woods and nearer to town, encouraging urban flight, developing policies to promote industrialization of the North, attempting to eradicate subsistence living, all of these policies came from a deep-seated eugenics-inspired Spencerianism, a paradigm quite popular in America in the early half of the twentieth century, echoes of which can still be heard throughout university halls today.

"When it comes to resetting an entire community," Wehrwein wrote, "it will be found that there is not only submarginal land but there are also submarginal people."(57) In fact, he believed, along with Ely and others, as Kates writes "that both peoples and soils could be rank-ordered as to their fitness for agriculture."(58) Those who were "fit" for the soil were to be encouraged to enter the agricultural realm. Ely and Morehouse strongly advocated for selecting settlers "with the intelligence necessary to grasp farm problems, and at least a small amount of capital with which to start."(59)

One government official in Wisconsin's Douglas County in 1934 referred to families who were squatting on land as "more or less undesirable and shiftless."(60) To support his own views, Wehrwein reported an observer as saying the settlers in the cut-over area were "the result of generations of eugenic carelessness, they lack the fiber to do anything for themselves . . . The way they live is bound to breed degenerates."(61) In a personal letter in 1922, Lovejoy wrote to another forester that if the Northwoods was not subjected to stiff management, it would continue "breeding paupers and morons and fires."(62) This sort of thinking perfectly reflected the eugenics mores of the time.

The terms themselves were also used by the American eugenicist movement during this era. Poverty, the American eugenicists believed, was genetic, and to prevent the spread of "bad" genes to future generations, "paupers and morons" as well as other "undesirables" and "degenerates" should be forcibly sterilized. Recently there have been some reports on the forced sterilizations of Native American women in this country. They were victims of the eugenicists' racist and classist visions. Their non-Native rural neighbors with lower incomes were often victims as well. In Michigan alone, 2145 people were forcibly sterilized between 1907 and 1940.(63)

Like the term "savage," these perceptions of lower income Northwoods residents, Native, mixed-blood, and non-Native, were indicative of an extreme racism and classism on the part of these urban experts. These experts were not quacks with small followings, however. Rather, they were highly respected for their work. The Wisconsin Historical Society describes Wehrwein as "[w]idely known as an expert in land utilization, rural zoning, soil conservation, forest taxation, and public land management."(64) Further, the highly regarded conservationist author, Aldo Leopold, wrote Lovejoy's obituary. In it he celebrates his friend's life in many ways including offering up his favorite Lovejoy witticisms including the term "carrying capacity." In discussing this term, "[t]he ultimate question," Leopold quotes directly from one of Lovejoy's letters, "is not how to step up human carrying capacities per habitat but what sort of humans we want to have around at all."(65) From perspectives such as these grew land policies that not only ignored the right of people to live off the land in subsistence lifestyles but actually set out to destroy those subsistence lifestyles and, in its place, encouraged an industrial use of the land for profit.

What, then, have been the long-term effects of this industrialization of the Northland?

Ecological Health of the American Northwoods in Modern Times

Governmental policies intent on industrializing the North, the subsequent corporate practices employed here, and the social engineering schemes to ensure the Northwoods became a profit-producing part of the American industrial economy have exacted their toll on the land. This toll is paid heavily by the plant, animal, and human communities that make up the Northwoods today.

Wildlife

Wisconsin environmental activist/sociologist Al Gedicks writes, "The Chippewa, along with the other Indian nations in northern Wisconsin, already suffer a disproportionate environmental risk of illness and other health problems from eating fish, deer, and other wildlife contaminated with industrial pollutants like airborne polychlorinated biphenyls (PCBs), mercury, and other toxins deposited on land and water."(66) According to former Lac Courte Oreilles tribal chair Gaiashkibos, "I hear the Great Lakes is one of the seven wonders of the world. You can't drink the water out of Lake Superior. There's young children that will never be able to taste the fish out of those lakes. There's advisories that women of childbearing age and pregnant mothers cannot consume certain species of fish out of the Great Lakes."(67)

Until the advent of industrialization, the Anishinaabeg and other rural northerners did not have to worry about mercury, PCBs or other such industrial contaminants in the fish. However, "[s]ince 1982, the DNR has tested 700 of the [Wisconsin's] 15,000 lakes [for mercury-contaminated fish]; usually one out of the three lakes makes it on the advisory list," wrote Gedicks back in 1993.(68)   The mercury and other heavy metal pollution "gets worse every year, as it is cumulative," writes LaDuke.(69) Anishinaabe activist Walt Bresette was very upset about this; "I refuse to eat the fish and I refuse to let my family eat the fish because of the toxins," he said.(70) "You may be surprised to know," writes LaDuke in 1999, "that almost every lake in northern Minnesota has a Fish Consumption Advisory for it. You can only eat one walleye per week or month if you are a woman of childbearing age in many of those lakes because of PCBs or mercury."(71)   In recent years, the numbers of mercury-contaminated lakes has risen drastically in all three of the northern Great Lakes states.

"Virtually all the mercury in these [Wisconsin] lakes comes from the sky," says DNR scientist Carl Watras.(72) Gedicks writes, "The major sources of the mercury in rain and snow are latex paints and emissions from coal power plants. [Further, i]n the upper peninsula of Michigan, the White Pine copper mine and smelter [was] sued by the National Wildlife Federation and the Michigan United Conservation Clubs for emitting mercury, lead, and arsenic over the waters of nearby Lake Superior at five times the legal limit."(73)

General Chemical Contamination

If mercury contamination is not enough, around the year 2000, "[f]ish from Lake Michigan show[ed] levels of dioxin more than 100,000 times higher than the surrounding water, plants and sediment," writes LaDuke, adding, "The pulp and paper industry ranks as the leading source of dioxin exposure to the public—a direct consequence of the use of chlorine bleaching in their processes."(74)   The Environmental Protection Agency considers dioxin "the most potent carcinogen ever tested in a laboratory," according to LaDuke.(75) In addition, dioxin is a bio-accumulator, meaning it is a fat-soluble chemical found in greater concentrations higher up the food chain.(76)

As human beings are at the top of the food chain in most areas, this is of major concern to our own species. Northern Minnesota and Wisconsin as well as the Upper Peninsula of Michigan are home to several paper mills including mills in Duluth, Minnesota; Rhinelander, Wisconsin; and in Michigan in Quinnesec, Escanaba, and on the old K.I. Sawyer Air Force Base near Marquette, Michigan. According to LaDuke, "If you live in the Great Lakes region, your body burden of dioxin may be two to three times greater than that of someone living on the West Coast. Both weather patterns and clustering of Chemical plants produce this additional exposure."(77)

While the North battles mercury and dioxin, other forms of industrial pollution also continue to crop up. Most recently, in August 2007, the Environmental Protection Agency (EPA) was called in to handle dangerous lead levels in Torch Lake near Lake Linden, Michigan on the

Keweenaw Peninsula.(78)   The EPA On-Site Coordinator, Brian Kelly, said it was "an urgent problem" as the "extremely high levels of lead" were 200 times higher than acceptable levels.(79) Torch Lake is home to several Superfund Sites(80) produced by the copper mining and related activities that took place in the area from the 1890s to 1969.(81) These activities dumped approximately "200 million tons of copper mill tailings" into Torch Lake where it is believed the contaminated sediments reach up to seventy feet in thickness in some areas of the lake.(82)

Further south on the Keweenaw Peninsula, "billions of pounds of stamp sand waste was deposited into Keweenaw Bay" along a beach belonging to the Keweenaw Bay Indian Community (KBIC) near Baraga, Michigan.(83) These waters are traditional fishing and recreation waters for the Ojibwe. A 2000-2001 study by the U.S. Army Corps of Engineers found that six billion pounds of stamp sand had been deposited both above and below the water along KBIC's Sand Point shoreline.(84) The stamp sands came from a copper ore processing plant some four miles up the bay that had operated in the early 1900s.(85) While KBIC took it upon itself to do what it could to clean up the brownfield by covering the thirty-five acres of stamp sands with clean soil,(86) the contaminants, essentially pushed under a rug, appear to be here to stay, yet another lingering effect of the industrial colonization of the American Northwoods.

Wild Rice

Wild rice is a major cultural as well as subsistence staple for the Ojibwe. Today, however, industrial chemical pollution, the tourist industry, and the genetics industry threaten the survival of wild rice. As Thomas Vennum writes, wild rice "does not tolerate chemical pollutants" and is highly sensitive to water levels.(87) "It used to be you would get lost in the rice on that lake [Big Rice Lake, Minnesota]," says Russell Warren, a ricer for twenty years, "They used to have to put flags up at the landings, so you could find your way back. It's the fertilizer [from agricultural operations], and the runoff, that ruins the crop."(88) One Anishinaabe man from Wisconsin, Paul Buffalo, also "suggest[s] that artificial fertilizers (runoff from nearby farms) and a decline in the quality of the air have been responsible for less bounteous crops today" in his area of the northwoods.(89)

Others point to the tourism industry as an additional cause in the decline of the wild rice. Anne M. Dunn, Anishinaabe elder and storyteller, in describing a walk she took one day briefly mentions "[w]ild rice stalks that have somehow survived the heavy motor traffic." (90) Vennum writes, "In recent years the rice crop has shown signs of deterioration, and the increase of motorboat traffic, mostly by non-Indians fishing for sport in the sloughs, has been suspected as one culprit. . . . Excessive boat speeds can effect wake damage to the wild rice plant, to say nothing of water pollution by gasoline engines."(91)   Vennum further cites

144

incidents where non-locals, who bought vacation homes on the shores of wild rice lakes, "frequently weeded out the rice and prevented Indians from harvesting" so that they, the vacationers, could sportfish, motorboat, and waterski to their heart's content.(92)

Additionally, wild rice now faces the threat of bio-piracy or genetic research and the subsequent corporate patenting of life-forms as discussed by LaDuke in this volume. Former Lac du Flambeau tribal chair, Tom Maulson, offers this advice: "Mother Nature handles her own reproduction and we shouldn't try to fool her. I think Indian people understand that better than the scientists who are doing this work. Don't mess with Mother Nature."(93)

The Forests

While the wild rice of the northern forests is under siege from industrial society, so too are the northern forests themselves. The Anishinaabeg are of the forest. They have been part of the forest community for hundreds of years. "[O]ur roots are in the land of the forests," writes Ojibwe storyteller Ignatia Broker, "[t]he trees are the glory of the Gitchi Manito."(94) "We, the Anishinaabeg, are a forest people, meaning that our creation stories, instructions, and culture, our way of life are entirely based in the forest, from our medicine plants to our food sources, from forest animals to our birchbark baskets," says LaDuke.(95)

Continuing this forest culture can be very difficult in today's industrially-impacted north. "Sometimes, it takes tribal members days, or even months, of walking through the woods examining birch trees before finding the right tree. The variety of birch bark seems to be declining considerably," writes Great Lakes Indian Fish and Wildlife Commission (GLIFWC) forest ecologist Karen Danielson.(96)   Don Chosa, a former ricing chief for the Keweenaw Bay Indian Community, commented that it is difficult to find the right sort of birch bark needed for rice processing these days as the birch tree population has declined.(97) A study done by the GLIFWC/USDA Technical Working Group in 2003 confirms this showing that since the early 1980s, the number of paper birch in the ceded territories of Michigan, Wisconsin, and Minnesota has declined.(98)

In many ways, this is indicative of the northern forests in general. In a report written for GLIFWC, Stephen White, Jr. and Danielson write that "[l]ess than one percent of the original forest which existed prior to the cutover period remains.(99) The present state of the landscape is a fragmented matrix of small stands of relatively mature forest surrounded by younger stands of larger successional forest, along with human development such as housing, highway networks, agriculture, and industry.(100)" Along with logging, they cite acid rain, climate change, and increased ozone concentrations at ground level as factors that have added and will add to the decline of trees and plants in the northern forests.(101)

Ojibwe elders are concerned about trees in general. In an article on a meeting between Ojibwe elders and the U.S. Forest Service, Rasmussen writes,

Since the cutover of ceded territory lands from the mid 1800s to around 1910, young hardwood tree species have dominated the landscape. Routine timber sales through-out the Twentieth Century created forests that never reached maturity. Only a small amount of old growth has survived, tucked away in scattered stands and in protected forests like federal wilderness areas.(102)

One Bad River elder, Sylvia Cloud commented, "I see a slaughter of everything growing in the forest. Did you ever see babies survive without grandmothers and grandfathers? What's going to happen when you take away all of the [mature trees]?"(103)

In blatant disregard to the Anishinaabeg and the earth, unsustainable logging practices that result in destroyed forests and forest communities continue. In research interviews conducted by GLIFWC, Anishinaabe elders identified trees and understory plants affected by logging: zhingwaak (white pine), mitigomizh (red oak), wiigwaasi-mitiig (paper birch), ininaatig (sugar maple), apakwanagemeg (red pine), giizhik (white cedar), wiigob-atig (basswood).(104) Plants the Anishinaabe elders identified as endangered by logging included odatagaagominagaawanzh (blackberry), minagaawanzh (blueberry), waagaag (ferns), and wiinisiibag (winterberry).(105) Elders cited "increased light, temperatures, drought conditions, and competing vegetation" as factors caused by logging that have led to a decline in understory plants.(106)

According to GLIFWC's Danielson and White,

Modern logging practices continue to influence the environment and affect the complex ecological relationship of plant abundance and regeneration, insects, disease, nutrients, and herbivory. Log-ging often results in a reduced amount of coarse woody debris. . . . The lack of coarse woody debris has been implicated in the lack of reproduction of kaakaagiwanzh (eastern hemlock), giizhik (white cedar), and other species.(107) Many forested areas have been replanted and managed as monoculture plantations for pulp and paper production; this practice has resulted in a loss of biodiversity.(108)

"New" Industrial Threats to the Northwoods

Unfortunately, instead of merely having to deal with the offal of old industries, the North faces a series of new industrial threats. For example, corporations interested in uranium mining are seriously exploring the western side of Michigan's Upper Peninsula. Further,

146

pressures to increase logging in the National Forests as a means to boosting county revenues are mounting.

The opening of a metallic sulfide mining district in the Upper Peninsula of Michigan is being spearheaded by Kennecott, a subsidiary of the British Rio Tinto. Kennecott has submitted an application for opening a metallic sulfide mine just north of Marquette in wild lands that boast terrific blueberry harvests and excellent fishing streams. Further, according to the Michigan Department of Natural Resources, the local Salmon Trout River is thought to be the only remaining area of natural coaster brook trout reproduction in Michigan.(109) The Michigan Department of Environmental Quality (DEQ) has given the application its preliminary approval and awaits only the public's final input this fall, as required by law. As public input has already revealed an overwhelming opposition throughout the application process, it is widely presumed that the DEQ will approve the permit despite a groundswell of citizen opposition.

Metallic sulfide mining is one of the most persistently and dangerously polluting forms of mining. In pursuit of metals such as copper and nickel, the mining process exposes sulfide ores to water. The primary concern is that the mine tailings will come in contact with water through rainwater or some other form of moisture. When moisture mixes with the sulfide ore it creates sulfuric acid. This acid mine drainage (AMD) would be a disaster for the surrounding bodies of water (streams, rivers, lakes, groundwater, wetlands). The citizen-initiated metallic sulfide mining moratorium that was signed into law in Wisconsin April of 1998 forbade any metallic sulfide mining in the state unless a metallic sulfide mine somewhere in the U.S. or Canada could be found that had operated for 10 years and been closed for 10 years without contaminating the surrounding area. Such a mine has yet to be found. Further, once the tailings from a metallic sulfide mine come in contact with water, the danger does not fade with the passage of time. AMD can remain toxic for thousands of years.

Electrical power transmission also threatens the Northwoods in a complex web of ecological and cultural tragedy that can be traced from the Northwoods to the Pimicikamak Cree in Manitoba. A high-voltage (345 kV) line known as the Arrowhead-Weston is currently under construction in the rural areas between Wausau, Wisconsin and Superior, Wisconsin. Ojibwe tribes, farmers, and other rural dwellers have fought this line since the early 1990s, but to no avail. Concerns over electromagnetic fields (EMFs) and stray voltage (technically ground currents produced by harmonics(110)) associated with high-voltage transmission lines echo the concerns voiced by others around the nation who are threatened with the construction of high voltage transmission systems in their own backyards.

Long distance transmission of electricity results in the loss of 50% of the electricity transferred between point of production and point of use(111) often producing stray voltage. Stray voltage is particularly problematic with "the proliferation of computers, variable speed motors and other equipment that generate[s] non-linear loads."(112) As it travels through the ground, this stray voltage follows the best conductor available: usually water. As living beings, such as humans, cattle, and other animals are mostly composed of water, we can end up as electrical conduits in areas heavy with stray voltage. Although expert studies done by power corporations disagree, dairy farmers have long argued that stray voltage adversely affects their dairy herds, causing serious muscle spasms and decreased milk production particularly during stray voltage surges.(113)

The transmission lines themselves often involve maintenance that lies heavily on the land, such as the spraying of pesticides to keep vegetation from interfering with the transmission corridors.

Electrical power production has long been a private for-profit industry. Since 2001, however, the building of high-voltage transmission lines themselves became a for-profit industry as well. American Transmission Company (ATC) is the first utility company founded solely to deal in the transmission of electricity between various states.(114) This means the transmission of power, the majority of which is intended for urban areas, has become yet another for-profit industry to invade the rural northland, potentially transforming the north into a whole new sort of resource colony. ATC has even begun its propaganda in support of its energy colonization of the Northwoods. Radio stations in northern areas slated for ATC activity air ATC ads lauding the corporation's supposed contributions to building "better" communities. As ATC is responsible for the Arrowhead-Weston line, Wisconsin's rural residents would strongly disagree.

The Pimicikamik Cree would also vehemently disagree, for in building the Arrowhead-Weston, ATC connects Wisconsin to the Minnesota grid. This grid imports power from Manitoba-Hydro, thus providing Manitoba-Hydro access to a large market: urban areas in the United States. The megadams generating this electricity are built on lands traditionally used by the Cree for subsistence hunting and fishing. The flooding of three million acres in building these mega-dams has drowned hunting grounds, diverted major waterways, and led to serious mercury contamination of the waters and thus the fish that are a staple in the Cree diet.(115)

ATC's activities in northern Wisconsin and Michigan's Upper Peninsula will increase Manitoba-Hydro's available market, and, ironically, will link the American Northwoods' electrical consumption to the destruction of the Pimicikamak Cree's traditional subsistence lifestyle. With the prospect of increased consumer demand with the Arrowhead-Weston (coupled with the constant increase in luxury energy use across the nation), Manitoba-Hydro is looking to further decimate Cree lands

148

and traditional subsistence lifestyles by adding to its already massive hydro-complex in the Cross Lake area of Manitoba.

If this is not enough, some urban-based alternative energy proponents have made serious suggestions about building industrial scale windfarms in the rural American Northwoods. While windpower is a great source of alternative energy, it can quickly become a non-green energy source if, like the supposedly alternative energy of megadams on Native lands in Canada, it is built on a scale that results in the colonization of rural areas to produce energy for distant urban centers. The rural areas of Sault Sainte Marie, Ontario, Canada, were recently subjected to this colonization: the Prince Wind Energy Project was completed in 2006 with 126 wind turbines covering a whopping 20,000 acres.(116)

Building industrial-scale windfarms with their accompanying high-voltage, long-distance transmission lines in the American Northwoods is only one more way of industrially-colonizing the money-poor north for the sake of a wealthier, more urban south.

Conclusion – Traditional Knowledge As a Solution

"We have got to stop poisoning our land, and our air, our water, and rain," says Lac Courte Oreilles member Ron Winters,

> One time the rain used to bless us, now it poisons us because they are mining and   putting things in the air and they are endangering my children. They are putting me on that endangered species list. Whatever that bureau is that makes that list, I'd like to be on that list. I'm part of the land here. I'm part of the trees, the water, I'm part of that. I'm Anishinabé.(117)

Thus far, the robber barons have virtually had their way with the American Northwoods, taking from us what they pleased largely because rural Northerners haven't the financial independence or political clout to prevent them from doing so. Despite this, or perhaps because of it, there is a growing movement interested in revitalizing the old ways by learning the traditional knowledge of our Native and non-Native ancestors and adapting it to today. This traditional knowledge involves not only learning the skills required for hunting, fishing, gathering, and farming but it also involves learning the values necessary for protecting the land for all our relations, present and future.

"The difference between a white man and an Indian is this," LaDuke quotes a Central American Indigenous leader as saying, "A white man wants to leave money to his children. An Indian wants to leave forests."(118) There are non-Natives, too, who want to leave forests to their children, real forests. You'll find many of these people in the Northwoods. As long as there are people who make the land a way of life and not simply a recreational pastime, or worse, an industrial resource, we have the hope and the knowledge to protect our land from further ravages by industrial civilization. As Okanagan activist-artist, Jeanette Armstrong, writes, "I know how powerful the solidarity is of peoples bound together by land, blood, and love. This is the largest threat to interests wanting to secure control of lands and resources."(119)

By understanding who we are as people of the land through a knowledge of our past as well as our present, we can come together, as part of the human community of the Northwoods to resist further industrial invasions of our homeland. We must continue listening to the trees, the animals, the waters so that we can protect this piece of Turtle Island, this part of paradise on Earth. After all, Native, mixed-blood, and non-Native, we are aki anishinaabeg. We are the people of the land.

◊ ◊ ◊ ◊ ◊ ◊

Aimée Cree Dunn, a lifelong resident of the northern Great Lakes area, is currently an adjunct instructor for Northern Michigan University's Center for Native American Studies and Department of English. Her teaching and research emphasize a connection to place, the international Indigenous experience, rural perspectives and traditional ecological knowledge. Although there is no group officially recognized as such, she considers herself Northwoods Metís.

Notes

(1) John Bodley, Victims of Progress, 4th ed. (Mountain View, CA: Mayfield Publishing Company, 1999), 12.
(2) The term "subsistence" is used to refer to an economy whose activities directly provide food, shelter, clothing, medicine and other things necessary to a good and healthy life. It should not be taken to imply that "subsistence" means barely scraping along, barely surviving. "Subsistence" relates to that which directly provides for a good and healthy life and is to be distinguished from the capitalistic and communistic economic models.
(3) Henry R. Schoolcraft, Narrative Journals of Travels from Detroit Northwest through the Great Chain of American Lakes to the Sources of the Mississippi River in the Year 1820 (1821 rpt. NY: Arno Press, Inc., 1970), 97-98.
(4) Ibid., 100.
(5) Ibid., 130.
(6) John Mohawk, "Subsistence and Materialism," in Paradigm Wars: Indigenous Peoples' Resistance to Globalization, ed. Jerry Mander and Victoria Tauli-Corpuz (San Francisco: Sierra Club Books, 2006), 27.
(7) Ibid., 26-27.
(8) John Bodley, Victims of Progress, 20.

150

(9) John Bodley, Anthropology and Contemporary Human Problems (Mountain View, CA: Mayfield Publishing, Co., 2001), 8.

(10) A few days into the voyage, the Native guides nicknamed Schoolcraft Paw-gwa-be-can-e-ga   meaning, according to Schoolcraft's journal, "destroyer of rocks."   Henry Schoolcraft, Narrative Journals, 166.

(11) The Institute for the Development of Indian Law and Cook Christian Training School, "L'Anse Chippewa Treaty 1842," in U.P. Indian Treaties: Treaty Rights Workshop (1975), 12.

(12) Ibid., 12.

(13) The Institute for the Development of Indian Law and Cook Christian Training School, "Second L'Anse Chippewa Treaty 1836," in U.P. Indian Treaties, 3.

(14) Mark Keller, The Chippewa Land of Keweenaw Bay: An Allotment History (Baraga, MI: Keweenaw Bay Printing Department, 1981), 7-8.

(15) The Institute for the Development of Indian Law and Cook Christian Training School, "Text of 1842 Chippewa Treaty," in U.P. Indian Treaties, 25, emphasis added.

(16) Mark Keller, The Chippewa Land, 13.

(17) Ibid., 13.

(18) Great Lakes Indian Fish and Wildlife Commission. Sandy Lake Tragedy and Memorial. http://www.glifwc.org/Publications/SandyLake_Brochure.pdf (accessed September 9, 2007).

(19) Mark Keller, The Chippewa Land, 15-16.

(20) Ibid., 20.

(21) Charles E. Cleland, The Place of the Pike (Gnoozhekaaning): A History of the Bay Mills Indian Community (Ann Arbor, MI: University of Michigan Press, 2004), 22-26.

(22) Ignatia Broker, Night Flying Woman: An Ojibway Narrative (St. Paul, MN: Minnesota Historical Press, 1983), 117.

(23) Ibid., 117.

(24) Jim Northrup, Walking the Rez Road (Stillwater, MN: Voyageur Press, Inc., 1993), 137.

(25) Ibid., 143.

(26) George S. Wehrwein, "Goals in Land Use Policy," Journal of Farm Economics (1938): 245.

(27) Ibid., 245.

(28) James Kates, Planning a Wilderness: Regenerating the Great Lakes Cutover Region (Minneapolis, MN: University of Minnesota Press, 2001), 158.

(29) Ibid., 148.

(30) Ibid., 101.

(31) Charlie Otto Rasmussen, "Reflections from Bucko Teeple: Horses on the ice; vigilantes on the beach," Mazina'igan, Ziigwan (Spring) 2007, 10.

(32) The danger, though diminished, still persists as sometimes can be seen at boat landings come spearing time.

(33) In various Canadian provinces, however, the Metís have recently had subsistence rights recognized.

151

(34) George S. Wehrwein, "An Appraisal of Resettlement," Journal of Farm Economics (1937): 199-200.

(35) P.S. Lovejoy, "Segregation of Farm from Forest Land," Journal of Forestry, XVII, No. 6 (October 1919): 645.

(36) Ibid., 645, emphasis added.

(37) Ibid., 645.

(38) Ibid., 639-640, emphasis added.

(39) Richard T. Ely and Edward W. Morehouse, Elements of Land Economics (NY: MacMillan Company, 1924), 118.

(40) Ibid., 51, emphasis added.

(41) James Kates, Planning a Wilderness, 158.

(42) George S. Wehrwein, "Goals in Land Use Policy," 240.

(43) Ibid., 241.

(44) George S. Wehrwein, "Enactment and Administration of Rural County Zoning Ordinances," Journal of Farm Economics (1936): 522.

(45) George S. Wehrwein, "Goals in Land Use Policy," 241.

(46) George S. Wehrwein, "Enactment and Administration," 514, 521.

(47) Ibid., 514.

(48) P.S. Lovejoy, "Segregation of Farm from Forest," 627.

(49) James Kates, Planning a Wilderness, 158.

(50) George S. Wehrwein, "Enactment and Administration," 522.

(51) James Kates, Planning a Wilderness, 158.

(52) Ibid., 103.

(53) Ibid., 103.

(54) Ibid., 105-106.

(55) Ibid., 98.

(56) Ibid., 106.

(57) George S. Wehrwein, "An Appraisal of Resettlement," 197.

(58) James Kates, Planning a Wilderness, 149.

(59) Richard T. Ely and Edward W. Morehouse, Elements of Land Economics, 306.

(60) No citation given, James Kates, Planning a Wilderness, 158.

(61) No citation given, James Kates, Planning a Wilderness, 158.

(62) James Kates, Planning a Wilderness, 48.

(63) Edwin Black, War Against the Weak: Eugenics and America's Campaign to Create a Master Race (NY: Four Walls Eight Windows, 2003), 123.

(64) Wisconsin Historical Society, "Term: Wehrwein, George Simon," Dictionary of Wisconsin History, http://www.wisconsinhistory.org/dictionary (accessed August 29, 2007).

(65) Aldo Leopold, "Obituary: P.S. Lovejoy," The Journal of Wildlife Management, 7, No. 1 (January 1943): 128.

(66) Al Gedicks, The New Resource Wars: Native and Environmental Struggles Against Multinational Corporation (Boston, MA: South End Press, 1993), 167.

(67) Gaiashkibos, "Where are all the hellraisers?", Midwest Treaty Network Forum (Madison, WI: May 1990), quoted in Al Gedicks, New Resource Wars, 168.

(68) Al Gedicks, New Resource Wars,, 194.

(69) Winona LaDuke, "Don't Cheapen Sovereignty," The Circle (March 1996), rpt. In The Winona LaDuke Reader (Stillwater, MN: 2002), 192.

(70) Al Gedicks, New Resource Wars,, 194.

(71) Winona LaDuke, Building with Reservations, lecture at the Association of Collegiate Schools of Architecture National Conference (Minneapolis: 1999), rpt. in The Winona LaDuke Reader, 194-195.

(72) Will Fantle, "Fishing for Trouble," Isthmus Newsweekly (June 5-11, 1992):8, quoted in Al Gedicks, New Resource Wars, 194.

(73) Al Gedicks, New Resource Wars, 194-195.

(74) Winona LaDuke, "Dioxin, Incinerators and Breast Milk," Ojibwe Akiing (May 31, 2000), rpt. in The Winona LaDuke Reader, 23.

(75) Ibid., 22.

(76) Winona LaDuke, "A Seventh Generation Amendment," Ojibwe News (October 4, 1996), rpt. in The Winona LaDuke Reader, 275.

(77) Ibid., 275.

(78) Jane Nordberg, "Torch Lake contamination 'an urgent problem,'" MiningGazette.com,   August   7,   2007, http://www.mininggazette.com/stories/articles.asp?articleID=8073 (accessed September 5, 2007).

(79) Ibid.

(80) Brenda R. Jones, "Torch Lake Superfund Site Remediation Monitoring: Fall, 2002 Sampling Overview and Results," United States Environmental Protection Agency, http://wupcenter.mtu.edu/education/great_lakes_ecology/ torch_lake/Overview_Torch_Lake_Superfund_Remediation_Project.ppt (accessed September 5, 2007).

(81) Michigan Department of Environmental Quality, The Superfund Program in Michigan: Fiscal Year 2006 Legislative Report: Summary of Hazardous Substance Cleanups Funded by the Comprehensive Environmental Response, Compensation, and Liability Act (CERCLA), 1980 PC 96-510 As Amended by the Superfund Amendments and Reauthorization Act (SARA), 1986 PL 99-499 and the Small Business Liability Relief and Brownfield Revitalization Act, 2002 PL 107-118 (March 2007), http://www.michigan.gov/deq (accessed September 5, 2007), 137.

(82) Ibid., 137.

(83) "EPA recognizes KBIC's brownfield cleanup at Sand Point in Baraga County," Mazina'igan, Dagwaagin (Fall) 2007, 10.

(84) Ibid., 10.

(85) Ibid., 10.

(86) Ibid., 10.

(87) Thomas Vennum, Jr., Wild Rice and the Ojibway People (St. Paul, MN: Minnesota Historical Society Press, 1988), 14, 20.

(88) Winona LaDuke, "Under the Wild Rice Moon," Minneapolis Star Tribune, September 19, 1999, rpt. in The Winona LaDuke Reader, 30.

(89) Thomas Vennum, Jr., Wild Rice, 288.

(90) Anne M. Dunn, Grandmother's Gift: Stories from the Anishinaabeg (Duluth, MN: Holy Cow! Press, 1997), 73, emphasis added.

(91) Thomas Vennum, Jr., Wild Rice, 285-286.

(92) Ibid., 286.

(93) Charlie Otto Rasmussen, "Wild rice genetic research scrutinized by some Ojibwe tribes: Protestors rally at U of M," Mazina'igan, Summer 2002, 1.

(94) Ignatia Broker, Night Flying Woman, 10, 32.

(95) Winona LaDuke, "Like Tributaries to a River," Sierra, November/December 1996, rpt. in The Winona LaDuke Reader, 61.

(96) Karen Danielson, "GLIFWC and USDA Forest Service collaborate on birch bark monitoring protocol," Mazina'igan, Winter 2003-2004, 4.

(97) Donald Chosa, personal interview, November 19, 2003.

(98) Karen Danielson, "GLIFWC and USDA Forest Service collaborate," 4.

(99) Lee E. Frelich, "Old forest in the Lake States today and before European settlement," Natural Areas Journal 15 (1995): 157-167, quoted in Stephen White, Jr. and Karen Danielson, Threats to Wild Plants in the Ceded Territories (Odanah, WI: Great Lakes Indian Fish and Wildlife Commission, 2002), 3.

(100) James E. Meeker, Joan E. Elias, and John A. Heim, Plants Used By the Great Lakes Ojibway, Odanah, WI: Great Lakes Indian Fish And Wildlife Commission, 1993, quoted in Stephen White, Jr. and Karen Danielson, Threats to Wild Plants in the Ceded Territories (Odanah, WI: Great Lakes Indian Fish and Wildlife Commission, 2002), 3.

(101) Stephen White, Jr. and Karen Danielson, Threats to Wild Plants in the Ceded Territories – Project Report 02-01 (Odanah, WI: Great Lakes Indian Fish and Wildlife Commission, 2002), 16.

(102) Charlie Otto Rasmussen, "Tribal elders, Forest Service convene talking circle at Bad River," Mazina'igan, Winter 2003-2004, 4.

(103) Ibid., 4.

(104) Stephen White, Jr. and Karen Danielson, Threats to Wild Plants, 8.

(105) Ibid., 8.

(106) Ibid., 8.

(107) David J. Mladenoff and Forest Stearns, "Eastern hemlock regeneration and deer browsing in the Northern Great Lakes Region: a re-examination and model simulation," Conservation Biology 7 (1993): 889-900, quoted in Stephen White, Jr. and Karen Danielson, Threats to Wild Plants in the Ceded Territories (Odanah, WI: Great Lakes Indian Fish and Wildlife Commission, 2002), 15.

(108) Stephen White, Jr. and Karen Danielson, Threats to Wild Plants, 15.

(109) Save the Wild U.P., Coaster Brook Trout in Danger, http://www.savethewildup.org/blog/coaster-brook-trout-in-danger/ (accessed September 5, 2007).

(110) Kurt Gutknecht, " 'Stray voltage' seen as 'electrical pollution,'" special rpt. of article in Wisconsin Agriculturist, August 1999, 2.

(111) Winona LaDuke, Making the Connections Between Dams, Transmission Lines, and Mines, Midwest Treaty Network, http://www.alphacdc.com/treaty/winona2.html (accessed September 5, 2007).

(112) Kurt Gutknecht, " 'Stray voltage,' " 5.

(113) Ibid., 4.

154

(114) American Transmission Company, Key Facts,
http://www.atcllc.com/A9.shtml (accessed September 5, 2007).

(115) Aimée Cree Dunn, "Making the Connection: Bears, Dams, Mines
and Powerlines," Northwoods Wilderness Recovery,
http://www.northwoodswild.org/newspro/viewnews.cgi?id=EEuuu
kkuAyxOyQvlwn.

(116) BeyondFossilFuel.com, Canada's Largest Windfarm,
http://www.beyondfossilfuel.com/windpower/canada.html
(accessed September 5, 2007).

(117) Ron Winters, Speech to Protect the Earth Gathering and Pow-Wow
(Lac Courte Oreilles, Hayward, WI: September 1991), quoted in Al
Gedicks, New Resource Wars, 169.

(118) Winona LaDuke, "I Heard the Owl Call My Name: Indian Forests,
the Endangered Species Act, and Endangered Cultures," Fall 1993,
rpt. in The Winona LaDuke Reader, 99.

(119) Jeanette Armstrong, "Community: 'Sharing One Skin,' " in
Paradigm Wars, 39.

Bibliography

American Transmission Company. Key Facts. http://www.atcllc.com
/A9.shtml (accessed September 5, 2007).

Armstrong, Jeanette. "Community: 'Sharing One Skin'". In Paradigm
Wars: Indigenous Peoples' Resistance to Globalization. ed. Jerry
Mander and Victoria Tauli-Corpuz, 35-39. San Francisco: Sierra Club
Books, 2006.

BeyondFossilFuel.com. Canada's Largest Windfarm. http://www.
beyondfossilfuel.com/windpower/canada.html (accessed September
5, 2007).

Black, Edwin. War Against the Weak: Eugenics and America's
Campaign to Create a Master Race. NY: Four Walls Eight Windows,
2003.

Bodley, John. Anthropology and Contemporary Human Problems.
Mountain View, CA: Mayfield Publishing Co., 2001.

Bodley, John. Victims of Progress. 4th ed. Mountain View, CA:
Mayfield Publishing Company, 1999.

Broker, Ignatia. Night Flying Woman: An Ojibway Narrative. St. Paul,
MN: Minnesota Historical Society Press, 1983.

Chosa, Donald. Personal interview. November 19, 2003.

Cleland, Charles E. The Place of the Pike (Gnoozhekaaning): A History
of the Bay Mills Indian Community. Ann Arbor, MI: University of
Michigan Press, 2004.

Cree Dunn, Aimée. Making the Connection: Bears, Dams, Mines and
Powerlines. Northwoods Wilderness Recovery.
http://www.northwoodswild.org/newspro/viewnews.cgi?id=EEuuu
kkuAyxOyQvlwn.

Danielson, Karen. "GLIFWC and USDA Forest Service collaborate on
birch bark monitoring protocol." Mazina'igan, Winter 2003-2004, 4.

Dunn, Anne M. Grandmother's Gift: Stories from the Anishinaabeg.
Duluth, MN: Holy Cow! Press, 1997.

Ely, Richard T. and Edward W. Morehouse. Elements of Land Economics. NY: MacMillan Co., 1924.

"EPA recognizes KBIC's brownfield cleanup at Sand Point in Baraga County." Mazina'igan, Dagwaagin (Fall) 2007, 10.

Fantle, Will. "Fishing for Trouble." Isthmus Newsweekly, June 5-11, 1992. Quoted in Al Gedicks. The New Resource Wars: Native and Environmental Struggles Against Multinational Corporations. Boston, MA: South End Press, 1993.

Frelich, Lee E. "Old forest in the Lake States today and before European settlement." Natural Areas Journal 15 (1995): 157-167. Quoted in White, Stephen Jr. and Karen Danielson. Threats to Wild Plants in the Ceded Territories. Odanah, WI: Great Lakes Indian Fish and Wildlife Commission, 2002, 3.

Gaiashkibos, "Where are all the hellraisers?" Midwest Treaty Network Forum. Madison, WI: May 1990. Quoted in Al Gedicks, The New Resource Wars: Native and Environmental Struggles Against Multinational Corporations. Boston, MA: South End Press, 1993, 168.

Gedicks, Al. The New Resource Wars: Native and Environmental Struggles Against Multinational Corporations. Boston, MA: South End Press, 1993.

Great Lakes Indian Fish and Wildlife Commission. Sandy Lake Tragedy and Memorial.
http://www.glifwc.org/Publications/SandyLake_Bro chure .pdf (accessed September 9, 2007).

Gutknecht, Kurt. " 'Stray voltage' seen as 'electrical pollution.' " Special rpt. from Wisconsin Agriculturist, August 1999.

Institute for the Development of Indian Law and Cook Christian Training School, The. "L'Anse Chippewa Treaty 1842." In U.P. Indian Treaties: Treaty Rights Workshop. 1975.

Institute for the Development of Indian Law and Cook Christian Training School, The. "Second L'Anse Chippewa Treaty 1836." In U.P. Indian Treaties: Treaty Rights Workshop. 1975.

Institute for the Development of Indian Law and Cook Christian Training School, The. "Text of 1842 Chippewa Treaty." In U.P. Indian Treaties: Treaty Rights Workshop. 1975.

Jones, Brenda R. Torch Lake Superfund Site Remediation Monitoring: Fall, 2002 Sampling Overview and Results. United States Environmental Protection Agency. http://wupcenter.mtu.edu/ education/great_lakes_ecology/torch_lake/ Overview_Torch_Lake_Superfund_Remediation_Project.ppt (accessed September 5, 2007).

Kates, James. Planning a Wilderness: Regenerating the Great Lakes Cutover Region. Minneapolis, MN: University of Minnesota Press, 2001.

Keller, Mark. The Chippewa Land of Keweenaw Bay: An Allotment History. Baraga, MI: Keweenaw Bay Printing Department, 1981.

LaDuke, Winona. "Building with Reservations." Delivered: Association of Collegiate Schools of Architecture National Conference (Minneapolis: 1999). Rptd. in The Winona LaDuke Reader: A

Collection of Essential Writings. Stillwater, MN: Voyageur Press, 2002: 44-54.

LaDuke, Winona. "Dioxin, Incinerators and Breast Milk." Ojibwe Akiing (May 31, 2000). Rpt. in The Winona LaDuke Reader: A Collection of Essential Writings. Stillwater, MN: Voyageur Press, 2002: 20-24.

LaDuke, Winona. "Don't Cheapen Sovereignty." The Circle (March 1996). Rptd. in The Winona LaDuke Reader: A Collection of Essential Writings. Stillwater, MN: Voyageur Press, 2002: 191-194.

LaDuke, Winona. "Like Tributaries to a River." Sierra, November/December 1996. Rpt. in The Winona LaDuke Reader: A Collection of Essential Writings. Stillwater, MN: Voyageur Press, 2002: 55-64.

LaDuke, Winona. Making the Connections Between Dams, Transmission Lines, and Mines. Midwest Treaty Network. http://www.alphacdc.com/treaty/winona2.html (accessed September 5, 2007).

LaDuke, Winona. "I Heard the Owl Call My Name: Indian Forests, the Endangered Species Act, and Endangered Cultures." Fall 1993. Rptd. in The Winona LaDuke Reader: A Collection of Essential Writings. Stillwater, MN: Voyageur Press, 2002. pp89-99.

LaDuke, Winona. "A Seventh Generation Amendment." Ojibwe News (October 4, 1996). Rpt. in The Winona LaDuke Reader: A Collection of Essential Writings. Stillwater, MN: Voyageur Press, 2002: 273-276.

LaDuke, Winona. "Under the Wild Rice Moon." Minneapolis Star Tribune, September 19, 1999. Rpt. in The Winona LaDuke Reader: A Collection of Essential Writings. Stillwater, MN: Voyageur Press, 2002: 28-34.

Leopold, Aldo. "Obituary: P.S. Lovejoy." The Journal of Wildlife Management, 7, No. 1 (January 1943): 125-128.

Lovejoy, P.S. "Segregation of Farm from Forest Land." Journal of Forestry, XVII, No. 6 (October 1919): 627-646.

Meeker, James E., Joan E. Elias, and John A. Heim. Plants Used By the Great Lakes Ojibway. Odanah, WI: Great Lakes Indian Fish And Wildlife Commission, 1993. Quoted in White, Stephen Jr. and Karen Danielson. Threats to Wild Plants in the Ceded Territories. Odanah, WI: Great Lakes Indian Fish and Wildlife Commission, 2002, 3.

Michigan Department of Environmental Quality. The Superfund Program in Michigan: Fiscal Year 2006 Legislative Report: Summary of Hazardous Substance Cleanups Funded by the Comprehensive Environmental Response, Compensation, and Liability Act (CERCLA), 1980 PC 96-510 As Amended by the Superfund Amendments and Reauthorization Act (SARA), 1986 PL 99-499 and the Small Business Liability Relief and Brownfield Revitalization Act, 2002 PL 107-118 (March 2007), http://www.michigan.gov/deq (accessed September 5, 2007).

Mladenoff, David J. and Forest Stearns. "Eastern hemlock regeneration and deer browsing in the Northern Great Lakes Region: a re-examination and model simulation." Conservation Biology 7 (1993):

157

889-900. Quoted in White, Stephen Jr. and Karen Danielson. Threats to Wild Plants in the Ceded Territories. Odanah, WI: Great Lakes Indian Fish and Wildlife Commission, 2002, 15.

Mohawk, John. "Subsistence and Materialism". In Paradigm Wars: Indigenous Peoples' Resistance to Globalization. ed. Jerry Mander and Victoria Tauli-Corpuz, 26-28. San Francisco: Sierra Club Books, 2006.

Nordberg, Jane. "Torch Lake contamination 'an urgent problem.' " MiningGazette.com. August 7, 2007. http://www.mininggazette.com/ stories/articles.asp?articleID=8073 (accessed September 5, 2007).

Northrup, Jim. Walking the Rez Road. Stillwater, MN: Voyageur Press, Inc., 1993.

Rasmussen, Charlie Otto. "Reflections from Bucko Teeple: Horses on the ice; vigilantes on the beach." Mazina'igan. Ziigwan (Spring) 2007: 10+.

Rasmussen, Charlie Otto. "Tribal elders, Forest Service convene talking circle at Bad River." Mazina'igan, Winter 2003-2004, 4.

Rasmussen, Charlie Otto. "Wild rice genetic research scrutinized by some Ojibwe tribes: Protesters rally at U of M." Mazina'igan, Summer 2002, 1.

Save the Wild U.P. Coaster Brook Trout in Danger. http://www.savethewildup.org/blog/ coaster-brook-trout-in-danger/ (accessed September 5, 2007).

Schoolcraft, Henry R. Narrative Journals of Travels from Detroit Northwest through the Great Chain of American Lakes to the Sources of the Mississippi River in the Year 1820. 1821. Rpt. NY: Arno Press, Inc., 1970.

Vennum, Thomas, Jr. Wild Rice and the Ojibway People. St. Paul, MN: Minnesota Historical Society Press, 1988.

Wehrwein, George S. "An Appraisal of Resettlement." Journal of Farm Economics (1937): 190-202.

Wehrwein, George S. "Enactment and Administration of Rural County Zoning Ordinances." Journal of Farm Economics (1936): 508-522.

Wehrwein, George S. "Goals in Land Use Policy." Journal of Farm Economics (1938): 237-246.

White, Stephen Jr. and Karen Danielson. Threats to Wild Plants in the Ceded Territories. Odanah, WI: Great Lakes Indian Fish and Wildlife Commission, 2002.

Winters, Ron. Speech to Protect the Earth Gathering and Pow-Wow. Lac Courte Oreilles Reservation, Hayward, WI: September 1991. Quoted in Al Gedicks. The New Resource Wars: Native and Environmental Struggles Against Multinational Corporations. Boston, MA: South End Press, 1993, 169.

Wisconsin Historical Society. "Term: Wehrwein, George Simon." Dictionary of Wisconsin History. http://www.wisconsinhistory.org/ dictionary (accessed August 29, 2007).

Traditional Ecological Knowledge and the Science of Wildlife Management: Motivations for Tribal Wildlife Biologists to Protect Traditional Species

Joel Geffen

Introduction

Traditional ecological knowledge generally refers to the ways that indigenous peoples gain and use knowledge associated with the particular environments in which they live. Traditional ecological knowledge is obtained over literally innumerable generations. If it is to survive, it must be maintained by current generations and passed on to future generations.

> Indigenous knowledge (IK) and "traditional" knowledge are terms that describe knowledge specific to a given culture or society . . . Traditional knowledge is acquired by local people through the accumulation of experiences and informal experiments, and through an intimate understanding of the environment in a given cultural context.

> Traditional ecological knowledge (TEK) is a construct within IK that focuses more on a local culture's conceptualization and interactions with their biotic and abiotic environment. TEK encompasses everything from cursory awareness of natural histories associated with local wildlife to cultural norms for land management and resource allocation (Becker and Ghimire 2003: 1).

Many native organizations today promote TEK. Among them are the Indigenous People's Restoration Network, the Gwitch'in Environmental Knowledge Project, and the Native American Fish and Wildlife Society.

This paper focuses on the work of tribal fish and wildlife biologists-- those individuals working for and enrolled as or descendants of members of tribes. Their professional activities, while rarely directed overtly toward the practice of traditional ecological knowledge, can be understood in terms of accentuating and reclaiming such knowledge as they work to restore and maintain habitats and species.

They incorporate TEK with modern scientific epistemologies and practices. For them, the preservation and maintenance of habitats and species is aimed at the preservation of culture. That culture--or, more

159

properly, cultures--is grounded in attitudes of respect for the so-called biophysical world.

That respect is grounded in the conviction that the world is populated by spiritual entities filled with consciousness and capable of deliberate action. These entities are moral beings. They are part of humankind's moral community, and are to be treated as such. For most tribal biologists, it seems to me, their practice of science--which includes TEK-- is underlain and guided by their spiritual and/or religious beliefs and values. Significantly, for many, species and habitat restoration efforts are at least in part motivated by historical and enduring memories of genocidal policies and actions on the part of the larger American population.

Genocidal Histories and the Maintenance Identity in the Pacific Northwest

I begin with a quote from Russell Means, a well known member of the American Indian Movement (AIM). On October 12, 1992, Means spoke about genocide. He said:

> All my life, I've had to listen to rhetoric about the United States being a model of freedom and democracy, the most uniquely enlightened and humanitarian country in history, a "nation of laws" which, unlike others, has never pursued policies of conquest and aggression. I'm sure you've heard it before. It's official "truth" in the United States. It's what is taught to school children, and it's the line peddled to the general public. Well, I've got a hot news flash for everybody here. It's a lie. The whole thing's a lie, and it always has been. Leaving aside the obvious points which could be raised to disprove it by Blacks and Chicanos and Asian immigrants right here in North America . . . there's a little matter of genocide that's got to be taken into account right here at home. I'm talking about the genocide which has been perpetrated against American Indians, a genocide that began the instant the first of Europe's boat people washed up on the beach of Turtle Island, a genocide that's continuing right now, at this moment. Against Indians, there's not a law the United States hasn't broken, not a Crime Against Humanity it hasn't committed, and it's still going on (Means, qtd by Ward Churchill, A Little Matter of Genocide, 1997: ix).

Experiences of genocide--understood as occurring through armed conflict, Euro-American diseases, boarding school traumas and transformations, and the impacts of the Termination Policy--are crucial to understanding some of the most important motivations for tribal biologists to utilize TEK.

Before discussing TEK, therefore, it may be helpful to briefly review native history in the Pacific Northwest. Since "time immemorial," native peoples in the Pacific Northwest have been acquiring knowledge of the

160

land and its inhabitants. While avoiding romanticizations, it is nonetheless true that they lived in mutually-supportive ways with "nature."

Rituals were performed to give thanks for gifts of food from salmon, elk, huckleberry, and other beings. It was understood that proper respect would encourage the continuing availability of these and other foods and medicines.

The levels of "take" were limited. Resources were managed for the benefit of the larger community--the community of people and non-human people as a whole. With limitations on "take," for instance, and with proper rituals, it was understood that salmon would willingly give themselves to the people. Gifts of respect were reciprocated with gifts of respect.

Lives of inland peoples such as the Yakama, Umatilla, and Nez Perce revolved around what anthropologists later called "an annual round." From villages usually located in proximity to salmon-bearing rivers and streams, people would travel to pick roots, hunt, and fish in season. Over the course of the year, beginning in the early spring, they would move to increasingly higher elevations as foods became more available there, and less available with onset of hotter weather below. After huckleberry harvests in the fall, they would return in large numbers to their villages along the watercourses.

This began to change dramatically with the arrival of ship-borne explorers in the latter eighteenth century and with land-based expeditions such as that of Lewis and Clark in the first decade of the nineteenth century. Diseases in their wake annihilated in many instances upward of 80% of village populations. Within a generation or so, missionaries were settling throughout the region. They introduced a new religious view of course, but also new plants, animals, and ways of relating to them. Cattle were for profit.

Settlers followed. By the mid-nineteenth century pressures for Indian land were so great that the U.S. government negotiated treaties throughout the region. Most tribes agreeing to treaties ceded approximately 90% of their traditional lands.

Reservations were created--as were contemporary tribal identities based on the "nation" model. Many people moved willingly or unwillingly from the Columbia River and its major fish-bearing tributaries onto reservations. Movements were restricted. Religious practices were restricted. And in boarding schools such as Chemawa, Oregon, the use of language and traditional clothing was also restricted. Land was divided and allotted.

All of this had significant and detrimental impacts on traditional land uses and knowledge. Although treaties guaranteed the use of "usual and accustomed places," new non-native landowners were not particularly open to the presence of natives. Furthermore, on the Columbia River, fish wheels and other technologies were utilized to harvest tremendous numbers of salmon--much to the detriment of native peoples.

Inland, reservation agents promoted new land uses such as logging and livestock raising for native peoples. By the early twentieth century, major irrigation systems were established--with significant impoverishment for native peoples.

Child mortality was skyrocketing. In 1928 the Meriam Report detailed problems with the boarding schools in particular, and with reservation living conditions in general. The picture was not a pretty one.

Despite all this, many people did maintain some level of traditional knowledge. And many continued to harvest roots, fish for salmon, and hunt for elk and deer. Reservation lands were used, as were time-honored "usual and accustomed places" along the rivers. People continued to participate in traditional spiritual and religious practices. Of course, some of those practices changed over the years as Christian influences modified them. Significantly, however, they persisted.

Persistent too was the association of "Indian" or specific tribal identity with those land use practices and associated spiritual and religious beliefs. Those practices and beliefs received a much-needed and unfortunately short-lived boost during the Great Depression. Indian Commissioner John Collier encouraged traditional native ways and helped end the ravages of the Dawes Act and boarding schools.

Within ten years, the Yakama Nation began commercial logging on a large scale. So did other forested reservations in the region. Ideas of nature taught in the boarding schools on the Judeo-Christian model were bearing fruit.

Logging was done in hopes of benefiting the native community. However, there were no management plans that incorporated concern for traditionally valued plants, animals, or places. TEK was important for families and individuals, to be sure. But it did not come into play on the level of policy and tribal resource management--perhaps because tribal management was effectively synonymous with federal (BIA) management.

This remained the case through the Termination Policy period of the 1950s and early 1960s. Yet, faced with termination, Northwest tribes began protesting through "fish-ins" along the Columbia and other rivers (Johnson, Champagne, and Nagel, 1997: 288).

The activities of Hank Adams exemplify this period of activism in the Northwest. In 1964, Adams was at Nisqually, declaring that the natives have a primary right to the salmon. The main issue, he said, was "the state's allowing non-Indians to catch 13 million salmon last year while throwing Indians into jail for catching any--and prohibiting some treaty tribes from harvesting any salmon or steelhead at all" (Valendra "National coexistence", 2005: 75).

In 1968 Hank Adams became director of the Survival of the American Indians Association. He and others actively battled for native fishing rights. He was frequently arrested. So were others—some far to the east of Nisqually on the Columbia River. In 1968 the travails of David Sohappy led to the court case Sohappy vs. Smith. He was cleared of any wrongdoing. Like Hank Adams, he continued the fight for Indian rights to traditional resources.

In 1974 Federal district judge George Boldt declared that treaties gave natives rights to catch half the harvestable salmon in Washington's waters. Three years later, in 1977, four treaty-fishing tribes -- the Umatillas, Yakamas, Nez Perce and Warm Springs -- joined forces to create a political entity capable of negotiating for an equitable share of the salmon harvest and for the right to be considered equals in the management of the habitat.

TEK is based in the understanding that humans are intimately linked, physically and spiritually, with other conscious entities--plants and animals . . . and sometimes apparently non-animate entities such as water, rocks, and sky. This view is evident in comments made by CRITFC officials. The Columbia River Inter-Tribal Fish Commission has worked very hard to restore a salmon fishery lost over the last hundred years or so. Dams, habitat degradation, and excessive commercial harvests have all taken a heavy toll.

In 1999, newly elected executive director for the Columbia River Inter-Tribal Fish Commission offered some comments about Native American survival needs:

> I see overwhelming odds today," he said. Big money, political power. However, the federal government and this country has a legal and moral obligation to the tribes to protect the salmon now and forever . . . Parallels between Indians and salmon are identical. We're tied; one in the same. We have a spiritual connection that most people can't understand. We have memories and traditions. People have for too long ignored that link, but we will continue to promote healthy streams, healthy fish and healthy people (Phinney, 1999: 1).

Having survived genocidal policies visited upon them through war and assimilation and/or termination, native peoples today are seeking ways to survive through co-management of resources - resources of traditional value. Through restoration of habitats and the maintenance of species that use those, tribal biologists work to preserve what they understand to be the cultural integrity of their people.

163

Let me give you some examples from a study I conducted during the summer of 2001. To try and determine how spiritual and/or religious beliefs influence the scientific practice of fish and wildlife biologists, I interviewed over 50 such biologists across Washington State, Oregon, Idaho, and Montana. Interviewees included nearly equal proportions of men and women. Ages ranged from 23 to 78. Employers included tribal, state, federal and private organizations.

Umatilla male (approximately 26 years old)

Traditional ecological knowledge is remembered though "social memory," which is the long-term communal understanding of the dynamics of environmental change, and the transmission of the pertinent experience" (Davidson-Hunt and Berkes, 2003: 2).

Ann Garibaldi and Nancy Turner noted the value of linking restoration efforts to those species having high cultural significance to the local communities concerned.

> If we begin our conservation and restoration efforts by focusing on cultural keystone species, both social and ecological integrity may be enhanced. Once local people begin to reconnect to their landscape through the conduit of species that have high importance to them, they will play a much more active role in ecosystem conservation and restoration, including the conservation of ecological keystone species.

They continued: "We anticipate that linking conservation and restoration to cultural concerns will result in an upward spiral of increasing effectiveness in maintaining and restoring both human and ecosystem health" (Garibaldi and Turner, 2004: 14).

Their comments are reflected in the thoughts and actions of a Umatilla biologist. Nez Perce background. Grew up on the Umatilla Reservation. Got a degree in Fisheries Management from the University of Idaho, Moscow. He works for the [Umatilla's] Pacific Lamprey Project.

I found the program to be interesting: lamprey are not generally considered by the American public to be a worthwhile fish to save. To Umatillas, I learned, they are however. He told me:

> [Lamprey are] a natural part of the ecosystem. They're not in here and originally they were in here. They are a vital component to the ecosystem. They provide a food supply for salmonids and they're also a cultural resource for our people. And the practice itself means a lot to me for a social gathering, teaching . . . Time to teach youth, more interaction between adults and youths. I think there's more to it than just putting them back so that they can restore nature or restore the ecosystem.

164

For this biologist, the ecosystem issues are vital. It is of the utmost importance to preserve biodiversity. Restoring lamprey habitat, restoring lamprey, through education and social interaction, and restoring communication and concern about traditional cultural resources to his people are all tightly interwoven for him.

I asked him what the consequences might be if biodiversity is not protected and present trends with lamprey and salmon in the Pacific Northwest continue. "Extinction," he replied. "Extinction of species and a way of life . . . if that species is gone, so is that interaction with the species such as salmon. So the way of life with salmon which is fishing has ended if you don't have fish to fish for."

According to him, protection of this resource was directly related to protection of family interactions. Maintenance of one leads to maintenance of the other. In his view, protecting the lamprey simultaneously protects Umatilla traditional culture. It does so by preserving the family interactions that revolve around fishing for and processing lamprey. His personal values help motivate him to engage in habitat restoration for this fish.

At times, some TEK scholars say, there is "two-way intergration or synergy between two knowledge frameworks . . . local indigenous knowledge and globally oriented conservation knowledge based on western science" (Becker and Ghimire;, 2003 4).

This certainly held true for all the people I interviewed. Scientific objectivity is important to the Umatilla biologist. He said:

> I believe science is laid out to be objective in order to lay out the pros and cons of the problems . . . I think it is important so you don't make biased decisions . . . that's what I'm here for. To lay out the information and in the best objective format that I can give and then have those people make the management decisions based on that objectivity.

He uses science to achieve his personal goals. However, religious beliefs play a role. This is not antithetical to TEK.

Jeanette Wolfley observed that "values embodying our cultural and religious beliefs are necessary for any engagement process . . . " (Wolfley, 1999: 300). This biologist was brought up loosely as a Catholic. Also exposed to Presbyterianism.

"But as an adult I have come more to focus on the Native American spirituality, such as there's a spirit in everything and that those animals and plant life, and I mean the ecosystem, held in such a high regard as my life." Nature is sacred. "Sacred - I think that's a great word for it. It is very special in my heart . . . Nature is my religion. Those interactions with hunting and fishing and the family that goes along with that."

"[M]y family's conflicted . . . [M]y mom's side, they're not very strong on their Native American beliefs and how they can preserve our culture. And I think it has to do with integrity versus preservation. And preservation seems to be more of a -- it is a positive direction. But I think integrity is -- first for me is what I'm saying is right now at this time in my life maybe five years from now I'd see preservation in the main way. But I think integrity meaning this first, this culture first for now because so much has been lost and that's the voice that needs to be strongest." I asked if any of his ideas related to genocide of Indian people.

"I agree," he said without hesitation. "I believe that's been taking place. I mean, look at me. I mean I'm a perfect example of it. You pretty much assimilated people out of existence. I don't know if that's right. I think there are certain steps that should have been taken to preserve a human race . . . I mean the assimilation and trying to say, look, this -- we're these sorts of people -- Cayuse, Umatilla, Walla Walla. We've got a set of beliefs and to keep us having some identity that we recognize as us."

Yakama female (43 years old)

According to TEK principles, other, non-human lives matter; they are important. In accord with many indigenous traditions, those lives deserve respect. "The worldview of reciprocal relationships between humans and ecosystems underlies caretaking traditions among indigenous peoples" (Long, Tecle, and Burnette:, 2003: 9).

This biologist is motivated to do scientific work on behalf of owls, at least in part, because of her traditional background--involving these principles. She explained:

> I guess what draws me towards the work I do today, is my parents instilled in me to respect all the created, like foods, animals, I guess, the trees, water, everything that is nature to people, for us to respect that due to they were placed there for one reason or another before we, as Indian people, came here to the earth. That is the reason why I -- we grew up in the mountains, and we've gathered foods, we've preserved food. We've pretty much relied on that as our subsistence in our younger years, until the modern world came about. And now it's just a battle to preserve all of that.

One of the most important personal values for her is the desire to preserve traditional cultural practices and beliefs. Traditional practices define her identity as a Yakama--indeed, as an Indian woman. She told me:

> I can tell you until I'm blue in the face how important it is, but you will never understand unless you've actually did those stages to

166

know the feeling when that time comes when you first went and did your -- picked your first berry or did your first root digging. Or like with the men, it's like when they did their first fish, their first hunt, their first kill. You know, unless you experience that, then you can kind of maybe relate to how important it is to the Indian people.

The consequences of biological extinctions, according to her, are severe. Not only are plants and animals threatened, but so are the (Native) people who depend in various ways upon them. She told me: If you let the foods disappear and the animals disappear, and the consequences would be that there would be no more Yakama Indians, there would be no more Yakama people. Just basically the people themselves would -- I mean, they may not, you know, disappear, but their traditional and cultural values will disappear. So them being an Indian would disappear. So that would be the consequence.

Despite her worry that Native could "disappear" if their traditional foods become extinct, Patty does not frame this in terms of genocide. According to her, genocide was real enough in the lives of Indians in the past. Additionally, genocidal experiences continue to have impacts upon Yakama life in the present. But now, she says, the problems are internal; the threat is inside. "The Yakama have internalized the way that modernization is taking over traditional ways." Tragically, enrolled members are now sometimes the greatest advocates of land use practices that contribute to the erosion of cultural practices and knowledge.

Mother Nature is the land, plants, and animals. But The Creator gave life by forming them. She is to nourish them--using traditional knowledge and science.

Nez Perce man (45 years old)

Worked as a forester for the BIA. Then went to school at OSU and obtained a bachelor's degree in forestry. Spent over seven years working for Washington State DNR in western Washington as a forester. Finally, he moved back to the Nez Perce Reservation as head of the tribe's Department of Natural Resources. Five years later he ran for Council and served two terms.

He very much wants to sustain Nez Perce traditions. For him, sustaining those traditions have everything to do with reacquiring lands lost to whites during the tumultuous years of the late 1800s. That land was taken from them in the 1860s following the discovery of gold. Resistance to forcible removal led to battles, and then to a 1,500-mile retreat that ended in loss. When Chief Joseph surrendered, just 30 miles south of the Canadian border, members of his band were sent far away.

"So we was that Nez Perce occupancy in Northeast Oregon had just gone to zero overnight, even though we maintained our treaty rights, our rights to hunt and fish, pasture animals there. But the presence of the Nez Perce over time was just almost as a visitor in our homeland. We'd go over there, hunt and fish. Few tribal members lived there. It was really important for us to gain a foothold, to truly return as a landowner."

But what is the importance of a "foothold"? Existence, that's what. "This is what some of the elders have stated to me," Jamie explained, "is that as Indian people, if we lose our language and if we lose our relationship with the land, we lose our identity as Nez Perce. We become indistinguishable. We become, gosh, basically strangers in our own ancient homeland."

TEK includes the assessment of resource use so that individuals and communities both benefit. You get lost with the science," this biologist said.. "You can't get lost with the science. You've got to maintain that relationship with the community which you serve. And it's a bigger community. It's not a fish community or an Indian community. It's one community." "What I do for the sake of the fish is also for the benefit of the community. And what I can do for the benefit of the community is always -- should translate as it's good for the fish."

Traditional ways offer productive paths of ecological restoration. "Passing on cultural traditions also sustains the collective action needed for successful restoration work by providing a vision for restoration, a sense of place and community, and guidance for decision-making" (Long, Tecle, and Burnette, 2003: 10). For this biologist, pro-tection of nature equates with protection of culture. "[S]ustainability of the fish means sustainability of the Nez Perce, the sustainability of our fishing culture, of the language, our access, the traditions that go with it."

Genocide issues: "You lose the connection to the land, you lose our language, and we're no longer the Nez Perce people. And that's extinction. And it's not saying that we all, as Nez Perce, must be physically dead. It's just that we have no sense of our past, no sense of a culture, no sense of the language that makes us unique."

Happily for the Nez Perce, they have successfully acquired old traditional-use lands in northeastern Oregon. And on those lands they seek to restore and maintain traditionally valued habitats and species. He uses a blend of science and religious values. It seems that for him, TEK is "biology with a heart."

Conclusions

Traditional ecological knowledge is based on the conviction that other, non-human lives matter; they are important. They deserve respect. Traditional ecological knowledge is based in the understanding that humans are intimately linked, physically and spiritually, with other conscious entities--plants and animals . . . and sometimes apparently non-animate entities such as water, rocks, and sky.

Tribal biologists often deal with degraded environments and depleted species. The restoration of ecological integrity, and say over how lands containing those ecological places are managed, is seen by many native peoples as essential to maintaining what they understand as their cultural integrity. It is essential to long-term survival.

The work of fish and wildlife biologists can certainly be understood in terms of traditional ecological knowledge--especially as it is blended with modern science-- as they work to restore and maintain habitats and species. For tribal biologists in particular the preservation and maintenance of habitats and species is aimed at the preservation of culture.

Toward this end, for most it seems, their practice of science is underlain and guided by their spiritual and/or religious beliefs and values. Through the restoring habitats and maintaining species, tribal biologists seek to re-pair and maintain cultural integrity of their people, and to open pathways of greater physical, emotional, and spiritual health for future generations to come.

◊ ◊ ◊ ◊ ◊ ◊

Joel Geffen worked as a forester for the U.S. Forest Service, and later as a forest archaeologist and land-use historian for the Yakama Nation, before receiving a doctorate in Religious Studies from UC Santa Barbara. He is working on a second doctorate in Geography at UCLA. His areas of specialization are American ideas of nature and contemporary Native American issues. He has written about the values held by fish and wildlife biologists, the role of religious and spiritual beliefs in resource management, and Native American views of ecological restoration and species protection.

References

Becker, C. D. and K. Ghimire. 2003. "Synergy between traditional ecological knowledge and conservation science supports forest preservation in Ecuador." Conservation Ecology 8(1): 1. [online] URL: http://www.consecol.org/vol8/iss1/art1. Accessed February 23, 2014.

Davidson-Hunt, I. and F. Berkes. 2003. "Learning as you journey: Anishinaabe perception of social-ecological environments and adaptive learning." Conservation Ecology 8(1): 5. [online] URL:

http://www.consecol.org/vol8/iss1/art5/. Accessed February 23, 2014.

Garibaldi, A. and N. Turner. 2004. "Cultural keystone species: implications for ecological conservation and restoration." Ecology and Society 9(3): 1. [online] URL: http://www.ecologyandsociety .org/vol9/iss3/art1/ . Accessed February 23, 2014.

Johnson, Troy, Champagne, Duane, and Joane Nagel. 1997. American Indian Activism and Transformation: Lessons from Alcatraz. University of Illinois Press, Chicago.

Long, J., A. Tecle, and B. Burnette. 2003. "Cultural foundations for ecological restoration on the White Mountain Apache Reservation." Conservation Ecology 8(1): 4. [online] URL: http://www.consecol. org/vol8/iss1/art4/. Accessed February 23, 2014.

Means, Russell. qtd. by Ward Churchill in A Little Matter of Genocie: Holocaust and Denial in the Americas 1492 to the Present, 1997.

Phinney, Wil. 1999. "CRITFC chooses Sampson." Confederated Umatilla Journal. March 31.. v. 7, n. 3, p. 1.

Valandra, Edward C. 2005. "National coexistence is our Bull Durham: Revisiting "The Indian Today'. In Yetman, Norman and Marion Dyer, eds. David Katzman, author. American Studies. Special Issue with Indigenous Studies Today. Vol. 46, Issues 3-4: Mid-American and Kansas University, Fall/Winter.

Wolfley, Jeanette. 1999. "Ecological Risk Assessment and Management: Their Failure to Value Indigenous Traditional Ecological Knowledge and Protect Tribal Homelands." In Contemporary Native American Cultural Issues. Duane Champagne, ed. AltaMira Press, Walnut Creek, CA.

◊ ◊ ◊ ◊ ◊ ◊

PART IV – ENVIRONMENTAL DEGRADATION AND THE INDIGENOUS RESPONSE: THE GREAT LAKES AND BEYOND

Native Americans in the Great Lakes/St. Lawrence River Basin: Treaties, Laws, and Environmental Issues

Scott Perez

Introduction

The St. Lawrence-Great Lakes drainage system covers a vast amount of land in Northern United States and Southern Canada. The watershed comprises 518,500 square miles (1,344,000 km2), representing 25% of the fresh water supply on earth (Beck & Litteljohn 2000) and is approximately 2,340 miles long (3700km), making it the 17th longest system in the world (St. Lawrence Centre 1996). Only the polar ice caps contain more fresh water. This large system encompasses a wide variety of ecological zones and landscapes. From the northern pine forests, to the rich prairies, to the bedrock expanses of the north shore, life takes on many forms. More than 10% of the population of the United States and over 25% of the population of Canada live in the Great Lakes/St. Lawrence River Basin (GL/SLRB) Large concentrations of industry can be found in the area, including nearly 25% of Canada's agriculture production and 7% of the United States' (Environmental Protection Agency 2006.) The basin also is home to more than 100 Native nations or tribes and thousands of Native people living in its cities and rural areas.(1)

The water found here is the key to our lives. It is a physical necessity for all life. The economies of the region and the nations depend on it. Over the last 250 years, this very dependence on the water has led to its degradation. From the time of the first white settlements, the water was used not only to sustain life, but as a sewer to get rid of the wastes produced by towns, cities and industries. Land use practices led to excessive runoff and erosion. The opening of the St. Lawrence Seaway led to further problems; from ending the runs of Atlantic salmon to opening a gateway for invasive species. For years, water quality has been a main issue in this region. Despite apparent abundance, we now face threats to water quantity. The commercialization of water, growing human population, and the effects of global climate change are only a few of the problems now before us (Environmental Protection Agency 2006.)

Often lost among the environmental and legal concerns of water issues, both here and throughout North America, is the fact that to the Native peoples of Turtle Island, this is more than environmental and legal concern. Water is also more than a physical need. It is part of the culture and spiritual beliefs of Native peoples. It is part of history and the

173

creation story. The water, the land, and the air are all part of life and cannot be separated. It is important to understand this, and remember it. (2)

The Physical and Biological Setting

Geologists tell us that the Great Lakes have been formed over millions of years. Some of the oldest rock in the world is found in the area of the Canadian Shield, forming the northern and northwestern parts of the basin. The same rock can also be found in the Adirondack Mountains of New York where it has been uplifted and is the source of several tributary rivers to the system. The seas that once covered the area left deposits which eventually became many of the rock and mineral formations found in the region. A series of glaciers over millennia scoured out valleys from early rivers to form the Great Lakes. They also pushed and deposited rock and soil in seemingly random patterns throughout the area, giving rise to the landforms we see today from the craggy rocks and deep gorges to the level plains (Environmental Protection Agency 2006.)

The climate of the region has pervasive effects on life around the lakes. This climate is affected by winds and moisture coming from outside of the region and altered by the presence of the lakes themselves. The cooler, dry air is predominant in the northern areas of the basin, while warmer, moist air coming from the Gulf of Mexico prevails in the south. The blending of the air masses causes significant rainfall throughout the basin. During the summer, the lakes warm. As winter sets in, this warmth moderates the temperatures along the lake shores. As this warm, moist air rises, it collides with the arctic cold and the famous "lake effect" snows are formed. During the spring, the lakes tend to keep the adjoining land cooler than the surrounding areas (Environmental Protection Agency 2006).
.
This moist climate and the landforms combine to produce a wealth of wetlands in the region. These wetlands serve many purposes and are important to the overall health of the ecosystem. Wetlands control erosion and flooding, slowing the speed of water runoff. They are also referred to as the "kidneys" of the system, filtering pollutants and excess nutrients from the water before it flows to the streams or recharges the groundwater. Fish and wildlife depend on these wetlands for food, habitat and resting places for migrating waterfowl, habitats for animals such as the beaver and muskrat, and hatcheries and nurseries for many fish, reptiles, and amphibians. Many endangered species depend on the wetlands for at least part of their lifecycle (Environmental Protection Agency 2006.) The wetlands are also home to many of the medicinal and culturally significant plants of the Native peoples.

Before European arrival, the southern part of the basin was covered with great stands of hardwoods, including oaks, maples, and others. These stands were interspersed with large areas of grasslands which resembled

174

the tall grass prairies further west. In the northern section of the basin, where the soils are thinner and sandier, vast stretches of pines and other conifers abound, interspersed with bogs and other wetlands. The land was home to a great number of plant and animal species. Birds were found in great abundance and it has been said that there were over 180 species of indigenous fish in the Great Lakes/St. Lawrence system. The waterways, wetlands, and forests were heavily populated with furbearing animals, a fact that would play heavily in the history of the post-contact landscape. Today, there are only remnants of these natural systems and the biodiversity they supported to be found. Over the last 20 years, more of the landscape has started converting back to its original state as more farm land is abandoned and conservation agencies buy more land for habitat protection (Environmental Protection Agency 2006.)

The Native Peoples

It has been estimated that the population of the Great Lakes Basin was possibly 117,000 people in 1500 (Environmental Protection Agency 2006.) Besides the people living in the basin, many more passed through the area, using the St. Lawrence River and Great Lakes as a water route for both trade and warfare. Oral tradition has many stories about such interactions in ancient times, including the story of the Peacemaker who journeyed from the Upper Great Lakes to the Haudenosaunee (Iroquois) lands to unite the tribes.

The Native peoples lived in scattered towns throughout the basin. Hunting and fishing were important to the people, as was agriculture and gathering of wild foods. Many of the peoples grew the Three Sisters of corn, beans and squash along with sacred tobacco. The town would clear fields and plant, living in the same place for 10 to 20 years. As the soil became less fertile, the people would clear new fields and move the town, allowing the old fields to remain fallow and regenerate.

The peoples hunted large and small game. Moose and deer were important and in some areas, buffalo and elk could be found. Furbearing animals were used for food and winter clothing. Fish of all kinds were used, with sturgeon, now rare, being of particular cultural importance to many communities. Nuts, berries, roots and other wild plants were gathered in season for use as food or medicine. Wild rice became a staple of many of the tribes, particularly in the Upper Great Lakes. Ceremony and thanks accompanied all aspects of agriculture, hunting, and gathering.

These patterns and ways of life continued for centuries, adapting and changing as new ideas were introduced and changes of locality and environment demanded. While the people used the landscape to provide their livelihood, it was done with respect for the land and water, both in the physical and spiritual sense. Changes would come rapidly starting in the 1500's with the coming of the Europeans.(3)

175

Euro-American Settlement

The arrival of non-Native people to the region started a process of rapid and unprecedented change to the land and the Native peoples. European products and demand for furs changed the lifestyles of the Natives in many ways. Diseases previously unknown on this continent decimated the people who had no immunity to them. Native populations dropped by an estimated 50 to 90%. Warfare did further damage with the French and English, and later the Americans and English fighting over control of the land and the waters, and the people who lived there (Richter 1992.) After the American Revolution, the Great Lakes and part of the St. Lawrence River became the boundary for the new United States and the British holding Canada. During the War of 1812, the British and Americans again fought over this region. Two years later, they both claimed victory and the boundary remained the same (Environmental Protection Agency 2006.) The Natives often took sides in these conflicts, hoping to gain an advantage and preserve some of their land and way of life. No matter which side they took, or who won the wars, the Native peoples paid a heavy price in the end. The land was taken through a variety of means and the peoples were scattered and settled into small portions of their original homelands. Others were forced entirely from the area.(4)

Over the next century and a half, development proceeded quickly in the area. The waterways became the commercial highways for the new Euro-American nations. Commercial fishing also took root in the basin. Lumber, wheat, iron ore, lead and coal were just some of the major resources that were developed in the area and shipped along the water highway. Ports, industry and manufacturing grew apace. The basin became the heart of American and Canadian growth in the 19th and 20th centuries (Environmental Protection Agency 2006).
Environmental Degradation:

The agricultural and industrial growth of the region had a devastating effect on the environment. Commercial fishing and hunting also caused much harm. The earliest logging occurred to facilitate agriculture and to build the homes and structures needed for the growing population. By the 1830's commercial logging started, first in Canada and then in the border states of the U.S. The deforestation opened the land to erosion both from water and wind. As the land eroded, the smaller bodies of water were changed and clogged by siltation. Western agriculture bore little resemblance to the agriculture of the original inhabitants. Fields were much larger and made up of a single crop. As time went on, the size of the fields has increased even more. Wetlands have been drained and tiles and ditches installed to hasten the runoff of water. Pesticides and fertilizers are added to the soil. These changes have also led to deterioration of water quality throughout the region. Excess nutrients and other chemicals runoff of the land are carried to the waterways by the systems of tiles and ditches. The wetlands that once would have filtered and slowed these waters are no longer there (Environmental Protection Agency 2006.)

Urbanization and growth of industry have had a similar, and often more destructive, effect on the waters of the basin. Pollution from chemicals used in the industrial processes has caused serious problems throughout the region. Paving, ditching, draining and chemical use from urban growth have exacerbated this situation. Up until the mid 1900s, it was common for urban areas to drain sewage directly into rivers and streams, all of which would find its way into the Great Lakes and the St. Lawrence River. Once they enter the Great Lakes system, these pollutants can remain for years, even generations. The Great Lakes, particularly in the upstream end of the system are deep and the rate at which they drain to the sea is relatively slow.(5) The water stratification found in the lakes during the summer, reduces the rate at which the pollutants are diluted. Many settle to the bottom and become a long term part of the system. Others find their way into the food chain, being taken in by the smallest of creatures and accumulating in the systems of the larger creatures as they feed upon the smaller (Environmental Protection Agency 2006.)

Some of the greatest environmental problems in the system have come about since the opening of the St. Lawrence Seaway in 1959. The Seaway was built to allow ocean going cargo ships access to the Great Lakes and to provide electricity. A system of dams and locks was constructed along the St. Lawrence River and around Niagara Falls between Lakes Ontario and Erie. The construction entailed massive dredging in places along the river and in the lake ports. The dams have caused other areas to be flooded (Patch and Busch 1984.) In the past several years, business interests have called for the Seaway to be enlarged to allow for the newer, larger ocean going vessels, a move being contested by environmental groups, some cities and towns, and Native communities.

The St. Lawrence River has borne the brunt of the environmental problems from the Seaway. For example, 110 wetland plant species found along the St. Lawrence before the construction of the Seaway, were not found in surveys taken after the project completion (Patch & Busch 1984.) Similarly, dams are responsible for the alteration of natural water fluctuation which is one of the major causes of damage to aquatic wildlife. The movement of fish is also greatly restricted by dams. Due to the multitude and duration of various stresses caused by dams, short-lived fish species may eventually become dominant while long-lived fish, such as lake sturgeon, are compromised (SLC 1996.)

The case of pollution at the Mohawk reservation of Akwesasne is well-known and documented. Up-river industry, attracted by the cheap electricity from the Seaway project, severely polluted the land, air and water for years with PCB's, heavy metals, and fluoride. In testing on the reservation, many animals were found to be contaminated. Among those affected were the snapping turtles, an animal of cultural and spiritual significance to the people. Not only were the contamination levels in the Akwesasne snapping turtles the highest found, but these concentrations were among the highest ever recorded in the tissues of free-ranging animals. One turtle trapped had levels so high, I had to be classified as toxic waste (Grinde and Johansen 1995.)

Other environmental problems associated with the Seaway have become common throughout the Great Lakes system. Large oil and gas spills have thankfully been fairly rare. But low-level spills are common. The biggest issue has been invasive species, both plant and animal, which are brought into the Great Lakes basin in the ballast water of the ships. Zebra mussels, round gobi fish, and invasive common reed grass are just a few examples. These non-native species out-compete the indigenous species and radically alter the ecosystems. They do not remain only in the Great Lakes but radiate outwards into tributaries and water bodies throughout the system. Even though the economic costs alone associated with invasive species are in the billions of dollars (Environmental Protection Agency 2006) the Federal governments of the United States and Canada have so far refused to take any meaningful steps in prevention. The cost of loss of plants and animals important to the Native peoples cannot be calculated by any scientific or economic framework.

Treaties

During the early years of interactions between the Native peoples and the European/Americans, treaties were signed between the groups, usually involving the Native peoples ceding more and more land to the newcomers. In most of the treaties, there was a section stating that the Native people would maintain the right to fish and hunt on all ceded land that had not become private property. The Robinson Treaty of 1850 is just one example (Indian and Northern Affairs Canada 2006.) Dams and pollution have made the right to fish a moot point in some areas.

In 1905, the International Waterways Commission was formed by the United States and Canada to look at water levels and flows in the Great Lakes system. The main purpose was in relation to hydropower projects and it had little to no jurisdiction over pollution or any other environmental issues. The Boundary Waters Treaty was signed in 1909 by the two countries. The treaty created the International Joint Commission (IJC) with the authority to resolve disputes over the joint water resources. The commission consists of three members from each of the federal governments. There was no mention of a place for any of the sovereign nations of Native peoples who might have been affected by these issues (Environment Canada 2006, International Joint Commission 2006.)

The Great Lakes Water Quality Agreement was signed in 1972 by President Richard Nixon of the United States and Prime Minister Pierre Trudeau of Canada. The agreement committed the two countries to

178

clean up waste waters from communities and industry in the basin and to control pollution. In 1978, the agreement was amended to include restoration and maintenance of the ecological integrity of the Great Lakes ecosystem. Again these treaties involved the governments of the U.S. and Canada. In 1987, another agreement was signed as an adjunct to the original treaty. Known as the 1987 Protocol, this agreement placed emphasis on human and aquatic ecosystem health. An ecosystem approach, including non-point contaminant sources, and community involvement were introduced in this agreement (Environment Canada 2006.)
Today:

We can now look back and see how some things have changed in relation to the Great Lakes/St. Lawrence Basin. The extreme pollution that we faced over the past two centuries has decreased due to stricter environmental laws and controls. Remediation efforts have been undertaken throughout the system. Private individuals, Non-Governmental Organizations (NGO's) such as the Nature Conservancy and Great Lakes United, Tribal, local, state, provincial, and federal governments have taken a hand in the process. The IJC sponsors research and is working with representatives of the Native communities (International Joint Commission 2006.) The proposal to enlarge the Seaway seems to have lost its steam, at least for now, and there is a proposal under consideration to allow only "lakers" (non-ocean going cargo ships) west of the port at Montreal. People are taking quality of life and recreational values of the area more seriously. Town meetings are being held throughout the basin to discuss the issues of the day. In October, the United States passed the Great lakes Fish and Wildlife Restoration Act (The Nature Conservancy 2006.)

But we still face potential problems. Some business and politicians favor privatization of our waters. The Great Lakes would become a source of water to be sold to the highest bidder under their idea. One plan has been put forth to build a pipeline and send water from the Great Lakes to the Southwestern U.S. where cities like Phoenix are outgrowing their own water supplies (Great Lakes Directory 2006a.) Some wetlands and other environmental regulations have been relaxed in the U.S. And in 2006, there were large die-offs of fish and waterfowls which can be traced directly back to invasive species and diseases brought in through the Seaway (Great Lakes Directory 2006b.)

The restoration of the basin still has a long way to go. Fish, animals and plants that the Native peoples have used for centuries for cultural, spiritual, and medical practices are still rare in many places. The Great Lakes/St. Lawrence system is of great importance as a physical entity and in its spiritual significance. On Native lands, the people are working to protect and restore the environment using a blend of Western science and traditional Native practices. Many of the major issues involved beyond the Native lands and waters will be worked on through the legal systems of the United States, Canada, and the states and provinces. It is my hope that the legal profession can move in the direction of the environmental work by looking at traditional Native law to form a new set of laws, valuable not only on Native lands, but to all of Turtle Island and that environmental research and remediation efforts throughout the region take into consideration the vast knowledge and deep connections of the people who have lived in the region for thousands of years.

◊ ◊ ◊ ◊ ◊ ◊

Scott Perez was a PhD Candidate in Cornell University's Dept. of Natural Resources/American Indian Program when this was written. He is now a Consultant and Educator working in the environmental and cultural fields.

Notes:

(1) It is difficult to find a source that gives an exact number of nations or tribes within the Basin. Many groups are not recognized by the U.S. or Canada and therefore do not show up on any official records or maps. Estimates run from 70 to over 100 groups. I have chosen the over 100 after talking to Frank Ettawageshik, Tribal Chairman of the Little Traverse Bay Bands of Odawa Indians, Michigan, who has been a leader in uniting Native communities to protect their rights and the environment of the GL/SLRB.

(2) The Haudenosaunee Environmental Task Force has prepared a paper that covers many of the issues discussed in this article. Other Native nations, organizations, and communities also have statements on water.

(3) There are many written and academic sources for the pre-contact era usually drawn from the journals of the early European explorers or archeological investigation. More recently, Native academics have taken a hand in writing their own history. I have been privileged to hear the stories over the years from the elders of several nations.

(4) There is not room, nor is it the purpose of this paper to document the history of Native/white relations during this period. There is much written on the subject and each community has their own story to tell. It is enough to say that the colonial process was devastating to the Native peoples. However, the resurgence of Native pride and the growth of Native communities is evidence that the peoples have persevered and are on the way to reclaiming their sovereignty and rights on Turtle Island.

(5) The rate of release into the Lower Great lakes is currently on the increase. As this was being written, it was announced by U.S. environmental researchers that Lake Superior will probably drop to a record low level this fall (2007). Although drought is considered to be a factor, a Canadian research group says that the dredging of Michigan's St. Clair River has seriously exacerbated the problem,

acting like a bathtub drain. As the volume and velocity of the water flowing through increases, it further erodes the channel which again increase the flow from the Upper Great Lakes. More information on this and other issues facing the Great Lakes can be found at Great Lakes Directory, http://www.greatlakesdirectory.org/.

References:

Beck, G.G. and Litteljohn, B. 2000. Voices for the Watershed. New York: Ithaca.

Environment Canada. 2006. Great Lakes Water Quality Agreement. Webpage: http://www.on.ec.gc.ca/greatlakes/default.asp?lang=En&n= FD65DFE5-1   Site visited October 20, 2006.

Environmental Protection Agency. 2006. The Great lakes: An Environmental Atlas and Resource Book. Webpage: http://www.epa.gov /glnpo/atlas/index.html Site visited October 12, 2006.

Great Lakes Directory, 2006a. Great Lakes Water Privatization. Webpage: http://www.greatlakesdirectory.org/great_lakes_water_ export.htm Site visited October 20, 2006.

Great Lakes Directory. 2006b. Great Lakes Exotic Species/Great Lakes Invasive Species Webpage: http://www.greatlakesdirectory.org/ great_lakes_exoticinvasive_species/great_lakes_exotic_invasive_ species.htm Site visited October 20, 2006.

Grinde, Donald E. and B.E. Johansen, 1995. Ecocide of Native America: Environmental Destruction of Indian Lands and People. Santa Fe: Clear Light Publishers.

Indian and Northern Affairs Canada. 2006. Webpage: http://www.ainc-inac.gc.ca/pr/trts/rbt2_e.html   Site visited October 20, 2006.

International Joint Commission. 2006. Webpage: http://www.ijc.org/en/home/main_ accueil.htm Site visited October 20, 2006.

Patch, S. P. and W-D. N. Busch, eds., 1984. The St. Lawrence River: Past and Present: A review of historical natural resource information and habitat changes in the International section of the St. Lawrence River. Buffalo: U. S. Army Corps of Engineers.

Richter, D. K. 1992. The Ordeal of the Longhouse: the peoples of the Iroquois League in the era of European colonization. Chapel Hill: University of North Carolina Press

St. Lawrence Centre. 1996. State of the environment report on the St. Lawrence River. Volume 1: The St. Lawrence ecosystem. Environment Canada – Quebec Region, Environmental Conservation, and Editions MultiMondes, Montreal.

The Nature Conservancy. 1997. Great Lakes In The Balance: Protecting Our Ecosystem's rich Natural Legacy. Chicago: The Nature Conservancy. Online version: http://www.epa.gov/glnpo/ecopage/glbe/glbal.html Site visited January 10, 2007.

The Nature Conservancy. 2006. The Nature Conservancy Celebrates the Passage of the great Lakes Fish and Wildlife Restoration Act. Webpage: http://www.nature.org/wherewework/northamerica/greatlakes/press/glfwra.html   Site visited October 20, 2006.

◊ ◊ ◊ ◊ ◊

The People and the Planet: Health Access and Crises in the Great Lakes Region

Reddog Sina

For decades, there has been a glacially slow move toward accepting the reality that the Earth is in a state of declining health. Highly conservative scientists myopically argued that natural cycles are contributing to (if not causing) the problems that currently affect the ozone layer, air quality and composition, and innumerable animal and plant species. And while the most powerful nations in the world have been justifiably vilified for failing to take responsibility for their nations' (and domestic corporations') contributions to environmental degradation, leading nations have also escaped public criticism resulting from their treatment of human populations which may be considered most closely tied to the environment. For more than five hundred years, ongoing institutionalized Euro-American mistreatment of Indigenous North, Central, and South Americans has mirrored the systematic destruction of the environmental world, predominantly in the cause of natural resource extraction, and to a lesser extent because of some bigoted notion of the Christian God's will.

Contrary to the arguments of Jared Diamond and Shepard Krech, indigenous peoples across the world have the most outstanding track records of environmentally-friendly cultural practices, predominantly because of their uses of soft technologies and their lack of waste resulting from industrial and post-industrial technologies. To sum up their impact on the environment, it is safe to say that damage done was generally repaired within seasons, or, in rare cases, human generations or lifetimes. This is a far cry from the damage currently being done by developing and industrialized nations that will require recoveries spanning geologic time to reestablish some level of balance.

Unfortunately, because Native people often self identify as being attached to the Earth Mother by an umbilicus, and because we see ourselves as part of the original ecosystem, and because our traditional world view opposes the dominant Euro-American model (or Cartesian, Enlightenment, or Western - take your pick) which is based in humankind being separated from the environment, Aboriginal people are thought of as canaries in an environmental coal mine. While this notion is dehumanizing because of the implied intent to use us as living indicators of the nearness of the point of no return, there is some benefit to this metaphor. If, instead of thinking about Aboriginal people as caged song birds (which is hopelessly demeaning), we think about Aboriginals as those who benefit least from the "advantages" provided by the post-industrial world, then our compromised socioeconomic position as a group may indicate the future of the broader population. As the population group with the lowest income, least employment, and worst public health, we become the front end of the impending tsunami of social disarray that corresponds with environmental degradation. This notion becomes a good place to begin a discussion of Indigenous health in the Great Lakes, a place where land use, water access, and multinational industrial concerns square up with public health issues – and as usual, Aboriginal peoples seem to lose out. This area is also representative of the problems affecting Indigenous North America as a whole because the industries (farming, manufacturing, tourism, etc.) that are the economic backbone of the region have such an impact on Indigenous people.

I think it's very easy to fall into a discussion of genocide and ecocide when starting off in a discussion of the history of the Indigenous people of the Americas, and that discussion is better left to people who understand its intricacies far better than I (such as Ward Churchill). As a health care provider, I am predominantly concerned with the provision of health care not just as a component of treaty agreements, but really as a function of human social obligation across the U.S. and Canada, and specifically in the Great Lakes region. In essence, I see healthcare as a lynchpin that holds societies together, and as a means of defining some of the problems that face a people as a whole. Health care represents a starting point to many of the best available strategies to avert both environmental and human disasters, so my goal here is to define some of the problems facing Native People is a way of contextualizing the bi-national approaches to the human impact of environmental problems.

My discussion will focus on the International Great Lakes region, which I will define as the Province of Ontario on the north side of the border (although arguments might be made for including Quebec because of the St. Lawrence Seaway and even Manitoba because its waters contribute to Minnesota and the Great Lakes), and the states of Illinois, Indiana, Michigan, Minnesota, New York, Ohio, Pennsylvania, and Wisconsin to the south. These areas, which have been subdivided out by political expediency rather than according to regional difference, make up the northern and southern borders of a more naturally-defined area, the Great Lakes watershed.

Thinking about the region as a single bioregion lends credence to the claims of the people of the Three Fires (Odawa, Ojibwe/Chippewa, and Potawotami) that while there are more than 1000 nations of Indigenous peoples in Canada and the U.S., the majority of the peoples of this region are from one language and cultural group – they are largely one people. Public health statistics from both sides of the water seem to support this claim, and also illustrates the need for cross-border solutions to the problems affecting both Indigenous people and the environment.

When we talk about the Native population of the Great Lakes watershed, it helps to understand some basic information about who these people are, and how their group relates to their larger numbers. Because population trends change much more quickly than most people realize, these numbers can only be used to guide, and are not absolute. To begin, according to the 2000 US Census, American Indians and Alaska Natives nationally made up approximately 1.5% of the US population, of which about 70% lived off tribal/federal lands.(1) Similarly, Statistics Canada reports that Aboriginal peoples made up about 1.7% of Ontario's total population, but off-Reserve populations outnumbered on-Reserve and Crown Land occupation for the first time in 2003.(2)

As of 2001, 90% of the approximately 292,000 Métis lived west of Ontario, with 70% residing in urban and metropolitan areas.(3) The trend among native people on either side of the water is to move toward the cities, where there is greater likelihood of employment and other social opportunities, including improved access to health care.

One of the significant measures of long-term health care access is life expectancy. Those groups who expect to live longer do so for a number of reasons, and one of the main reasons is health care access. Life expectancy on either side of the Great Lakes is lower among Aboriginal people, and the population breakdown varies significantly among the Native and non-Native peoples. The average life expectancy for registered Indian males in Canada was 7.6 years below the general population, and 5.8 years below the national average for women.(4) At the same time, the Indian Health Service reported in 2006 that life expectancy in the U.S. was also lower, although the difference was not as dramatic (2.4 years lower on average).

Because we know that socioeconomic pressures have effects on life expectancies, this seems to have a larger effect upon life expectancy than method of health care provision; these two populations, which are served by entirely different health care infrastructures, demonstrate the effects of seemingly similar stresses as compared to the general population surrounding them.

When you add into the equation the population breakdowns by age group, the trends become even more clearly parallel. In Ontario, Aboriginal people under the age of 25 make up 45% of the Native population. In the U.S., 44% are under 25 years old. This is in comparison to the 33% and 35% of Ontario and the U.S. among the total population. In all four populations, about 30% are in the group of 25-44 year-olds.

Above the age of 44, however, the numbers begin to change drastically, showing a much shallower decline among the late middle aged and elderly in the general populations: among the 45-64 group, U.S. and Ontario general populations make up 24% of the total (each) whereas for U.S. Native the numbers drop to 20% and among Ontario Aboriginals it drops to 18% of the total population. Among the elderly (older than 64), the difference in population makeup becomes even more apparent, as elders make up 4% and 6% in Ontario and the U.S., respectively, as compared to 12% of the general population in both places.

As Figure 1 indicates, there is a clearly parallel age breakdown between the Aboriginal and General populations in the U.S. and Canada. While there may be many different reasons for this (Education levels, employment statistics, economic circumstances, crime rates), I will focus on public health. What follows is a detailed look at the similarities of these populations, especially demonstrating how they share collective deviations from their countries' general population health trends. I will argue that these divergences are manifestations of inherently flawed Indigenous health care policy, indications of a larger devaluing of Indigenous people as a whole, and reflection of social policies that have similar impacts on the environment.

Winona LaDuke, the Ojibwe Journalist/Activist/Vice-Presidential Candidate, is infamous for having described Indian Country as the Fourth World, a place where there is little economic development, severe employment shortages, and an utter lack of hope. Common wisdom suggests that while these other issues are perhaps less common in urban aboriginal communities, what both groups share is decreased health care access, despite bi-national federal policies that guarantee health care to Indigenous People. While there may be many different ways to measure health access, among the most useful is to compare health indicators between the target and general populations, which as a group can create a picture of broad health care trends. I will look at several such indicators, including incidence of preventable diseases, disease prevention rates (such as immunization rates), and rates of physician visits.

When we look at preventable diseases, some are considered lifestyle-dependent, such as type II diabetes, which is largely preventable with adequate exercise and dietary control. While there is certainly a genetic component to non-insulin dependent diabetes, studies have shown that it is relatively low. In comparison, heart disease has a much more demonstrable genetic component, but people who develop it are speeded along in the process by poor diet and exercise habits. Tuberculosis is increasingly a disease that occurs among immunosuppressed people or those who live in comparative poverty. HIV is almost completely preventable with adequate education, abstention from sharing needles, and engaging in safe sexual practices, and even when an individual is infected, the progression to full-blown AIDS generally occurs only when people are not treated with very expensive anti-retroviral drugs – in an ideal world it should rarely happen.

All of the above diseases are considered preventable with adequate care and education, and yet their prevalence in Indian country demonstrates frightening trends. In the U.S., American Indians are 1.3 times more likely to have AIDS than Caucasians; have three times higher rates of type II diabetes; have eight times higher rates of tuberculosis; and are half again as likely to die from heart disease.(5) In Canada, Aboriginal people represent 15% of new HIV and AIDS infections; have 3-5 times higher rates of type II diabetes; have 8-10 times higher tuberculosis infection rates; and have a 1.5 times higher rate of heart disease.(6) Heart disease is the top killer in both countries, and that its occurrence is closely tied to high cholesterol levels from poor diets.

Type II (non-insulin dependent) diabetes is a direct result of obesity; it is considered a risk equivalent to heart disease, which means that diabetics have an equally high risk of heart attack as anyone with coronary artery disease. A decade ago, tuberculosis was thought to be nearly eliminated from North America, and yet new and highly drug-resistant strains are emerging as dangerous public health threats. As I noted above, AIDS is utterly preventable, and yet its rates of spread seem to be highest among young people, the poor, and communities of color; when people belong to two or three of these groups, their chances of contracting HIV and converting to AIDS are substantially increased.

186

All of these statistics indicate a lack of basic primary care for people who are old enough to control their health conditions. Unfortunately, this lack of care crosses generational lines.

One of the ways this is manifested is in infant mortality. According to the Centers for Disease Control, U.S. Indigenous Peoples have infant mortality rates of approximately nine per one thousand, as compared to less than six among Caucasian infants.(7) In Canada, the 1999 rate for Aboriginal Peoples was 8.0 per one thousand births, as compared to the general population's 5.5. While the medical evidence supporting the efficacy of prenatal care is equivocal in uneventful pregnancies, there is clear evidence to support necessity of prenatal care if a pregnancy is high-risk. This is a clear example of the damage done by a systematic inattention to preventative care. Perhaps a better example come with looking at the public health conditions of slightly older children, and the well-documented means by which a well-designed and implemented system of preventative care can make a huge difference in their lives individually and as a group.

When we look at the health of children, there are deeply concerning statistics relating to the most basic disease prevention: immunizations. In the U.S., American Indian and Alaska Native children are vaccinated at lower rates than non-Hispanic Whites and are well below the national average for three of the most important immunization series for children: 6% less for Measles, Mumps, and Rubella (MMR); DTP (Diptheria, Tetanus and Pertussis) and Polio.(8) Furthermore, only 62% of Children <3 are fully immunized.

Perhaps the most damning statistic is that, in 2002, despite getting their information directly from Indian Health Service, the US Centers for Disease Control only had statistics for MMR and Varicella vaccinations, but not for Polio, DTP, and Hemophilus influenza B.(9) Considering the yearly reports of death because of influenza, and resurgence of previously-controlled diseases such as pertussis and polio, the absence of statistics are an indicator that there are serious gaps in the provision of preventative care to children.

The record-keeping problem is only a symptom of the real problem, lower immunization rates. Native children in the U.S. have twice the national rate of pertussis (Whooping Cough), seven times the rate of Rubella, more than two times the rate of Shigellosis, six-to-seven times the rate of Genital Chlamydia and higher rates of cervical cancer (which we know to be related to infection with certain strains of human papilloma virus). Furthermore, American Indian and Alaska Native children also had higher rates of allergies, asthma, ear infections or problems, learning disabilities, and teen pregnancy (although these numbers are declining rapidly).

One question to ask is how this happens when people meeting governmentally determined criteria for tribal membership are guaranteed free health care. Unfortunately, there is a difference between not charging for health care and making it available where patients can access it. In the U.S., one explanation for this disconnect is that most Native Peoples live in urban areas, but only 1% of the Indian Health Services budget goes to urban clinics. In general, urban

187

clinics are not supported by casino profits (although reservation-based clinics are more likely to be). In addition, even if a clinic is geographically accessible, Indian Health Service clinics have huge staffing shortages, and despite an emphasis on primary care at IHS facilities, primary care needs are largely unmet in the community as a whole.

In the U.S., while there is a roughly equal occurrence of emergency room visits and outpatient procedures (which suggests that acute and emergent issues are addressed), American Indians and Alaska Natives have about one quarter the number of office visits, which may explain the impact of long-term chronic disease on life expectancy, causes of death, and even quality of life. This is particularly a concern because of the impact of inaccessible care for people with chronic diseases and conditions, such as diabetes (and its associated conditions such as peripheral neuropathy), hypertension, high cholesterol, obesity, rheumatological diseases, chronic pain/headaches, and mental illness. On either side of the border, more than 50% of Native people are living with diagnoses of one or more long-term health condition. More than 10% of both countries' Native adults have diabetes mellitus, They have more than double the disability rate of the general population: more than 28% of 21-64 year-olds and more than 57% of those over 65 have disabilities.(10)

But when attempts are made to look at the health trends more closely, problems emerge. The 1999 data published by Health Canada indicates some of the problems with the way information (and, arguably care itself) is managed. While it is relatively easy to locate data relating to causes of death by disease coding for the Canadian population (including, by province), there is no easily attainable data available from Health Canada to make similar comparisons between First Nations and Ontario (or Canadian) causes of mortality. So while published reports contain data such as that appearing in Figure 3 (above), there is inadequate detail to draw any conclusions about the prevalence of many kinds of disease, including differentiating between coronary and cerebral circulatory disease, which has a huge impact the data's usability.

The method used to report mortality statistics fails to account for key information, such as that AIAN and First Nations each have a substantially lower rate of death per 100,000 than the US population, but a higher rate than Canadians (650 for AIAN, 800.8 for the US, 557.3 in Canada, and 662 in 1999 for First Nations). Health Canada admits that this adds a complication to looking at age-standardized data across different populations, which manifests in the following way: 27.1% of the general US population died from Heart Disease, as did 22.7% of AIAN, and 31.7 of Canadians, but the percentages of deaths tell a different story than what appears at first glance.

First Nations had rates of 32% of "circulatory disease" deaths, but this number combines heart disease with stroke (and possibly vascular diseases), a changing of definitions that creates confusion (looked at in this way, Canada has a "circulatory disease" mortality rate of 50%). Similarly, other information gets buried as well. Suicide numbers are folded into the accidental death and poisoning rates in Figure 3, which simultaneously impedes understanding the rates of each separately and prevents comparison to Canadian national numbers.

188

What hasn't been lost is a clear indication of certain trends that can at least be attributed to social environment. Around the Great Lakes to the north and south (and throughout much of the rest of the Turtle Island landmass), despite having lower rates of cancer and broadly-defined diseases of the heart and vasculature, Native people have shorter life expectancies that are undoubtedly related to higher rates of smoking, fatal accidents, and suicide.

Suicide remains a major concern among Native people in Canada and the U.S. According to Health Canada suicide rates are five to seven times higher for First Nations youth than for non-Aboriginal youth.(11) These numbers represent a disturbing trend, to be sure, but they lead to unjustifiable suppositions. They are much more reflective of reserve, rather than urban, populations, because ethnic identification is more easily tracked when people share the same background and family ties. But not all reserves are the same: there is wide variation in suicide rates depending upon language group, tribal council, or community. There are also many levels of intergenerational trauma(12) that may influence suicide rates, such as residential schools, rape, substance abuse, poverty, and environmental degradation. There are trends to note, however, and they are disturbing.

Young men (15-24) and Elder men (>65) have highest rates, with Bender (2003) reporting that 30% of men from one urban and one rural community had considered or attempted suicide.(13) Beals (2005)(14) also demonstrated that there are wide ranges of mood disorder and substance abuse prevalence among different American Indian Nations from different geographic areas. While there is no doubt that there is a history of Aboriginal mental health concerns that often relate to the fallout from a history of displacement, it must be noted that there is also a long history of poor record-keeping. Indian Health Service, as I've noted already, has very good statistics for the patients they see, but their service population is less than 50% of the American Indian population, and even the CDC admits that health statistics for American Indians and Hispanics (among other populations) are "underreported."

Similarly, Health Canada notes that they have done well at tracking Reserve populations, but they have largely failed at tracking treatment of urban Indigenous populations. While some of the historical trends in mental health are apparent, the larger picture is fuzzy and poorly defined and will remain so until communities become involved in studying themselves (and can therefore assure that the information that's reported is accurate).

Much has been written about suicide in Native communities, and the subject deserves more attention than can be afforded here in this essay. However, it should be noted that just as Health Canada grouped accidental death and suicide in their mortality statistics, suicide should be looked at within the context of the social environment in which it occurs. Some of the suicides, especially among young people, may actually result from risky behaviors, the kinds that emerge from living in an isolated area with few structured forms of entertainment. There is evidence that among Native youth there is substantial substance misuse, abuse and addiction, and that these behaviors increase the possibility of acquiring a disability, possibly by as much as 300%.

189

Mood altering substances do appear to be heavily influential in causing accidental death, possibly as much as 80% of the time. When petty crime, unprotected sex, sexually-transmitted infections and boredom are mixed in, the product may be dangerously explosive. What's worse, though, is when either the young or elderly are disenfranchised or dispossessed. There has been a sharp increase in gang activity in urban and rural communities, and this certainly stems in part from a prisoner of war mentality: no place to go, no jobs, no money, no hope, and the threat that the government will still take more away any day now. For elders, who have seen a lifetime of mistreatment at the hands of economic, political, religious, and educational power structures, it is no surprise that many reach their breaking point, especially if they believe their circumstances will only continue to degrade. Under such circumstances, many, many people may find themselves considering suicide.

In what must be among the most optimistic approaches to suicide, Health Canada reports that there are social circumstances that can help to curtail suicide rates. This may seem obvious, but when there is order and a social infrastructure, suicide rates decrease. There is clear evidence that perceptions of a community having self-determination--which is to say control of its own government, land claims, and cultural facilities--is a huge benefit to the mental health of a community. Furthermore, when the social safety net includes adequate health services and satisfactory police and fire protection, suicide rates will decrease as well.(15) Another way of saying this is that the mental health of the young and the elders in a community is a reflection of the mental health of the community as a whole.

This is the key connection that has to be drawn. For while it is damaging--even dehumanizing--to think of Aboriginal Peoples as canaries in a coal mine, sectors of each community certainly can be thought of that way for the rest of their communities. The health circumstances of the very young and the very old are fully enmeshed with the health of the community. And especially for Native People, the health of the community is deeply rooted in the health of the Earth in the place where they are located.

Many readers will see this as a stretch. But for a people who have nearly universally seen themselves as part of the earth and the inheritors of its stewardship, as the earth becomes sick, so do the stewards, and vice versa. Environmental degradation in the face of inadequate health care delivery is manifested much more obviously in Native public health than it is in mainstream Canadian or U.S. society. For urban communities, asthma and respiratory illness rates skyrocket in heavily air polluted neighborhoods and where people live in decrepit old buildings. Sepsis, learning disabilities, and other problems result from toxin and heavy metal exposure in unremediated waste dumps. In rural areas, poor reservations are targeted to house toxic waste that no one else will touch.

The long history of resource removal has brought arsenic and uranium exposure, loss of historical land use, loss of sacred sites, and loss of traditional food

190

sources. The accidental or purposeful dumping of Dioxins, PCBs and PBBs in the Great Lakes, the St. Lawrence Seaway, and northern waters has ruined fisheries, brought about loss of livelihood, and hastened whole communities down the path to diabetes, liver disease, and cancer. In a geographic area that has one of the world's largest contiguous supplies of fresh water, IHS reports that approximately 12% of AIAN homes do not have safe and adequate water supplies.(16) This is consistent with Statistics Canada's 2001 Aboriginal Peoples Survey, which reported that water in 1 in 8 Native homes was not safe to drink, and 15% reported that there were some times during the year when their water was contaminated.(17)

In all of these circumstances, it is impossible to draw a clear delineation between the environmental degradation and public health catastrophe. If you read Vine Deloria, Ward Churchill, Gregory Cajete, Winona LaDuke, Oscar Kawagley, Donald Grinde, Donald Fixico, even Jerry Mander, you will see health problems marking areas of environmental destruction. Each is representative of the other, because each is endemic to a cultural clash. When the need for raw materials to serve the western scientific economic agenda collided with the needs of the less powerful stewards of traditional Indigenous belief and practices (this could have been in 1492 or at any juncture since then) there was a permanent link established between the public health conditions of Aboriginal Turtle Islanders and the environmental health of Earth Mother herself. And this has not changed in more than half a millennium.

For twenty-five generations, the economics of resource extraction have been inextricably joined with the diminishment of Indian health. As long as there's been permanent Anglo influence on this landmass, Aboriginal people have been thought of as canaries in the coalmine. But more accurately, Indigenous people are the coalmine. And the coal. And the slag, the methane, and the ties upon which the rail tracks were laid. Aboriginals are the support beams and the iron that the tools of industry are shaped from. When the Earth Mother is sick, her children are sick as well. Let us hope that when the Native people are healed, so too will be our Earth Mother.

◊ ◊ ◊ ◊ ◊ ◊

Reddog Sina DO is of East Baffin Island and Greenlandic Polar Inuit ancestry. He is a graduate of the Michigan State University College of Osteopathic Medicine and is dually-boarded in Family Practice and Neuromusculoskeletal and Osteopathic Manipulative Medicine. He was one of the founding faculty of MSU's American Indian Studies Program, has spoken widely on the issues related to Aboriginal Health, and is very concerned over issues that affect the health of Indigenous Peoples. His medical training included rotations at the Sacramento (CA) Native American Health Center and American Indian Health and Family Services in Detroit, MI. Dr. Sina practices medicine at the Beals Institute in Lansing, MI.

Notes:

(1) http://www.census.gov/statab/www/sa04aian.pdf
(2) "Historical Trends – Registered Indian Population Ontario Region 1982-2005." Data from Indian Registry, First Nations and Northern Statistics section, Indian and northern affairs Canada. http://www.ainc-inac.gc.ca/pr/sts/htrip/ht-on_e.pdf. Accessed 12/26/07.
(3) Indian and Norther Affairs Canada. "Growing Up Meti". http://www.ainc-inac.gc.ca/connex/rcd5_e.html
(4) http://www.hc-sc.gc.ca/fnih-spni/pubs/gen/stats_profil_e.html
(5) http://www.4woman.gov/minority/americanindian/tb.cfm
(6) Health CAnada: http://www.hc-sc.gc.ca/fnih-spni/diseases-maladies/index_e.html
(7) http://www.cdc.gov/nchs/data/hus/hus06.pdf#029
(8) http://www.omhrc.gov/templates/content.aspx?ID=3029
(9) http://www.census.gov/statab/www/sa04aian.pdf , p. 120
(10) http://www.census.gov/statab/www/sa04aian.pdf p.39 and http://www.unicef.ca/portal/SmartDefault.aspx?at=1981
(11) http://www.hc-sc.gc.ca/fnih-spni/promotion/suicide/index_e.html
(12) http://www.hc-sc.gc.ca/fnih-spni/alt_formats/fnihb-dgspni/pdf/pubs/suicide/prev_youth-jeunes_e.pdf
(13) Eve Bender. Study Identifies Suicide Risk Factors In Native-American Youth Psychiatric News June 6, 2003. Volume 38 Number 11, 28. http://pn.psychiatryonline.org/cgi/content/full/38/11/28-a
(14) Beals, J. et al. Arch Gen Psychiatry 2005; 62:99-108
(15) Health Canada. Acting On What We Know: Preventing Youth Suicide in First Nations. http://www.hc-sc.gc.ca/fnih-spni/alt_formats/fnihb-dgspni/pdf/pubs/suicide/prev_youth-jeunes_e.pdf
(16) http://info.ihs.gov/Files/DisparitiesFacts-Jan2006.pdf

◊ ◊ ◊ ◊ ◊ ◊

The Wild Rice Moon

Winona LaDuke

Editor's note: Winona LaDuke was scheduled to give the Keynote Adress at the Earth Day conference, but a last-minute scheduling conflict made that impossible. This essay was adapted from The High Plains Reader, and reprinted here with permission:
<http://hpr1.com/feature/article/the_wild_rice_moon/>

In the din of a large auditorium, the wild ricers of the White Earth reservation gather nervously. And, with a great deal of humor and friendly competition. It is the wild rice lottery on the reservation, allocating ricing permits to some coveted lakes in the middle of the reservation, lakes governed by specific laws and part of the National Wildlife Refuge. A hundred and fifty or so ricers gathered, having dug ricing permits and tribal ID cards out of their pockets...

"I've been ricing for forty years on and off" says Bucky Goodman "We'll start probably in a little over a week. I'll start on Mitchell dam, start there and rice and if it's not good there I'll probably go onto one of the state lakes, but usually I just keep the rice for myself, so I'm not out there to see how much money I can make, just how many pounds I can get to finish... I'm getting up there in age where I don't want to be out there for hours at a time." Bucky rices with his wife.

Elsewhere, Spud Fineday tells me "I've been ricing ever since I was bitty". He hopes to haul in enough rice to feed his family and enough to sell to make some of the expenses for the fall and bitter cold of winter.

It is Manoominike Giiizis, the wild rice making moon of the Ojibwe - August and September's time when the "food which grows on the water" comes home to the people. Wild rice, or Manoomin, is the only grain indigenous to North America and is one of the greatest gifts imaginable to the land and waters. Where there is wild rice, there are Ojibwe or Anishinaabeg people, and where there are Anishinaabeg, there is wild rice. Indeed, it was a part of the Anishinaabeg migration story and set of prophecies where the people were instructed to "go to the place where the food grows upon the water."

A millennium later, the prophecies which formed the Anishinaabeg culture and way of life still remain. The Ojibwe or Anishinaabeg stretch across the northern part of five states and the southern part of four Canadian Provinces. With the exception of the far western reservations, where there is rice there are Ojibwe.

193

Manoomin is a supreme food for nutrition. It has twice the protein and fiber of brown rice, is the first solid food given to a baby (as Mazaan or broken rice), and is one of the last foods served to elders as they pass into the Spirit world. Wild rice is gluten free, and when served with blueberries, cranberries, and a meat, provides some of the most amazing cuisine from the continent.

There is no way to quantify the value of this food to the Anishinaabeg people. It is the most spiritual and essential of foods. This food feeds the belly and the soul, and is a major source of wealth for a people of the land and lakes. For these reasons, the Ojibwe struggles to keep wild rice are far ranging and have transitioned from warfare to treaties to battles in court room battles, regulatory hearings, and everywhere from the market place, University halls to corporate offices.

Historic territory battles over wild rice between the Anishinaabeg and their most honored enemies, the Dakota or Bwaanag, are legendary, and demarcate land throughout the north country from Sioux Lookout Ontario to the Brule River, Wisconsin and Battle Lake, Minnesota. The Anishinaabeg inland navy dominated the region, and wild rice, and was an essential part of the stamina of the people. It was a consistent source of food, and could keep well when parched, even over several years. The Anishinaabeg grew strong with wild rice. This is in sharp contrast to the European experiences with famine and starvation, the value of a diverse wild food which preserved for years cannot be understated.The diversity of wild rice stands in part attributes to the significance of this food as a secure source of nutrition. Wild rice grows in rivers, creeks, and a multitude of shallow lakes. Some manoomin stands tall, some short, some looks like a bottle brush while other rice looks like a punk rock hairdoo. The diversity of the wild rice in location and appearance meant that there would always be manoomin...somewhere.

With the coming of the Europeans, wild rice became a major source of trade and income for the Anishinaabeg of our region. A fawn skin of wild rice was worth about two beaver skins or four dollars around 1820. The price went up from there. Wild rice became an essential source of cash for the Ojibwe for over a hundred years, but soon became a source of competition with American industrial foods. It also represents a conflict of cultures.

At the turn of the last century, a set of anthropologists descended on the Ojibwe and other Native peoples, measuring heads, collecting songs and stories, and digging up more than a few cemeteries. Several came to the White Earth reservation. Frances Densmore, an ethnomusicologist far ahead of her time collected songs and stories and, a hundred years later, has left a legacy of writings still used by Anishinaabeg scholars and teachers in writing, schools and legal hearings.

Albert Jenks and Ales Hrliska were far less positive in their practice and legacy. Hrliska was a physical anthropologist who specialized in measuring cranial capacity, measuring heads and scratching skin to create eugenics based data on racial inferiority and classifications. Much of his data would be used to deprive the Anishinaabeg of land, although he did comment that the Anishinaabeg of White Earth were "pleasant." Dr. Albert Jenks joined with Hrliska, but his work from the University of Minnesota became focused on manoomin, noting, " the primitive Indians do not take production very seriously…In the case of wild rice, they could gather more if they did not spend so much time feasting and dancing every day and night during the time they are here for the purpose of gathering". Indeed, Jenks considered wild rice a major impediment towards the Ojibwe progress towards civilization, not understanding that the Anishinaabeg practice of feasting, praying and dancing was an essential part. "Wild rice …which had led to their advance thus far," he would write, "held them back from further progress, unless, indeed, they left it behind them, for with them it was incapable of extensive cultivation."

So it seems, the University of Minnesota found its mandate: to domesticate wild rice, if it could not domesticate the Ojibwe.

In 1968, with the help of the University of Minnesota, aggressive production of paddy wild rice production began. That year, it represented some 20 percent of the state's harvest. The suggestion that the Ojibwe were not assimilating into the mainstream economy was reiterated. A 1969 report to the Minnesota legislature, commissioned by the Minnesota Resources Commission, disparaged the Anishinaabeg relationship to wild rice as a "September Santa Claus", a "good berry Mardi Gras," and "the excuse and provision for a spending spree."

There were also corporate profits to be made. By 1973, paddy rice production had increased the state's yield from less than a million pounds to some 4 million pounds. The increase in production and subsequent interest by the larger corporations such as Uncle Ben's, Green Giant, and General Foods, skewed consumers' perceptions and altered the market for traditional wild rice. The new market produced a long grained black hard wild rice which, to this day, is presented as "real wild rice", a far cry from the soft brown and tan hues of a rice harvested from a lake and parched over a fire.

In 1977, the state legislature designated wild rice as Minnesota's official state grain – a move that may well have been the kiss of death for the lake based Ojibwe economy. Financed by an outpouring from the state coffers, the University of Minnesota began aggressively to develop a domesticated version of wild rice, and by the early 1980s, production of cultivated wild rice had outstripped that of the indigenous varieties. Then the industry moved to California. By 1983, California's crop, at 8.3 million pounds, easily surpassed Minnesota's, at 5 million pounds. By 1986, more than 95 percent of the "wild" rice harvested was paddy grown, the vast majority produced in northern California.

When the glut of paddy-grown wild rice hit the market in 1986, the price plummeted, dampening the emerging domestic market and devastating the Native wild rice economy. Lakeside prices crashed. This had a huge impact on the Ojibwe, who, having been forced into the cash economy, found that they had to compete with a man on a combine in California. The source of wealth which came from a fawnskin of manoomin was largely lost.

The Anishinaabeg fought back. First in protests, then in court. In 1988, Wabizii v. Busch Agricultural Resources was filed essentially on the issues of misleading advertising. Busch (a division of the beer conglomerate) marketed a product called Onamia Wild rice. White Earth plaintiffs, Mike Swan (Wabizii) and Frank Bibeau charged that this was a California grown paddy product "disguised as a Minnesota lake rice". A labeling law was passed as a result of the lawsuit. The law required that paddy grown wild rice be labeled as such in letters no less than 50% the size of the words wild rice. The problem was a loophole; the law did not apply in California, so 95% of the crop available can still be represented.

In the early part of this millennium, another battle ensued - this one on genetic engineering. Again the University of Minnesota appeared as the protagonist, seeking options to genetically engineer wild rice based on their success in "cracking the DNA sequence" of wild rice, or zizania aquatica. Met with opposition again from the Anishinaabeg in the form of protests, meetings and legislative hearings, the debate raged for most of a decade, resulting finally in state legislation in Minnesota prohibiting the introduction of any genetically engineered wild rice paddy stands without a full environmental impact assessment. Thus far, there is no genetically engineered "wild rice." Indeed, the two phrases seem quite oppositional.

The Mines and the Wild Rice

This decade a new set of threats has come to the Anishinaabeg and the wild rice. This time it is in the form of new mining proposals in the north country, from Michigan's Keewenaw Bay to the Boundary Waters of northern Minnesota. A new set of mining proposals revisit century old projects, as the world minerals market scrapes the bottom of the ore deposits .

Instead of the battles with Gatling guns and bows and arrows of a hundred and fifty years ago, today the Ojibwe and their neighbors on the lakes face a set of regulatory battles, at the center of which is wild rice. It's a simple set of chemical realities. Mining transforms aquatic ecosystems. Wild rice cannot grow in water high in sulfates. That is a fact. In all studies over the past fifty years "sulfate concentrations above …[l0 mg/L] are detrimental to the growth of wild rice". Mining changes that chemical balance. There are "no large and important natural and self-perpetuating wild rice stands where the sulfate ion content exceeded

196

10 ppm". In fact, the only studies which state otherwise are either in test paddies or paid for by industry.

Mines proposed in Minnesota include the Franconia Mine and the Polymet mine, both of which will create sulfide contamination of the water. To the east, a similar challenge to the famed wild rice of the Kakagan Sloughs of Bad River is found in the Gogebic Mine proposal, an iron mine which would tackle up to 20% of estimated U.S. iron ore resources. It is found in the Penokee Mountain Range of Wisconsin. In that state, mining proponents are seeking a rewrite of Wisconsin mining laws to allow for sulfide discharge into the pristine waters of the Bad River Watershed, Kakagan, and ultimately Lake Superior. Finally, a RioTinto Zincmine at Yellow Dog on the Keewanee Peninsula in Michigan will also impact the wild rice, sacred sites and the Ojibwe

Mining projects release sulfuric acid. The mix of air, water and bacteria means the sulfur will turn into sulfuric acid. This changes the pH of the water system, and liberates heavy metals including mercury out of the rock formation. That's why wild rice and mines do not co-exist.

Minnesota mining proponents alone have spent over $20 million including land, advertising and studies, and a 1500 page environmental impact statement. Turns out that money can't buy you a clean bill of health. This is to say that despite industry's money, for the first time in the past decade the EPA has donned a very negative E2 rating on the Polymet mine proposal.

Meanwhile, back on the reservation, a pick-up truck pulls up at the rice mill at Native Harvest on Round Lake. Eugene Davis and Tony Warren, tired, wet, and happy, have brought 300 pounds of rice off South Chippewa Lake. "This is the only job we can make $50 an hour at up here," says Eugene, a young man of 20. He doesn't mind the rain, either. "I like it when it rains out there. It's nice. You can't hear anything but the rain."

That quiet and peace is what brings the ricers back – along with the memories. I ask him if it matters that five generations of his family have riced on South Chippewa Lake. He smiles. "I like knowing that they was on the same lake. It makes me feel good."

The sweet smell of rice parching wafts through the dusty air. The shifting, creaking machines are ancient, some handmade: a 1940s Red Clipper fanning mill, a handmade thrasher, a 1980s set of George Stinson parching drums (a regional celebrity), a '50s vintage gravity table. Most new equipment is made for the big operations in California, not for here. The men fiddle with the machines, fine tune the gravity table. Then the rice pours out – a stream of dark green, tan, and brown grains. This is the perfection of the small batch, and the simple joy of this life.

To the ricers of White Earth, the Ojibwe Wild Rice Moon, Manoomini-kegiizis, is the season of harvest, a ceremony, and a way of life. "I grew up ricing," reflects Spud Fineday. "You get to visit people you haven't seen for a whole year, because just about everyone goes ricing."

For another year, the traditions, the ecosystems and Manoominike Giizis the Wild Rice Moon continues. The battles will rage on, in the genetic labs and in the mining corporate headquarters. The Anishinaabeg of White Earth, however, who have pulled their harvest tags, intend to rice.

◊ ◊ ◊ ◊ ◊ ◊

Winona LaDuke (Anishinaabe-kwe) is an internationally respected Native American and environmental activist. She began speaking about these issues at an early age, addressing the United Nations at the age of 18, and continues to devote herself to Native and environmental concerns, as well as political and women's issues. The Harvard-educated activist is the founding director of the White Earth Land Recovery Project, the co-chair of the Indigenous Women's Network, and the program director of Honor the Earth where she provides vision and leadership for the organization's Regranting Program and its Strategic Initiatives. In addition, she has worked for two decades on the land rights issues of the White Earth Reservation, including litigation. LaDuke also served as Ralph Nader's vice-presidential running mate on the Green Party ticket in the 1996 and 2000 presidential elections. In addition to numerous articles, LaDuke is the author of Last Standing Woman (fiction), All Our Relations (non-fiction), In the Sugarbush (children's non-fiction), and The Winona LaDuke Reader. Her most recent book is Recovering the Sacred: the Power of Naming and Claiming (South End Press). An enrolled member of the Mississippi band of Anishinaabe, LaDuke lives with her family on the White Earth Reservation in northern Minnesota.

◊ ◊ ◊ ◊ ◊ ◊

The Anishnaabeg Joint Commission

Aaron Payment, Cathy Abramson, Dean Sayers

Editor's Note: The St. Mary's River, forming at the outlet of Lake Superior, separates the US from Canada in this region. But, while it separates those two countries, the River is what unifies the Indigenous People who live along its banks. In the summer of 2006, extremely high levels of fecal coliform bacteria were detected, most likely from the discharge of untreated sewage from the treatment plant in Sault, Ontario. Given that the most serious levels were measured on the shores of Sugar Island, on the US side of the River, international jurisdictional issues arose. Four Indigenous nations held an interest in the polluted region, and, based on their level of concern, and the inaction of either the US or Canadian governments, these four Nations came together to sign a Treaty pledging the signatory Nations to preserve, protect, and restore the St. Mary's River. The three Tribal representatives listed above discussed the issue and the resultant Treaty at the Conference. The text of the Treaty is presented below.

TREATY BETWEEN THE SAULT STE. MARIE TRIBE OF CHIPPEWA INDIANS, and GARDEN RIVER FIRST NATION, and BAY MILLS INDIAN COMMUNITY, and BATCHEWANA FIRST NATION

Regarding the preservation, protection and enhancement of the waters of the St. Mary's River ecosystem

THE SOVEREIGN NATIONS OF THE SAULT STE. MARIE TRIBE OF CHIPPEWA INDIANS, AND THE GARDEN RIVER FIRST NATION, AND THE BAY MILLS INDIAN COMMUNITY, AND THE BATCH-EWANA FIRST NATION:

A. ACKNOWLEDGING that our collective ancestors have inhabited the lands surrounding the waters of the St. Mary's River since long before any current geopolitical boundaries were established; and
B. RECOGNIZING that the waters of the St. Mary's River have served, and continue to serve, as the life blood for the region which supports each of our collective Nations; and
C. REAFFIRMING our commitment and responsibility as protectors of the waters for the next seven generations and beyond; and
D. UNDERSTANDING that the waters of the St. Mary's River and its ecosystem have undergone significant abuse and mistreatment resulting from the introduction of toxic substances and aquatic alien invasive species; and

E. ACKNOWLEDGING that many of these toxic substances and invasive species enter the waters of the Great Lakes, including the St. Mary's River, from the air, groundwater infiltration, sediments in the lake and river beds, runoff of non-point sources, and shipping operations; and

F. AWARE that the governments of Canada and the United Sates, together with their respective political subdivisions, have established certain commitments toward the revitalization, preservation and protection of the waters of the Great Lakes, including the St. Mary's River, and

G. RECOGNIZING the need for strengthened efforts from each of our Nations to address the continuing contamination of the waters of the St. Mary's River ecosystem; and

H. CONTINUING to recognize the sovereign rights of each of our Nations and our ability to interact with other political bodies on a government to government basis; and

I. RECOGNIZING that our Nations are uniquely able to influence other governments to respond and take action because of our inherent sovereignty, and

J. REAFFIRMING the spirit of friendship, cooperation, and pledged commitment to work together to secure a healthy future for the Great Lakes, including the St. Mary's River, under the Tribal and First Nations Great Lakes Water Accord, signed November 23, 2004; and

K. CONCLUDING that our Nations' mutual interests regarding the St. Mary's River are better served when our Nations' efforts and influences are united to serve a common goal.

HAVE AGREED AS FOLLOWS:

ARTICLE I – PURPOSE

The purpose of this Treaty is to unite the efforts and influence of our Nations to restore and maintain the chemical, physical, and biological integrity of the waters of the St. Mary's River. In order to achieve this purpose, we agree that we will use maximum efforts to:

A. Develop programs and practices necessary for a better understanding of the St. Mary's River and its ecosystem; and

B. Eliminate or reduce to the maximum extent practicable the discharge of toxic substances and introduction of invasive species; and

C. Influence the Governments of the United States and Canada, and their respective political subdivisions and agencies, to abide by existing commitments to revitalize, preserve, and protect the waters of the St. Mary's River; and

D.. Encourage the Governments of Canada and the United States, and their respective political subdivisions and agencies, to develop additional programs and practices to achieve these results.

200

ARTICLE II – OBJECTIVES

Our Sovereign Nations shall work together on these general objectives pertaining to the St. Mary's River:

A. It is our collective goal that the waters of the St. Mary's River be free from:
1. Substances that settle to form objectionable sludge deposit or adversely effect aquatic life or waterfowl;
2. Floating materials such as debris, oil, or scum in amounts that are unsightly or deleterious;
3. Thermal pollutants that produce color, odor, or taste that interferes with beneficial uses;
4. Materials and thermal pollutants that produce harmful or toxic conditions to human, animal, or aquatic life and which interfere with beneficial uses;
5. Nutrients in amounts that create growths of aquatic life, which interferes with beneficial uses; and
6. Alien aquatic invasive species that are harmful to naturally occurring aquatic life or interfere with beneficial uses.

B. It is our collective goal that each of our Nations continue our respective cultural heritage and traditional teachings to promote understanding of the importance or protection of the waters of the St. Mary's River, as well as other waters of the Great Lakes, as the life blood of our region.
C. It is our collective goal to work together to identify specific objectives and strategies to achieve the general objectives we have identified.

ARTICLE III -- TRIBAL AND FIRST NATION JOINT COMMISSION

Our Sovereign Nations shall form a Tribal and First Nation Joint Commission. The Commission shall be comprised of one representative of each of our Nations to facilitate open communication between and coordination among each of our Nations.

A. The Commission shall:
1. Meet at least biannually;
2. Develop specific objectives to be accomplished;
3. Develop joint strategies for recommendation to each of our Nations' Governments; and
4. Investigate issues regarding chemical, physical, and biological integrity of the waters of the St. Mary's River and make recommendations regarding actions in response to these issues.

B. Any of our Nations may provide additional technical or financial assistance to the Commission, including staff or other resources. The commission may request such additional assistance; however, any additional assistance provided shall be at the sole discretion of each of our respective Nations.

C. The Commission has no authority to independently bind any of our Nations' Governments individually, except as specifically authorized by all Nations consistent with each Nations' respective laws.

SIGNED AT THE BAY MILLS INDIAN RESERVATION ON NOVEMBER 8, 2006.

◊ ◊ ◊ ◊ ◊ ◊

Cathy Abramson received her Associates degree from Lake Superior State University in Executive Secretary Studies in 1976. Following a hiatus to be a full-time mother, she returned to Lake State as a non-traditional student, and graduated in 1994 with a B.S. in Business Administration-Marketing. After her graduation, she worked for the Sault Tribe Education Division, as Program Administrator of the Johnson O'Malley Program, and as Program Director of the Youth Education & Activities Program. She was elected to the Sault Ste. Marie Tribe of Chippewa Indians' Tribal Council in 2004 as a Representative of Unit I, a position she still holds.

After serving eight years on the Sault Ste. Marie Tribe of Chippewa Indians Tribal Council, **Aaron Payment** was elected to the position of Chairman in 2004. He was elected, again, to the position of Chair in 2012. A Sault Tribe member, Aaron also has historic ties to the Garden River First Nation and the Little Travese Bay Band of Ottawa Indians. Aaron holds a Masters degree in Public Administration from Michigan State University. He also holds a Masters in Education Administration from Nortehrn Michigan University. He is currently completing a PhD Educational Leadership at Central Michigan University.

As Chief of the Batchewana First Nation, **Dean Sayers** signed a treaty regarding the preservation, protection and enhancement of the St. Mary's River ecosystem on November 8, 2006. The Treaty was also signed by the leaders of the Bay Mills Indian Community, the Sault Ste. Marie Tribe of Chippewa Indians, and the Garden River First Nation. The Four Tribes represent all of the Indigenous People of the area, and all four Tribes share jurisdiction over, and responsibility for, the entire St. Marys River watershed.

◊ ◊ ◊ ◊ ◊ ◊

The Tribal and First Nations Great Lakes Water Accord

Frank Ettawageshik

Editor's Note: Frank Ettawageshik, Chairman of the Little Traverse Bay Band of Odawa Indians at the time, was instrumental in developing and promulgating the Tribal and First Nations Water Accord. Chairman Ettawageshik gave a keynote address at the conference on this subject. The text of the Accord is presented below.

Tribal and First Nations Great Lakes Water Accord

Our ancestors have inhabited the Great Lakes Basin since time immemorial, long before the current political boundaries were drawn. Our spiritual and cultural connections to our Mother Earth are manifest by our willingness to embrace the responsibility of protecting and preserving the land and Waters.

Traditional teachings and modern science combine to strengthen our historical understanding that Water is the life-blood of our Mother Earth. Indigenous women continue their role as protectors of the Water.
Ceremonial teachings are reminders of our heritage, they are practices of our current peoples, and they are treasured gifts that we hand to our children.

When considering matters of great importance we are taught to think beyond the current generation. We also are taught that each of us is someone's seventh generation. We must continually ask ourselves what we are leaving for a future seventh generation.

We understand that the whole earth is an interconnected ecosystem. The health of any one part affects the health and well-being of the whole. It is our spiritual and cultural responsibility to protect our local lands and Waters in order to help protect the whole of Mother Earth.

Tribes and First Nations have observed with growing interest that the Great Lakes Basin governments of the United States and Canada have begun to share our concerns about the preservation of the quality and quantity of the Great Lakes Waters.

The eight States and two Provinces of the Great Lakes Basin entered into the 1985 Great Lakes Charter, Annex 2001, and have drafted an Interstate Compact and International Agreement to implement the provisions of Annex 2001. These agreements, however, make no provisions for including Tribes and First Nations as governments with rights and responsibilities regarding Great Lakes Waters. These agreements also assert that only the States and Provinces have governmental responsibility within the Great Lakes Basin.

Through international treaties and court actions, however, Tribes and First Nations continue to exercise cultural and spiritual rights of self-determination and property rights within traditional territories for our peoples and nations. Tribal and First Nation governments, like all governments, have the duty to protect the interests and future rights of our peoples. Since we have recognized rights and we are not political subdivisions of the States or Provinces, the assertion that the States and Provinces own and have the sole responsibility to protect the Waters is flawed.

Thus, the efforts of the States and Provinces to protect the Waters of the Great Lakes Basin are flawed because these efforts do not include the direct participation of the governments of Tribes and First Nations. This fundamental flaw endangers the interests of all of the inhabitants of the Great Lakes Basin and, ultimately, because of the interconnectedness of the worldwide ecosystem, endangers the interests of the entire earth.

It is thus our right, our responsibility and our duty to insist that no plan to protect and preserve the Great Lakes Waters moves forward without the equal highest-level participation of Tribal and First Nation governments with the governments of the United States and Canada. Merely consulting with Tribes and First Nations is not adequate, full participation must be achieved.

By this accord signed on November 23, 2004, at Sault Ste. Marie, Michigan, the Tribes and First Nations of the Great Lakes Basin do hereby demand that our rights and sovereignty be respected, that any governmental effort to protect and preserve the Waters of the Great Lakes Basin include full participation by Tribes and First Nations, and we also hereby pledge that we share the interests and concerns about the future of the Great Lakes Waters, further pledging to work together with each other and with the other governments in the Great Lakes Basin to secure a healthy future for the Great Lakes.

Signatories, and Tribal Affiliation:

AAMJIWNAANG
Darren Henry, Councilor

ASSOCIATION OF IROQUOIS AND ALLIED NATIONS
Chief Chris McCormack

AUDECK OMNI KANING
Peter Nahwegahbow

BATCHEWANA FIRST NATION
Chief Vernon Syrette

BEAUSOLEIL FIRST NATION
Rod Monague, Councilor

BIIJITWAABIK ZAAING ANISHINAABEK
Chief Mike Esquega

CHIEFS OF ONTARIO
Regional Chief Charles Fox

CHIPPEWAS OF NAWASH UNCEDED FIRST NATION
Geewadin Elliott

DELAWARE (MORAVIAN) NATION
Denise Stonefish

FIRST NATION OF CREES QUEBEC
Daisy Costas

FOND DU LAC
Eugene Reynolds

GARDEN RIVER FIRST NATION
Chief Lyle Sayers

GRAND TRAVERSE BAY BAND OF OTTAWA AND CHIPPEWA INDIANS
Robert Kewaygoshkum, Chairperson

HURON POTAWATOMI, INC.
Laura Spurr, Chairperson

KEWEENAW BAY INDIAN COMMUNITY
William E. Emery, President

LITTLE RIVER BAND OF OTTAWA INDIANS
Lee Sprague, Ogemaw

LITTLE TRAVERSE BAY BANDS OF ODAWA INDIANS
Frank Ettawageshik, Chairman

MAGNETAWAN FIRST NATION
Chief Wilmer Noganosh

MATAWA FIRST NATION
Noah Oshag, First Nation Delegate

M'CHIGEENG FIRST NATION
Chief Glen Hare

MISSISSAUGA FIRST NATION
Chief Bryan LaForm

MOHAWKS OF BAY OF QUINTE
Chief R. Donald Maracle

MOHAWKS OF AKWENSASNE
Chief A. Francis Boots

NISHNAWBE ASKI NATION
Deputy Grand Chief Dan Kooses

ONEIDA NATION OF THE THAMES
Chief Randall Phillips

POKAGON BAND OF POTAWATOMI INDIANS
Dan Rapp, Tribal Secretary

SAGAMOK ANISHNAWBEK
Chief Angus Toulouse

SAGINAW CHIPPEWA INDIAN TRIBE OF MICHIGAN
Chief Audrey Falcon

SAUGEEN FIRST NATION
Chief Vernon Roote

SAULT STE MARIE TRIBE OF CHIPPEWA INDIANS
Aaron Payment, Chairperson

SOKAOGAN CHIPPEWA
Tina Van Zile, Tribal Delegate

STOCKBRIDGE MUNSEE
Robert Chicks, Chairperson

THESSALON FIRST NATION
Chief James Wabigwan

UNION OF ONTARIO INDIANS
Grand Council Chief John Beaucage

WALPOLE ISLAND FIRST NATION
David White, First Nation Delegate

WASAUKSING FIRST NATION
Chief Joel King

206

WHITEFISH RIVER FIRST NATION
Esther Osche, First Nation Delegate

WIKIWEMIKONG FIRST NATION
Ron Manitowabi, Councilor

ZHIIBAAHAASING FIRST NATION
Chief Irene Kells

◊◊◊◊◊◊

Frank Ettawageshik lives in Harbor Springs, Michigan, with his wife, Rochelle. They have four adult children and five grandchildren. An Odawa (Ottawa) Indian from northern Lower Michigan, he grew up in Harbor Springs, on Little Traverse Bay, in the Odawa homeland of Waganakising (the Crooked Tree). He opened Pipigwa Pottery & Gallery in 1974 in Traverse City, Michigan. In 1989 Frank was elected to the board of the Little Traverse Bay Bands of Odawa Indians (LTBB) where he served as Vice-Chairman until April of 1991, then as Tribal Chairman through July of 1999 where he represented LTBB in its dealings with the State of Michigan, the United States, and other Tribes. He provided leadership in the passage of reaffirmation legislation by the United States Congress for Federal recognition of the Little Traverse Bay Bands of Odawa Indians. Frank was Chairman of the Tribe's Economic Development Commission from 2002-2003. In 2002, Frank became a founding partner in Michigan Tribal Advocates (MTA), established to advocate for tribal governments to the State of Michigan. When he was reelected Chairman of the Tribal Council in July of 2003, he relinquished his role in MTA. Frank was elected Chairman of the LTBB's Executive Branch serving from2005 to 2009 under the Tribe' new Constitution which separates the powers of the Legislative (Tribal Council) from the Executive (Chair and Vice-chair). He currently serves as the Executive Director of the United Tribes of Michigan and is the Chair of the Governing Board of the United League of Indigenous Nations. His forty years of public service includes being a Board Member of the Michigan Indian Education Council, the Crooked Tree Arts Center, Chippewa Ottawa Resource Authority, Great Lakes Resources Committee, the Tip of the Mitt Watershed Council, the Little Traverse Conservancy, the Board of Advisors for the National Trust for Historic Preservation in Washington, D.C., and a Research Associate for the Michigan State University Museum. As an artist and owner of Pipigwa Pottery, and through much research, Frank has worked to revive the making of traditional Indian pottery in the Great Lakes area, and through giving lectures, trainings and workshops throughout Michigan. In addition to creating pottery, Frank is a storyteller following the tradition passed down from his father.

Haudenosaunee Position Paper on the Great Lakes

Joyce Tekahnawiiaks King

Editor's Note: Joyce Tekahnawiiaks King is the Director of the Haud-enosaunee Environmental Task Force. She gave a keynote address concerning the Haudenosaunee views of the Great Lakes environment. These views reflected in this document are derived from many voices throughout Haudenosaunee Territory and are presented below.

Haudenosaunee Position On The Great Lakes -- Executive Summary

We, Haudenosaunee, remain indebted to the foresight of our Chiefs and Clan Mothers, who had the wisdom to negotiate an agreement that reaches into our lives today…

It is impossible to address the Haudenosaunee Position on the Great Lakes without examining Haudenosaunee Worldview: why is Haud-enosaunee philosophy different than their European counterparts who imposed colonization on this land? In order to answer this, a small history lesson is warranted.

The essay, in Part 1, speaks about principles learned from ancient teachings when the Peacemaker walked upon this land. Principles such as Giving Thanks, One Dish/One Spoon, and the guiding principles in the Great Law of Peace: Skennen (Peace), Ka'nikonriio (Righteousness), and Ka'satstensera (Strength).

Part II examines treaties made between the Haudenosaunee with the early colonial governments on how two diametrically opposed people would and could co-exist with each other on this land.

Part III welcomes a new beginning between the sovereigns, on a gov-ernment-to-government basis – between the colonial governments of the United States and Canada, with the sovereign nation of this land, the Haudenosaunee.

Part IV addresses Haudenosaunee Environmental philosophy and the work of the Haudenosaunee Task Force on the Environment (HETF).

Part V speaks on the Great Lakes issues affecting the Haudenosaunee. This includes an article by the late Dr. Barbara Gray "The Socio-Cultural

209

Impacts of Icebreaking Activities Associated with Seaway Shipping --
Summary of the Briefing Paper for the Mohawk Nation Council of
Chiefs.

Haudenosaunee Worldview

The Haudenosaunee have lived in peace and harmony with the natural
world as the indigenous inhabitants of Turtle Island/North American.
We have fought and struggled to preserve our homelands for the benefit
of the seventh generation yet to be born. We want our grandchildren
and their grandchildren to be able to enjoy and appreciate the earth-
based culture and bounty of the natural world.

As people upon this earth, we have a great responsibility. The Creator
has placed all things needed for our survival. As instructed by the
Creator, our responsibility is to protect and preserve all he has created
and to give thanks to Creation that assists our continued existence.
Naturalized knowledge systems of the Haudenosaunee have taught our
people about our homelands in the Great Lakes Basin. The Natural
Knowledge integrates physical, social and spiritual aspects of our
surroundings. As newcomers to North American, European colonists,
and the people to follow them into this land, must come to realize we
share one dish: resources that are dwindling as we speak. What remains
of renewable resources must be protected.

Treaties are the highest form of agreement between nations. Those
agreements are considered Treaties under international law. Treaties
exist between the Haudenosaunee and the United States of America,
and, Great Britain. The early formal relationships recognized the
Haudenosaunee and the United States of America as sovereign nations.
As a result, the U.S. Federal, State, County and private U.S. citizens have
a responsibility to respect the terms of the treaties their governments
made with the Haudenosaunee. As with U.S. forefathers,
Haudenosaunee sovereignty, jurisdiction and cultural lifestyles must be
respected. It must be impressed upon those now living:
Haudenosaunee hunting, fishing and gathering rights were never ceded
in treaties made with the United States.

Treaties between nations also carry a great responsibility.

Treaties are recognized internationally as agreements between nations.

Like treaties, a similar type of agreement is examined here, which is
known as the Winter's Doctrine. The Winter's Doctrine has been upheld
in the U.S. Supreme Court. This Doctrine gives Tribes waters rights and
the resources from water. Under the Winter's Doctrine, which is a series
of cases beginning with Winters v. U.S. 2017 U.S. 564 (1908), Indian
nations have a reserved right to an amount of water necessary to fulfill
the purpose of the reserved lands. These rights exist regardless if the
treaty, statute or executive order is absent of specific language securing

210

water rights. The rights are reserved, by implication, to sufficiently fulfill the present and future needs of the Indian reservation.

The Great Lakes Basin, which includes the St. Lawrence River, is a historic portion of Haudenosaunee hunting, fishing and gathering territory. The Great Lakes and surrounding land became an extensive part of the Haudenosaunee Territory when the Peacemaker[2] joined the Five Nations of the Haudenosaunee.

In the lessons learned from the Winter's Doctrine, the Haudenosaunee have legal rights and status that are superior, and exist beyond the legal status, beyond rights as advocated by the United States and Canada. Canada, being a derivative of British rule must respect treaties and agreements made under the British Sovereign. The Canadian Charter of Rights and Freedoms recognize indigenous inherent right. As such, the principals of the Winter's Doctrine are as applicable for indigenous (Haudenosaunee) rights in Canada as they would be in the U.S. case law.

No Sovereign entities can claim solitude and self-sufficiency without assistance from Creation or from one another. Whether we term ourselves as Haudenosaunee, or U.S. Citizens, or Canadian Citizens, as people within the ecosystems of North America, we must come to the realization there are different cultural values and different worldviews.

As people of Creation, we need to proceed beyond our restricted thinking and progress to a productive dialogue concerning the natural resources of this land. With this in mind, and as keeping the values of the generations before us, we, the Haudenosaunee, extend our hand in peace and friendship to the interested parties for the benefit of the Great Lakes Basin.

The Haudenosaunee People

Our people have an ancient tradition of nationhood that developed long before contact with the Europeans. Our traditional values are the basis for our social and political institutions, as well as our sense of our place within the natural order. Long ago, we developed our own answers to the questions the European philosophers and political theorists have been asking for centuries. Upon the continent of North America, prior to the landfall of the first European white man, a great league of peace was formed. The inspiration for the founding of the league came from a messenger. We call him the Peacemaker.

The Peacemaker was a spiritual being, fulfilling the mission of organizing warring Nations into a confederation, governed by Gianashanagowa, the Great Law of Peace. This is a long history. It is too long to recount here. Suffice to say, it is a great epic, the equal of any in the European tradition. It tells of war and destruction that culminated on the lake now called Onondaga. After many years of hard work, the Peacemaker gathered the warring leaders. These leaders were transformed into rational human beings by the wisdom of the Peacemaker's teachings, in a grand council, held circa 1142. In this grand council, the Peacemaker began to instruct them as to how the great league of peace would work.

The Peacemaker, re-organized, as was in the past, families into clans. According to oral history, leaders of the clans were raised. This enlightened teacher established that this league of peace would follow matrilineal families. The matrilineal families (clans) would have a clan mother. Thus, he established in Haudenosaunee law equal rights among genders. As duty directed them, the clan mothers "raised" the leaders of each clan -- two men, one the principal leader, and, the second, the principal leader's partner. The two were to work together for the good of the people. The Peacemaker called these two men 'Hoyanah' or the 'men of the good minds.' The leaders were to represent their clan in council. Thus was established the principle of representation for the people in government. Henceforth, the Peacemaker said, these men will be chosen by the clan mother, freely using her insight and wisdom. Any decisions would be ratified by full consensus of the clans, chiefs, and, Grand Council of Chiefs of the Five Nations.

Then he also made two houses in each Nation. One he called the Long House and the other he called the Mud House. The houses would work together in ceremony and council, establishing the inner source of vitality and dynamics necessary for community. At the same time, it was established that while in Grand Council, the house would be split into two separate sides. One side of the house was called the Younger Brothers, consisting of the Oneida and the Cayuga Nation and later, enlarged to include the Tuscarora. The other house was termed the Elder Brothers, consisting of the Mohawks, the Onondaga whom he made the Firekeepers, and the Senecas who were the Keepers of the Western Door. Thus, he established in North American, the principle of a bicameral form of government that continues up to this day.

This council still governs today. Its first duty is to carry on the sacred ceremonies. The second duty is to meet in council for the welfare of the people.

Now that the Peacemaker built the house, and the rafters of the house were the laws that he laid down. Once completed, the Peacemaker called us Haudenosaunee, the People of the Longhouse.

Part I: Principles

1.1 Haudenosaunee Thanksgiving Address

Whenever the Haudenosaunee gather, our meetings are started and ended with the Thanksgiving Address. We have presented an English summary of the Thanksgiving Address at the beginning of this document. "The Words That Come Before All Else" is how we see and understand the world. It has a deliberate structure to it. It starts with the people and moves outward and upward from the earth to the waters to the plants and four legged creatures to the bird life to the sky world and concludes with the Creator who made all life with nothing lacking.

The Thanksgiving Address reminds each person present that human beings are a small part of a much larger natural world. Its structure is meant to address and return thanks to each part of the natural world separately. After each part, the speaker states that "we who are gathered here have put our minds together for this purpose," and the assembled people indicate their agreement.

The Thanksgiving Address reminds those gathered that they have duties and responsibilities, not only to themselves, but also to the entire natural world and the rest of creation. The message is simple: as each part of the natural world continues to fulfill its responsibilities, so we, as humans, have our own responsibilities to fulfill to maintain the world as it should be.

1.2   Hiawatha Belt -- One Dish, One Spoon

The symbols presented in the wampum, more commonly known as the "Hiawatha Belt" represents the first international agreement between the different Haudenosaunee Nations. It signifies the union or confederacy of five Nations, from east to west: Mohawk, Oneida, Onondaga, Cayuga and Seneca.

Through oral tradition, the wampum is recited that peace will prevail in our lands. In the center of the wampum, a Tree of Peace is found. Underneath the tree, the Nations collectively agreed to bury hatred, bad thoughts and words that promote weapons of war. The Tree, a white pine, is the symbol of peace.

When the Peacemaker introduced the Great Tree of Peace, he talked about the tree having four white roots that spread peace in all directions. Any person or Nation would be able to trace the roots to its source and find protection under the Great Tree.

The wampum or treaty belt, also symbolized a concept of one dish/one spoon among the Haudenosaunee. Before this great Confederacy came together, many arguments arose. The Nations were fighting over hunting grounds. This led to bloodshed and Nation warfare as well as a loose organization based on warrior-based leaders. There was also inter-familial fighting.

The Peacemaker was born at this time of great despair. He cognized and proselytized the Great Law of Peace, establishing the three principles of Peace, Power and Righteousness within the concept of one dish/one spoon. All Haudenosaunee and other Indigenous Nations agreeing to accept the principles of the Great Law of Peace, also agree to the concept of sharing one dish and using one spoon.

"We shall now do this: We shall only have one dish (or bowl) in which will be placed one beaver tail and we shall all have co-equal right to it, and there shall be no knife in it, there would be danger that it might cut some one and blood would thereby be shed." (1)

Therefore, Natural Resources found on Mother Earth, would belong collectively. Symbolically, Natural Resources are in one dish: Nations would be eating out of this one dish: taking only what was necessary and leaving whatever was available for others and enough to propagate for the future generations.

At one time, there was a knife in the middle of the bowl, but this was a weapon and could become harmful to each other. When the Tree of Peace was planted, the weapons of war were buried. The knife was replaced by a spoon and bad feelings and bad intentions between Nations would be eliminated. Upon accepting this Great Peace, the Mohawks could then hunt in Oneida Territory and the Oneidas could hunt in Seneca Territory, provided hunters took only what was needed to feed their families.

The One Dish/One Spoon symbolizes our collective rights and flow from this agreement among the Haudenosaunee Nations. Ever since this treaty was enacted and the Confederacy of the Haudenosaunee was formed, no one person shall own the land since it belongs to everyone. It included the other beings in the natural world and the unborn generations yet to come.

1.3 -- Great Law: Guiding Principles

Sken:nen, Ka'nikonriio, Ka'satstensera

The principles of sken:nen, ka'nikonriio and ka'satstensera serve as the foundation and guiding force for the Haudenosaunee. Since the beginning of time, our Creator has related to all people to strive for peace. As individuals, communities and Nations, we must constantly strive to talk, live and breathe peace. Sken:nen (peace) is more that just the absence of conflict or war. It is engrained into our culture, spirituality: social and political foundations. Peace has been defined as "the active striving of humans for the purpose of establishing universal justice... True peace is the product of a unified people on the path of Righteousness and Reason - the ability to enact the principles of Peace through education, public opinion and political and when necessary, military unity. It is the product of a spiritually conscious society using its abilities of reason" (2)

214

When we work for peace, we develop Ka'nikonriio (a good mind) a good way of thinking. Kariwiio (the good word) is part of ka'nikonriio and refers to "the shared ideology of the people using their purest and most unselfish minds. It occurs when the people put their minds and emotions in harmony with the flow of the universe and the intentions of the Good Mind or the Great Creator. The principles of Righteousness demand that all thoughts of prejudice, privilege or superiority be swept away and that recognition be given to the reality that the creation is intended for the benefit of all equally – even the birds and animals, the trees and the insects, as well as the humans... Reason is seen as the skill which humans must be encouraged to acquire in order that the objectives of justice may be attained and no one's rights abused." 1

When we work for peace and a good mind, we develop Ka'satstensera (strength). Strength flows from the power of the good mind to use rational thinking and persuasion to channel the inherent good will of humans to work towards peace, justice and unity to prevent the abuse of human beings and mother earth.

Part II --Treaty Relationships

Treaties are the highest form of agreement between nations, the place that peoples, their laws and governments meet. The historical records show hundreds of formal councils between the Haudenosaunee and the French, British and Untied States governments in North America. The Agreements that flowed from each of these councils should be considered a 'treaty' under the laws of Canada or the United States. For the Haudenosaunee, these agreements are like stones in a river that mark a place in its flow – what has remained important is the relationships established by formal treaty between the Confederacy and other nations. Enduring symbols of those relationships, which embody peace, respect, trust and friendship, include the Silver Covenant Chain and the Two Row Wampum. Other treaties, which provide for all aspects of international relations, including war and peace, trade and commerce, criminal jurisdiction and extradition – All flow from the foundation established by those relationship.

For nearly two hundred years after the arrival of the Europeans in the Great Lakes region of North America, the process of treaty making was based on Haudenosaunee protocol. This was not surprising. The colonists were few and weak, and the process worked remarkable well. The result of Haudenosaunee council processes was a clear relationship and firm peace.

2.1 TWO ROW WAMPUM

The Two Row Wampum is a treaty created in the 17th century to record an agreement between the Haudenosaunee and the Dutch settlers in Eastern New York. The belt consists of alternating rows of purple and white wampum running the length of the belt. The two purple rows symbolize two vessels traveling the river of life together, side by side. One vessel, a ship, symbolized the Dutch. The other vessel, a canoe, symbolized the Haudenosaunee. The meaning behind this treaty belt brought together a concept of two vessels traveling the river together and as they travel side by side, they are to help each other, from time to time, as people are meant to do. The people are to stay within in each other's respective vessel.

The vessels are connected by three white rows of wampum. They symbolize three principles: sken:nen or peace, ka'nikonriio or the good mind, and ka'satstensera or strength. Between Nations, the words are extrapolated as peace, friendship and respect. These principles guide the Haudenosaunee in our relationships today. Peace requires action. We must have good communication to have a positive relationship. A good mind requires that we work towards common interests rather than focus on our differences: respect. Strength arises from following these first two principles and the relationship becomes healthy: friendship.

2.2 THE CANANDAIGUA TREATY OF 1794

The Canandaigua Treaty is also known as the Timothy Pickering Treaty and the George Washington Covenant Treaty. There is a wampum belt in the possession of the Onondaga Nation that is six feet in length. It has thirteen figures holding hands with two native figures. The two native figures are on both sides of a house that is in the center of the belt. This was made to commemorate the Treaty of Canandaigua in 1794. The Canandaigua Treaty was signed by the Chiefs of the Six Nations of the Haudenosaunee Confederacy and representatives for the United States government on November 11, 1794, and ratified January 21, 1795.

"George Washington sent out Timothy Pickering to meet with us. We gathered at Canandaigua, New York, in July of 1794. There for a six-month period we discussed the terms of an agreement between our peoples. Many issues were discussed during that six-month period, and these discussions were brought back to our separate nations. On November 11, 1794, we finally signed the treaty. This treaty was between the Haudenosaunee (the Six Nations) and the United States. Again, Article I states, 'Let there be peace and friendship between our two peoples." This treaty was ratified by the United States Congress and was signed by George Washington, the president of the United States.'" (3)

A Living Treaty

Every August, the federal government sends treaty cloth and salt to members of the Haudenosaunee. At one time, $4,500.00 bought a lot of cloth: calico, cotton prints, etc. Because there were no lawyers present in 1794, there was no cost of living clause. Today, only muslin cloth is purchased, but it is still important because it demonstrates the existence of this living treaty.

216

A Parallel Process

In the spirit of the Two Row Wampum, Article VII of the Canandaigua Treaty is interpreted as a parallel process: two legal jurisdictions. In the event of a crime, there is reciprocity in the treaty to address the crimes or wrongs of their respective Nation/society. The section states that in the event of a crime, the two parties will pursue prudent measures involving the president or the superintendent until some other "equitable' provision shall be made. Since the birth of the Canandaigua Treaty, the Haudenosaunee, through its Grand Council, have exercised this right through various letters to the United States President.

Citizenship

We are not citizens of the United States. We are citizens of the Onondaga Nation. We do not vote in your elections, nor are we a part of the Democratic or Republican parties. We do not accept federal funds from the United States. The funds and services that we do receive come to us as treaty obligations. As a sovereign nation, we do not accept the federal and state laws that violate the concepts and interpretations of our treaties, as we understand these treaties.

Our mandate of today is the same as it was yesterday. What we see today, we should preserve, so that our great-great-grandchildren will be able to enjoy the same things that we see today. If we have fresh water, then let there be fresh water three or four hundred years from now. If we have fresh air, then let there be fresh air. Let us live together in peace and harmony with each other, the forces of nature, and the environment, forever.

> Dawnaytoh,
> Chief Powless Jr., Onondaga Nation

2.3 -- THE JAY TREATY

In 1794, Washington nominated Supreme Court Chief Justice John Jay as an envoy to conclude a treaty of peace and commerce. Justice Jay negotiated a definitive treaty of friendship, commerce, and navigation with Britain. The Jay Treaty solved some of the most important matters of dispute between the two nations. The Treaty was ratified June 24, 1775. The appropriations were finally made, but only after one the greatest political debates in American history.

Article III of the Jay Treaty provided and assured the Indians free and unrestricted passage and trade across the border. It was later reaffirmed in the Treaty of Ghent (1814).

Many scholars make note that the Jay Treaty was abrogated during the War of 1812. However, looking at the historical records, speeches and interviews were made with various officials involved during the war's closure. Hence, the Treaty of Ghent was reached. By all accounts, the rights of the Haudenosaunee Nations in the Jay Treaty provisions were reaffirmed in the Treaty of Ghent. Henry Clay, one of the U.S. negotiators at the Treaty of Ghent, described what he was absolutely certain Indian rights under the Treaty of Ghent. Furthermore, he noted that the Indian nations had the right 'quietly to possess and enjoy its lands, subject to no other limitation than that, when sold, they can only be sold to the United States."

Part III -- Into a New Beginning

The United States and the Haudenosaunee have co-existed for over two centuries. During this time, the relationship between us has, at times, been strained and adversarial. In building a relationship with those of other nations, we recall the words of the Two Row Wampum: what should be between us is Peace, Friendship and Respect. What is actually and presently between us are legal issues, grievances, hurt and frustrations.

Today, we send you greetings and extend our hand in peace and friendship in promoting mutual respect between two Nations living within this river of life, side by side and in parallel paths.

3.1 -- Three Bare Words

As giving thanks was the first step in peoples coming together, the condolence is second. When nations met, they would condole each other, to raise up and clear each other's minds, thoughts and bodies of distractions before they could get down to the business of peace. The strings used by the nations to perform the condolence at the beginning of Treaty Councils are the descendants of the Peacemaker's first strings, as well as of those used within the Confederacy to preserve and promote the peace.

The Ceremony of Condolence is the threshold to peace. A clear, rational; 'good' mind accepts peace as a matter of reason. The Good Mind accepts and welcomes the unity of nations brought together in peace.

Each of the 'words' of the Condolence describes a particular hurt that has come from the grief and loss. Then the speaker explains how that hurt has affected the people who are gathered together. Then through his words, he removes or heals the hurt and grief. The condolence is a healing for troubled minds.

The 'very few words' are also called the "Three Bare Words". They are to clear they eyes, ears and throat of those who have traveled. They are 'bare' because they are preliminary and are usually spoken without wampum (that is the speaker's hands are bare.) The Three Bare Words are also the first three parts of the 'full' condolence ceremony.

Afterwards, the hosts take the visitors by the hand, in affection. They bring them to the place of council. There, the words of condolence are spoken:

Today, we have joined to put our minds together, but before this council can proceed we need to offer you condolence. The Ceremony of Condolence is the threshold to Peace. The Good Mind, a clear and rational mind, accepts peace as a matter of reason. The Good Mind accepts and welcomes the unity of our nations brought together in peace.

Your eyes are constantly shedding tears for the ones who have departed, who have been gathered to the Creator's land. Because of these tears, you can no longer see your brothers clearly, and your ability to see the world around you have been affected. With this word, we wipe the tears from your eyes, so that you may once again see clearly.

The grief and sorrow you are suffering have stopped up your ears, so that you can no longer hear clearly what is being said to you. With this we once again open your ears, so that you can hear clearly what is being said.

Your throats have been stopped up with grief, so that you are no longer able to speak. With this we once again open your throats, so that you will be able to say what you wish, without obstruction.

With the purest white deerskin, the insides of your bodies are cleaned of any impurities that may have lodged there, so that you can go about your lives in comfort and peace.

The memory of the people who have departed sometimes takes the form of the sight of blood on the space where you sit as Chiefs. With this we remove the bloodstains from your mat and once again prepare a safe and comfortable place for you to sit.

In your sorrow and grief you sit in darkness in your minds. You cannot see your brothers who seek to raise your spirits once again. With this we remove the darkness you are seeing and feeling.

When you have suffered a great loss, you sometimes cannot see the sky above and around you: you are blind to the beauties of Creation. With this word we restore the sight of the sky to your eyes, so that you can gaze about in calm and beauty.

In your sorrow and grief the sun is lost to you and you can no loger feel his warmth and the light he casts about us. With this we restore the sun to the sky so that you can once again see the world around you.

You have traveled far, and your path has been difficult. There are thorns in your feet, and you are in pain from your journey. With this, we remove the thorns from your feet and once again make you comfortable.

The memory of the people who have passed away is refreshed in your minds whenever you pass their graves. With this we remove the sight of the graves and level the earth over them, so that their sight no longer disturbs your peace of mind.

When grief and sorrow strike the people, their fires are sometimes scattered, as their thoughts are in disarray. With this we gather together the embers of your fire and rekindle the fire so that it can once again give you warmth and light.

Not only a person's close family but all the people suffer when a respected person passes away. With this we once again raise up the minds of the women and the young men, that they may resume their responsibility of supporting and advising the Chiefs in their deliberations.

There are times when grief causes a person to behave in a way that is beyond reason, where they can injure or be injured by bad medicine. This can happen on earth, it is known to happen. With this we remove any shadow of insanity and all bad medicine from your minds, so that you can once again resume your place in our councils and our thoughts with a clear mind.

3.2 -- Silver Covenant Chain of Friendship Treaty

Oral and written tradition explains that when the British first met the Mohawks they took each other by the hand in friendship. Later, the British ship was tied to a tree with a rope. Since rope frays over time and the parties wished their friendship to be stronger, they replaced the rope with an iron chain. When the iron chain showed signs of rust, they replaced it with one of silver. When it was clear the tree could be shaken by high winds, and the Confederacy wished to expand the friendship, the other end of the chain was tied to the mountains on Onondaga, the fireplace of the Confederacy.

And later:
"We embrace this opportunity to rekindle the ancient council fore which formerly burnt as bright as the sun in this place and to heap on it so much fuel that it may never be extinguished and also to renew the ancient covenant chain with your, which you knew has always been kept bright and clean, without any stain or rust and which by this belt we now strengthen that forever hereafter you and we may have but One Heart, One Mind, One Body and One Belief.

By this Belt, we, the Twelve United Colonies renew the old Covenant Chain by which our forefathers in their great wisdom thought proper to bind us and you, our brothers, of the Six Nations together when they first landed at this place and if any of the links of this great chain should have received any rust, we now brighten it and make it shine like silver.

As God has put it into our hearts to love the Six Nations and their allies we now make the chain of Friendship so strong, we, hope through the favor and mercy of the good Spirit that it will remain strong and bright while the sun shines and waters run.

By this Belt we remove every difficulty that may be in the great road that runs through the middle of our Country and we will also clear up and open all the small roads that lead into the great one. We will take out every thorn, briar and stone so that when any of our brothers of the Six Nations have an inclination to see and talk with any of our brethren of the Twelve Untied Colonies they may pass safely without being scratched or bruised and we are further determined by the assistance of God to keep our roads open and free for the Six Nations as long as this earth remains." (4)

The Covenant Chain was more than a symbolic reference to the making of peaceful relations. It was also the actual confederation of Native nations and their allies, tied together with the colonies. To the Haudenosaunee, the Covenant Chain was the means by they could attach themselves to other Native American nations who were not in the confederacy, as well as the European colonists. The Covenant Chain was also a way to wipe the slate clean should there be transgressions.

The Covenant Chain of Peace, itself a metaphor for the preferred treaty relationship, is based upon the older metaphor of men linking arms as a show of peace. The links of a chain reminded the old timers of this linking of arms to show solidarity and peacefulness. A renewal of the commitments of a treaty agreement therefore became known as "polishing the chain" to remove any rust or dirt (metaphors for bad conduct) as a way of renewing the terms and spirit of the agreement.

There were said to be three links to the original chain, representing the concepts of peace, friendship and respect, forever. The Haudenosaunee believe that the Covenant Chain is an idea of a path that connects the two nations, a path that promotes peace, meaning that they are free to travel to each other to talk for help and support.

3.3 -- Re-Polishing the Silver Covenant Chain

Building Relationships Between the United States and the Haudenosaunee

"The League of the Haudenosaunee, more commonly known as the Six Nations (Mohawk, Oneida, Onondaga, Cayuga, Seneca and Tuscarora Nations, send its greetings to the men, women and children of other nations of this land. The league of the Haudenosaunee continues as a sovereign people on the soil it has occupied on Turtle Island since time immemorial, and we extend friendship to all who recognize our constitutional government and who desire peaceful relations". (Excerpt from the Haudenosaunee passport)

How We Will Dialogue With Each Other

Since the arrival of the Europeans on North America, the Haudenosaunee have strived to have peaceful relations with peoples from other nations. The protocols and processes underlying these relations have been embodied in instruments such as the Two Row Wampum, Silver Covenant Chain, and the Canandaigua Treaty of 1794.

The Haudenosaunee have had a relationship with the United States since the thirteen colonies were considering forming a union. On September 16, 1987, the 100th Congress passed a joint resolution acknowledging the contributions of the Haudenosaunee to the development of the United States Constitution.

Today, we need to take softest and cleanest cloth to polish the Silver Covenant Chain, to remove the tarnish that has accumulated over the years and to strengthen our relationship of peace, friendship and respect between the two confederacies: the United States and the Haudenosaunee. We need to brighten the Chain of Friendship as our forefathers did.

Our dialogue is a desire to maintain the peace between us. When we have peace, we can reach across the fire and greet each other in friendship. We need to respond to each other's differences and similarities in a respectful way. We need to recognize each other as sovereigns, respecting each other's customs, languages, and form of government.

As Haudenosaunee, we still speak our language, conduct traditional ceremonies and govern our people by a system installed centuries ago by the Peacemaker. Our spiritual and political system has not been separated. We have not entered the ship of the United States. We are Nations separate from the United States citizens as we keep our Nation citizenship within the Haudenosaunee. We are different from other people.

The younger generations will benefit from a renewal of the Silver Covenant Chain of Friendship and rekindling of our fires. Our youth will be proud of who they are and not feel hopeless for their future as a people. The youth of the United States can hold their heads up high knowing their leaders were keeping the promise of their forefathers in not breaking their promises to the Onkwehonweh (Native Americans).

It is proposed that this dialogue will provide the basis for the relationship the Haudenosaunee have with the United States. It will serve to educate your people on Haudenosaunee protocol and processes. It will, hopefully, bring consistency to an inconsistent relationship for the natural resources of this land.

222

Part IV: -- Haudenosaunee Environment

4.1 Environmental Philosophy of the Haudenosaunee

Today, we face new environmental issues our ancestors never had to consider. There were no polluting factories, gasoline stations, or human made chemicals like PCBs to harm the environment. Waterways followed their natural path. As people of this land, we took great care to keep the earth and its waters as pristine as possible, known in the past as common sense, known now as good environmental practices. There was no need for formalized environmental regulations. The challenge before us is finding ways to protect the natural world while preserving our unique relationship with it.

Over the past twenty years, the United States federal government has increasingly recognized the inherent sovereignty of Indian nations, their right to self-determination. Part of the inherent sovereignty of Indian nations is the power to create, regulate and assume primacy over environmental issues. The federal government recognizes this right by treating Indian tribes as states under numerous provisions of federal environmental laws.

4.2 Environmental Hazards and Impacts in Haudenosaunee Territories

Over the past five hundred years, the Haudenosaunee have observed and recorded the impacts of the European settlers on America. Our people tried to warn the colonists of their practices that do not sustain the earth and those practices will eventually destroy both ourselves and the newcomers. Like children possessed by a new toy, they the newcomers did not listen. The environmental destruction we see today is the result. Our communities have suffered the destruction of their natural resources. Our Nations have been confined to small tracts of land. Our Confederacy has been mocked by the young countries which do not understand the world. However, as more time passes, western society has begun to feel the limit or of our resources and the message of the Haudenosaunee has begun to be heard.

Knowledge long believed to be lost has exerted itself and the new science of ecology has resurged. Conservation and preservation are once again the principles of the modern day society, but still, arrogance of conventional science does not completely acknowledge the people who practice true conservation and peace.

Naturalized knowledge systems of the Haudenosaunee have taught how our people should to live in our territories. This knowledge system is based not only on experimentation and observation but also on feelings and emotions. The Haudenosaunee Knowledge System endeavors to integrated the physical, social and spiritual states into a cohesive force for the better of all and future generations. To this end, the

Haudenosaunee have vigorously advanced this knowledge which would progress our stance as an equal voice in the global systems

As early as the 1700's, histories indicate that our indigenous knowledge was very valuable to the colonial governments and people. This early knowledge had been meticulously tested over the centuries and proved correct. Our people have never been adverse to evaluating new technologies, rejecting those that are harmful and incorporating those that are useful. Western science is no exception. Our children have been trained in the sciences and tempered in the spirit of our people. Science and spirit are two very powerful tools to save the world.

4.3 -- Haudenosaunee Environmental Task Force

In 1992, in accordance with the Great Law of Peace, the Grand Council passed and agreed, based on Haudenosaunee protocols and cultural beliefs, to establish the Haudenosaunee Environmental Task Force (HETF). HETF is composed of delegates that include Haudenosaunee leaders, environmental technicians and scientists, chosen by each of the Haudenosaunee Nations who are committed to identifying environmental problems in their communities and working to find solutions to these problems.

The leaders of the Haudenosaunee have always considered three principles when making decisions: will a decision threaten peace, the natural world or future generations? The delegates of HETF have accepted these principles and use the following questions to guide us in our decision making:
What effect will our decision have on peace?
What effect will our decision have on the natural world?
What effect will our decision have on future generations?

The mission of HETF is to assist Haudenosaunee Nations in their efforts to conserve, preserve, protect and restore their environmental, natural and cultural resources; to promote the health and survival of the sacred web of life for future generations; to support other indigenous Nations working on environmental issues; and to fulfill our responsibilities to the natural world as our Creator instructed without jeopardizing peace, sovereignty or treaty obligations.

Part V -- Great Lakes Issues

"Seven generations, we really mean that. It often comes up against other current priorities, such as economic development. We have many issues to address, esp. development of the Seaway, cultural issues such as making baskets from cane grown in polluted waters and taken through the mouth, may not fall easily into the Great Lakes Governors nine priorities. The governor's nine points were preordained without our input..."

224

Oren Lyons, Haudenosaunee Environmental Task Force Political Co-Chair and Turtle Clan Faithkeeper representative making a statement to Mike Leavitt, U.S. EPA Administrator at a Great Lakes meeting with indigenous Nations/tribal leaders.

The Great Lakes are the largest body of freshwater on earth and holds approximately one-fifth of the world's freshwater. Lake Superior is the second largest lake in the world, after Lake Baikai. The Great Lakes system flows from Lakes Superior and Michigan, through Lakes Huron, Erie and Ontario and the St. Lawrence River into the Atlantic Ocean. The Lakes are connected by short narrows at Mackinac and by the St. Clair, Detroit and Niagara Rivers. These rivers have a very high flow rates.

There are approximately twenty-nine Native American Tribes in the Great Lakes area and the Great Lakes Basin. Within the 750 miles of land adjoining the Great Lakes, there are eight states and two provinces claiming jurisdiction. The Great Lakes hold 18% of the freshwater of the world.

As Haudenosaunee (Six Nations Confederacy), we live along one of the Great Lakes and/or within the Great Lakes Basin: from the St. Lawrence River to Lake Ontario.

5.1 -- The Great Lakes Charter - 1985

The charter states that only the State and Provinces have jurisdiction over the National resources of the Great Lakes. It avoids language about Native Nations who have signed treaties with the United States and Canada (Great Britain). The indigenous Nations, whether referred to as Tribes, First Nations, Native Nations, Native American, Indian or Haudenosaunee, have a shared jurisdiction over the waters.

The Charter's use of terms in the mission statement is commendable, such as "to conserve, preserve and protect the National resources of the Great Lakes Basin for the future generations". The terms are consistent with principles within Haudenosaunee philosophy. However, it stops short by only addressing new water diversions and does not address diversions which are currently existing.
Supplementary Agreement To The Great Lakes Charter (June 18, 2001) a.k.a. Great Lakes Annex -- Haudenosaunee Response

The philosophy of the Haudenosaunee is three-fold. We must look into the past to carry out the instructions given to us by the Creator. Secondly, we give thanks for the elements of Creation that include the plant life, the medicines, the fish, the waters and the air. Finally, under the law given to us by the Peacemaker, we use three principles: Peace, Power and Righteousness to implement the protection of creation's elements.

These are the principles of our forefathers. We exercise this and carry those thoughts into the present. The principles serve to remind us of the agreements we have made with other Nations and the agreements continue to be in force as international treaties. Those treaties are between two Nations: the Haudenosaunee and the United States and their successors, the Haudenosaunee and Great Britain and their successors. When those agreements were made, we used acceptable terms such as 'brothers, coexisting in the river of life on parallel paths.' Contained within the acceptable terms of the agreements are mutual peace, friendship and respect to live side by side.

The Haudenosaunee continue into the future, as instructed by the Creator, to protect those unborn faces yet to come and into the next seven generations.
As Haudenosaunee, we are citizens of our own Nations. We have never agreed to be citizens of the United States or Canada. Our land is not held in trust by the United States government or any State. We retain jurisdiction over our aboriginal territory, people, waters and the air as given to us by the Creator.

===================

The purpose of the Great Lakes Annex is to amend the Great Lakes Charter of 1985 to regulate and plan a decision-making process (G.L. Basin-wide) to withdraw or divert water from the Great Lakes.
The Annex to the Charter has resulted in a 'Proposal' consisting of two documents:
1. The Great Lakes Sustainable Water Resources Agreement ("the Agreement"), among the 10 Great Lakes States and Provinces, and,
2. The Great Lakes Basin Water Resources Compact ("the Compact"), an agreement among the eight Great Lakes States to join together in an interstate compact to enhance joint decision making about the use of the Great Lakes water.

An Agreement between Great Lakes government to regulate water withdrawals is a necessary reality and we thank those people who have begun to propose regulations.

World water shortages loom and efforts to sell the waters of our Mother Earth will be more common in the near future. We thank the United States Governors and Canadian Premiers for turning their attention towards this reality and we hope the regulations will be designed to protect those unborn faces yet to come.

The International Joint Commission (IJC) follows sound principles in their decision-making process. H.E.T.F.'s scientific co-chair sits on IJC scientific committee and the committee continues to produce excellent work.

226

The current agreement ignores the existing amounts of diversion and consumptive use of waters where the Haudenosaunee have a direct interest for customary uses, traditional practices and ceremonial purposes.

The Haudenosaunee Nations have never sanctioned the treaties and protocols in regard to the usage of Lake Ontario, Lake Erie, St. Lawrence River watersheds, and the greater Great Lakes Basin, beginning with the Boundary Waters Treaty of 1909 and ending with the Great Lakes Charter of 1985, of which the Great Lakes Annex of 2001 plans to amend.

The terms diversion and consumptive uses are too broad. They remain as ambiguous definitions that promote abuse beyond the existing constraints and may result in future lawsuits. As well, the uses create alternate paths for springs, lakes, rivers and streams to follow, sometimes being removed completely from the Great Lakes Basin. Our waters are already used to make profit for Private, State, Provincial, Federal and Crown interests, with large amounts of hydroelectric diversions from Lake Ontario, Lake Erie and the St. Lawrence River.

Haudenosaunee Nations should have been involved in drafting the Annex Proposal.

Some Nations were invited to the signing of the Annex, but no other consultation or participation was forthcoming. The governors and premiers face an uphill battle with the Haudenosaunee by presenting a proposal created behind closed doors with no prior consultation with Indigenous/First Nations governments. If there were true consultation, we would be engaged in devising the proposal before it is drafted, not in the 24th hour. The plan then could have been presented to the public and would receive much larger acceptance.

In the Treaties that preempt the Boundary Waters Treaty, the Haudenosaunee are a sovereign entity. The Federal government has a fiduciary responsibility to consult with the Haudenosaunee, on a Confederacy level. We are not to be treated as under State or Provincial jurisdiction that surrounds our Territory, but on a Federal level, government-to-government basis, Nation to Nation.
Indigenous Nations/Tribes throughout the Great Lakes Basin were not included in the process.

There is no mention of Indigenous Nations or their populations, who have a special relationship to the waters and land of the Great Lakes area. Indigenous Nations are established on rivers, streams and lakes flowing into the Great Lakes Basin.

The Annex only refers to new uses for withdrawal.

Existing usages are exempt. The Haudenosaunee have always used the Great Lakes Basin area for cultural and social purposes. The Annex fails to mention indigenous practices, loss of shoreline, destruction of fish spawning beds, polluted waters, diet change and the resulting epidemic increase of diabetes among indigenous populations. The Great Lakes Basin area is where we still retain the right to hunt, fish and gather in the customary manner accorded to our people and according to international treaty law.

The Winters Doctrine is the first international agreement on sharing water from the Milk River between the US and the Fort Belknap reservation. Haudenosaunee Nations, like most Indian Nations within the U.S., still have a strong case for protecting Indian interests in water quality and quantity impacts from off-territorial upstream interests, American or Canadian.

The Haudenosaunee should participate as an equal partner on the three groups appointed to develop the Annex Proposal, including the Water Management Working Group, the Advisory Committee and the Resource Group and Observers.

To our knowledge, there has been no participation by the Haudenosaunee in any of these three groups prior to the issuance of the Request for Public Comment. These groups have been working on crafting a proposal and guiding the public review process of the proposal for over two years and no consultation with the Haudenosaunee has occurred.

The information present in the "Request for Public Comment" is false because it does not apply in New York State, where the purported 'jurisdiction' has yet to engage in any consultation during the proposal development.

The July 19th Request for Public Comment states: "Finally, the individual jurisdictions have been engaging in ongoing consultation with their relevant Tribes and First Nations while this proposal has been developed." This is false information.

Although New York State surrounds Haudenosaunee Territory, we do not fall under New York State jurisdiction. Aside the fact that New York State and Wisconsin does not have the jurisdiction to dictate what happens in Haudenosaunee Territory, there has been no ongoing consultation. The same is true with Ontario and Quebec. Prior to a letter being generated from Gregory J. Allen, Senior Assistant Counsel to the Governor (Pataki) on July 20, 2004, there was no indication that New York State had any interest in consultation with the Haudenosaunee. A meeting was slated for September 21 at the Onondaga Nation Longhouse. The Haudenosaunee maintain that the engagement amounted to a briefing meeting and not a consultation session.

Jurisdiction is an inappropriate term and inconsistent within the Compact and the Agreement.

228

"Jurisdiction's Waters" is contained in the Definition of Terms of Agreement yet not addressed and clarified in the Compact. The use of the term is also inconsistent with Indian Law and Treaty Law whereby state, provincial, federal or crown governments have no jurisdiction over the Haudenosaunee.

Regarding water diversions and Indian Nations in Michigan and with respect to Haudenosaunee interests there are jurisprudence implications on the Annex. The Judge seems to justify water withdrawal via the Annex 2001 before the current proposal became enforceable.

It is in the best interest of the Great Lakes States and Provinces to include the Haudenosaunee in the discussions.

The Haudenosaunee reside in our sovereign territory within the Great Lakes Basin. In looking ahead, some entrepreneurs may pose a risk for New York State and Ontario/Quebec because neither the Charter, nor the Annex to the Charter applies to Indian territories. Should businessmen decide to sell surface water or groundwater from the Great Lakes but within an Indian reservation, disputes may evolve without full participation of the Haudenosaunee in these agreements.

CONCLUSION

Politically, Haudenosaunee Nations are sovereign entities that may not be party to a Charter amongst States and Provinces, much less an Annex to a Charter.

As indigenous people, we, the Haudenosaunee, are deeply concerned about the Great Lakes. As in the Great Lakes Governor's Council, we too are troubled by water/land/air pollution that affects this vast resource of our people. We are concerned about invasive species, ships emptying ballasts into the St. Lawrence /Great Lakes system, early icebreaking, expansion of the Seaway.

As well, as Haudenosaunee people, our traditions are the core of our society. We have never given up our rights to hunt, fish, and gather on our traditional Territories. Our rights need to be respected as guaranteed by Treaties signed between our forefathers and the fledgling United States. It is ridiculous to think we don't sit at the table with full authority over our own lands. We have presided over this territory from time immemorial and continue to take care of the resources the Creator has given to the Onkwehonweh (original people). We have competent people working on various environmental issues. Some are involved in the International Joint Commission and participate on various boards and committees for the sustainability of Mother Earth.

As part of the treaty agreements, we reserved the right to access and have free use of traditional waterways (and highways). The traditional waterways and highways need to be accessible and free to our people: currently, this is a matter that needs to be addressed.

We are asking for a review process on the Boundary Waters Treaty. At the very least, we would like to be assigned as a subject to a future annex of the Boundary Waters Treaty. The Haudenosaunee and other indigenous peoples don't fit under State/Provincial recommendations.

We know the issues and we have competent people to work on an Annex. We wish to work cooperatively on the issues that concern all of Creation and our unborn children seven generations into the future.

We await your response.
    Da nah tho
    Prepared by the Haudenosaunee Environmental Task Force

5.3 -- 2003 GREAT LAKES STRATEGY

The Great Lakes Strategy is supported by two concurrent bills: S1398 The Great Lakes Restoration Act and HR270 The Great Lakes Financing Act of 2003 (July 14, 2003)

The 2003 Great Lakes Strategy is designed to protect the resources of the Great Lakes Basin. With the backing of the U.S. Policy Committee, Thomas Skinner, Chair, 126 action items "articulates coordinated efforts of governmental partners (Federal, States, Tribes) in protecting and restoring Great Lakes." The core of the document focuses on the human population to "eat the fish, drink the water, swim at beaches, and [have] a healthy environment."

COMMENTS FROM HETF ON THE 2003 GREAT LAKES STRATEGY

The focus is on pollution, beaches (human health) and fish advisories. Initiatives take into account actions are progressing relatively quickly. However, in the areas that affects Haudenosaunee Territory, State of New York is lacking on project completion and/or lacks a monitoring system. Most of the initiatives within the Great Lakes Strategy will be completed by the deadlines, which does not consider all eight states. The initiatives are gauged by the number of on-going projects and not by participating states. In other words, some states may be doing the bulk of the projects whereas other states may be doing close to nothing. There is a discrepancy in the accountability of all states.

The Strategy makes a statement about jurisdiction to the states and provinces. It has not considered treaty rights and Federal policy which the states/provinces must adhere to.

The Haudenosaunee, as protectors and caretakers of the environment, would like to partner with the states and provinces.

230

The Great Lakes Strategy includes Tribes in the 300 page document, but did not consult with any tribes along the Great Lakes Basin. This should be rectified and their concerns addressed.

Strategy No. 37 is to improve understanding of exposure to health risks associated with consumption of fish and wildlife...and to follow fish advisories. We have seen from the past, in the community of Akwesasne, the fish advisories were effective. However, following the fish advisories and, in retrospect, omitting a clean source of protein, added to epidemic diabetes disease to the community. If fish advisories are implemented and followed, health practitioners need to also advise on healthy alternatives rather than leaving a community to make an uninformed decision to eating foods high in carbohydrates and sugars.

The Great Lakes Strategy makes an overall statement but no tracking systems are in place with no substance for progression to a cleaner, healthier environment.

Strategy No. 126 promotes Public Involvement in Great Lakes Program. The Haudenosaunee would like to be kept abreast of the any information in regards to the Great Lakes.

5.4 --SEAWAY ICEBREAKING ACTIVITIES

AKWESASNE MOHAWKS: The Socio-Cultural Impacts of **Icebreaking Activities Associated with Seaway Shipping -- Summary of the Briefing Paper for the Mohawk Nation Council of Chiefs, by Barbara Gray**

The integrity of the ice cover is of great importance to the entire natural world and has socio-cultural significance to the Mohawk people at Akwesasne. Icebreaking will disrupt the natural cycle of the river and will negatively impact the people and the natural order at Akwesasne. The people of Akwesasne are concerned that proper studies have not been undertaken to adequately determine the negative impacts of ice breaking activities in the St. Lawrence Seaway to the Natural World. Some studies exists that can be applied to ice breaking concerning fish and fisheries disruption, but more research needs to be conducted. In addition, an indigenous perspective is the holistically approach to include each of the beings within the environment, including the cultural needs of the Akwesasne people. The needs must be studied and protections put in place to protect them all.

The Mohawk people and migrating animals have continually used the frozen St. Lawrence River as an ice bridge. Forced destruction of the ice cover may weaken the ice in other parts of the St. Lawrence River, as well as impacting the ice on connecting rivers. That is: Under the ice, wakes may drown aquatic animals by flooding ice caverns (pockets) that these animals use for breathing and for traveling beneath the ice cover. It may also make the ice unsafe for humans as the frozen river is used as a roadway, ice-fishing activities and recreation use. Thus, ice breaking will jeopardize the socio-culture uses of the ice cover at Akwesasne.

The shoreline and shoreline vegetation, habitat and structures built along the shore will be highly impacted. In addition, the scouring of the riverbank and bed will churn up sediment; thus, exposing the environment and people to toxic chemicals. At risk are the breeding areas of animals and fish as well as impacts to sensitive medicinal plants that grow along and adjacent to the river that the Akweasronen depend on to keep the community healthy.

The Haudenosaunee environmental perspective requires thinking of the future generations. The waters have a natural cycle, with ice serving many functions that humans and the rest of the Natural World are interdependent on for their well-being and balance. Ice cover should be allowed to break up naturally. Nature should dictate the opening and closing of the Seaway shipping season, not humans. Icebreaking should not be used because the harms to the environment and to the community of Akwesasne far outweigh the economic benefits. An environmental injustice occurs when the people of Akwesasne and the natural world carry the burden of environmental and cultural impacts, for the economic benefits of others.

SEAWAY NAVIGATIONAL STUDY

HETF has a mandate from the Haudenosaunee Confederacy through a formal resolution by the Grand Council and is included in the United Nations document entitled: Haudenosaunee Environmental Restoration: An Indigenous Strategy to Human Sustainability" (1992).

From the Haudenosaunee comes a Traditional Knowledge System. TKS is a holistic approach to the ever-encompassing Natural World. Our Traditional Knowledge System is so imbedded that our philosophy and cultural lifeways are perpetuated in our actions despite the lack of understanding and sensitivity by governments that surround our communities.

Our culture is nature based. The Haudenosaunee have been given instructions from the Creator to give thanks by reciting the Ohenton Kariwatehkwen (Words That Come Before All Else). What does it mean? Give Thanks? The answer: Every part of Creation was made for sustaining humankind. Once we thank, acknowledge and understand this basic principal, mankind, you and I, will have the tendency not to overuse or waste resource. If you thank every part of Creation, you begin to realize the intricate connection with this web of Creation. So intricate, you become a voice, an advocate for the parts of creation that cannot defend itself from the abuse of mankind.

By using the framework within that Thanksgiving Address, here are a few impacts of the Seaway.

The People: impacts have been made to hunting, fishing, cultural use of the river and other impacts as addressed in this public hearing today.

Mother Earth: Destruction of the shoreline and upheaval of riverbed sediment.

The Grasses: important as a filtration system in wetland management, food and home to many creatures in the water. This also needs protection from shoreline erosion.

The Medicinal Plants: A vital component of Haudenosaunee well being and health, destroyed in places, by shoreline erosion.

The Fish: The drastic decline of eel populations – a medicine and a food to us.

There was also disruption to the sturgeon when dredged materials were emptied into their spawning beds. My dad is a fisherman and is over 6 feet tall. We have pictures of harvested sturgeon being taller than the fishermen. Today, sturgeon is approximately 3 feet tall. That is one foot for every ten years growth and the sturgeon are still recovering from the last grand plan of the Seaway. Where have they gone? They have been displaced from the St. Lawrence River to the St. Regis River. And you are talking about dredging again?

The Waters: Ship spills are not acceptable. You can't guarantee that inspections in Montreal will avoid a disaster in the St. Lawrence. Controlled water levels are unnatural and a detriment to aquatic life. The Great Lakes/St. Lawrence River is the largest drinking water system in North America.

The Birds: Our islands are protected nesting sites. Birds tend to naturally habitat in an area that is safe, undisturbed. We see endangered species nesting in our territory. The birds didn't need a Federal Protection Law to realize that Akwesasne is a safe haven for them. We welcome them to refuge in our Territory and we would like to keep them safe.

The Trees: Also a medicine, a source of food and a resource to us. It is a habitat for so many creatures. Shoreline erosion will harm trees in their path.

Since time immemorial, the Mohawk people have occupied this area as hunting/fishing/gathering stronghold. In 1755, it became a permanent settlement. As you see, we have the knowledge of this area. Certainly we knew this area long before the winds carried Jacques Cartier to Hochelaga (Montreal) in 1634. We have a lot to offer. We know this place. This is our Territory.

233

In 1957, the Seaway began construction. Mohawk lands were expropriated for NYPA dam and the Seaway. Our lands and burial sites were inundated. Other lands became unusable, fish habitat and navigational/migratory patterns destroyed.

So what were the benefits of the Seaway?
2. Easy transportation to and from Cornwall
3. Employment of local Akwesasronen

What are the negative effects of the Seaway to the Mohawks?
3. Port of Entry by U.S. and Canadian officials on our Territory. We have to go through two ports of entry on our land.
4. Environmental destruction of fish and wildlife and their habitat
5. Change of waterways (routes) used by our people
6. Severing of access to traditional waterways by the lock system and interconnecting damsInvasive species
7. Unregulated water withdrawals
8. Water level fluctuations

The Winter's Doctrine has been upheld in the U.S. Supreme Court giving Tribes water rights and resources from water. It is an area that has yet to be explored within the Mohawk communities along the St. Lawrence River and the Great Lakes Basin.

Setting the Winter's Doctrine aside, you are dealing with the Haudenosaunee Confederacy. These are not lands of your ancestors. We have jurisdiction over this area, as a Nation. When Quebec talked about separation, a Grand Council letter was sent the Prime Minister of Canada. This letter said if Quebec wants to separate, they can't take the land with them. It was never theirs to take: never Quebec's to begin with. The land belongs to the Haudenosaunee and the other indigenous people of that area. The land was never given up. If you look at the lands of the Tonawanda Senecas, the Onondagas, and the Mohawks, it was never placed in Federal Trust. It's still part of the Nation's Territory. (Administration for Native Americans summarizes defines this as 'tribal trust'.)

The Haudenosaunee are also concerned about Homeland Security. We are not terrorists: we are protecting our land, our environment – something the Seaway has not done in the past. Akwesasne has Homeland Security issues. We have ships going through our territory and no idea what shipments are going through our waters. The ship manifests are not public information. We have a right to know if shipments may be a threat to our people.

The St. Lawrence Seaway is protected by Treaties: The Boundary Waters Treaty of 1908 is one such treaty. However, there is a Treaty currently being disregarded: The Jay treaty – the Treaty of Amityville and Commerce which gives Haudenosaunee Nations free access and free

234

from tolls along waterways and highways in our traditional territory. This has never been abrogated, although some officials would like to tell you otherwise. But it is not so.

So why didn't we come forward during the early years of the Seaway. We did. The problem was a language barrier. To speak through a translator limits and misconstrues the issues you are trying to address. It didn't work in the 1957. But we know the English language, we have scientists, engineers, environmentalists, we have command of your language. It is clear the issues we are addressing and we would like to address them now.

How can we work together?

Consultation after final draft is completed, as with the Great Lakes Annex of 2001 does not promote dialogue. Meeting with indigenous Nations after the ink has dried is not called consultation. We can live side by side in this river of life. Your forefathers agreed to this, so did our forefathers. The United States and the British Empire entered into this protocol called the Two Row Wampum. And in the spirit of the two row, we can meet together and Polish this Silver Covenant Chain of Friendship so we may continue to live responsibly and to give thanks to the Natural World.

We can co-exist in this River of Life. We offer this solution: have a tri-national Study Partnership.

Da nah tho

◊ ◊ ◊ ◊ ◊ ◊

Joyce King is known as Tekahnawiiaks (Deh-gunna-wee-yuks). She is from the Mohawk Nation, Turtle Clan and a lifetime resident of the Mohawk Territory at Akwesasne. She has the experience of working with all three Mohawk governments in Akwesasne: the Mohawk Nation Council of Chiefs or MNCC (Traditional Mohawk Council of the Haudenosaunee Confederacy); St. Regis Mohawk Tribal Council (American elected council), the Mohawk Council of Akwesasne (Canadian elected council). During her employment with the MNCC she served as Managing Editor for Indian Time newspaper and managed the Akwesasne Notes Bookstore. In 1989, Joyce received an Order in Council as a 107 Justice of Peace (a Federal Canadian appointment under the *Indian Act*). In 2001, Joyce became the Cultural Researcher for the Haudenosaunee Environmental Task Force, which is mandated by the Haudenosaunee (Iroquois) Confederacy to protect and restore the environment. Two years later, she successfully became the Acting Director and two years later, the HETF Co-Chairs, Oren Lyons (Onondaga Nation, Political Co-Chair) and F. Henry Lickers (Seneca

Nation, Scientific Co-Chair) appointed her as the HETF Director. Joyce Tekahnawiiaks King is a Mohawk Educator and lectures throughout North America and has had the opportunity to present in Japan. She also was part of a documentary film "Cowjews and Indians..." filmed partially in Germany with three other Native Americans. Tekahnawiiaks is a supporter of the Akwesasne Freedom School and traditional teachings. As well, she is a certified New York State mediator.

Presently, Joyce is the Director of the Akwesasne Justice Department, Mohawk Council of Akwesasne.

Notes:
1 Jemison, Peter G. & Schein, Anna, Ed. Treaty of Canandaigua Clear Light Publishers, Santa Fe, NM 2000.
2 Akwesasne Notes, Mohawk Nation. Basic Call to Consciousness. Book Publishing Co. Summertown TN 1978.
3 Jemison, Peter G. & Schein, Anna, Ed. Treaty of Canandaigua (Introduction by P. G.Jemison) Clear Light Publishing Santa Fe, NM, 2000 p 30.
4 Statement made by the Commissioners appointed by the Twelve United Colonies to make a treaty with the Six Nations at the City of Albany on Friday, the 25th day of August, 1775.

◊◊◊◊◊◊

PART V -- VISION FOR THE FUTURE AND CONCLUSION

Traditional Knowledge Revival Pathways (TKRP)

Victor Steffenson

Editor's Note: Victor Steffenson, a descendent of the Gulf People of Cape York, is the project leader of the Traditional Knowledge Revival Pathways (TKRP) project in Australia. Victor made the Main Keynote address at our Earth Day Conference, stepping in for Winona LaDuke who was unable to attend the conference due to a scheduling conflict. The material below is adapted from the TKRP website, active at the time of the conference. They seem to be active on FaceBook, now.

TKRP -- Building pathways for community development through revival of traditional (indigenous) knowledge within contemporary society.

The Traditional Knowledge Revival Pathways (TKRP) was developed from the aspirations of Indigenous Elders, to preserve and recognize Traditional Indigenous Knowledge. With the guidance and instruction of our Aboriginal Elders, we are supporting them to collect information that will be beneficial for County and Community, both in the present and the future.

The project was initiated in 2001, by the aspirations of the Kuku Thaypan Elders who wanted their knowledge, beliefs and practices recorded and preserved for present and future use by their families and youth.

The Kuku-Thaypan Elders, now known as Dr George Musgrave, Senior, and Dr Tommy George Senior, are situated in the Cape York region of Far North Queensland, Australia. For many years these Elders have tried to pass on their knowledge, have it secured, and have it put into practice to sustain the future of country and community. This was seen as a matter of urgency for a local North Queensland man by the name of Victor Steffensen, who has been engaged with the Kuku-Thaypan Elders since 1991. After years of trial and error, in the year 2000, the team found an opportunity to develop a unique methodology of recording and demonstrating Traditional Knowledge using digital video and computer storage equipment. With very little funding and resources, the team started recording knowledge for no arranged payments. Knowing that it was a job that was to be done urgently, it was initiated from the heart.

Opportunities to preserve and value Indigenous Traditional Knowledge are endangered by the range of problems within our Environment and Communities today. Avenues for the preservation of Traditional

239

Knowledge are fading and are at risk of being lost altogether. Loss of Traditional knowledge will result in a decline of Indigenous Identity and a severe reduction in the recognition and understanding of an invaluable Sustainable Knowledge System. TKRP is endeavoring to rescue this knowledge, for the benefit of Community and Country, before it is too late. A re-focus of Indigenous Knowledge is a multi-layered healing aspiration of TKRP, which steers the direction of the project towards traditional ways of dealings.

The majority of Indigenous Elders in Communities understand the problems in Community and Country and bear the frustrations of not being able to re-apply traditional values. Current environmental strategies and community aid programs are tied by government red tape and funding guidelines that proceed to ignore and disadvantage Indigenous based initiatives. The Elders have voiced many concerns to government and industry relating to the lack of cooperative management regimes, and the lack of recognition of their inherited knowledge system as being of true value to contemporary outcomes. There is no doubt that in today's society Elders need new tools and assistance to pass on their traditional values to younger generations. To support this, there is the need for collaborative recognition from other authorities currently responsible for land and community management.

The TKRP is based on (1) ensuring the survival of cultural knowledge; and (2) the opportunity to demonstrate practices that have the ability to 'innovate' contemporary management and community outcomes for the benefit of all generations to come. TKRP seeks to support Indigenous Elders to mentor the process of Indigenous Knowledge Research and recording throughout the Cape York Peninsula region. TKRP is rapidly spreading its recording and mentoring methodology into other regions. The project has a demonstrated record of success, with a focused methodology, that has been built over time. The Project is achieving the following:

1. Transfer of Traditional Knowledge from the Elders to their young people based on the traditional methods as determined by the Elders.
2. Digitally recording this Traditional Knowledge before it is lost forever.
3. Storing knowledge onto multi-versions of a digital knowledgebase.
4. Incorporating traditional knowledge in cooperative land management strategies and building this practice into "Best practice principles" in all land management.
5. Building and improving the profile of Indigenous Knowledge and its appreciation with other land managers and users both nationally and internationally (for example, pastoralists, government, and the general public).
6. Creating practical action, research-driven, projects as live case studies to better collaborative land and community management.

240

TKRP is continuing to develop by assisting the Elders to conduct their own research on their own terms. The Elders need vital assistance to pass on their knowledge and most importantly, to practically implement their inherited cultural responsibilities in a race against time to rehabilitate our communities and environment.

Methodology

All of the operations and components developed by TKRP are done with the permission granted by the Elders and Traditional Owners. The project's methodology has been developed with the protocols of the Traditional Way of managing and applying cultural knowledge and practices. TKRP follows a system of methods which encompass the cultural process of the project. This method of process is necessary for the project's successful implementation. Choices made during the project's development are respectful of Aboriginal cultural processes, their mores, and ways of teaching and learning. Therefore, the project methodology seeks to respect and retain the integrity of the transfer of Traditional Knowledge from Elders to youth. The developing process of adopting Clan groups into the methodology of the project is based on recognizing the Elders as the Mentors.

Most Elders recognize other related Clan groups, within their traditional kinship system, and share the same views and strategies for revitalizing their youth and culture. The project ensures that the Elders have the leading role of demonstrating the project into new areas, so that it produces a positive introduction for other Clan groups to take on the methodology of TKRP trustfully, cost efficiently and in good time. The way that clan groups are initially encouraged to undertake the project is not through dollars and promises, but by realizing the importance of working with their own Elders and Country to do what they can, while they still can. With developing success and no definite promises, TKRP is working towards strengthening this resource and training component that supports the operations and implementation of TKRP into other areas.

The Traditional Knowledge Revival Pathways supports Communities with the recording of their own knowledge, on their own terms, through the methodology developed and mentored by Indigenous Elders. It is important to assist the communities with their recording process in order to develop consistent methods that support the recognition of traditional knowledge values in a contemporary setting. This section allows the communities to introduce themselves and exhibit their personal progress along side other communities that are undertaking the methodology.

All of the operations and components developed by TKRP are done with the permission granted by the Elders and Traditional Owners. The project's methodology has been developed with the protocols of the Traditional Way of managing and applying cultural knowledge and practices. TKRP follows a system of methods which encompass the cultural process of the project. This method of process is necessary for the project's successful implementation.

Choices made during the project's development are respectful of Aboriginal cultural processes, their mores, and ways of teaching and learning. Therefore, the project methodology seeks to respect and retain the integrity of the transfer of Traditional Knowledge from Elders to youth. The developing process of adopting Clan groups into the methodology of the project is based on recognizing the Elders as the Mentors. Most Elders recognize other related Clan groups, within their traditional kinship system, and share the same views and strategies for revitalizing their youth and culture.

The project ensures that the Elders have the leading role of demonstrating the project into new areas, so that it produces a positive introduction for other Clan groups to take on the methodology of TKRP trustfully, cost efficiently, and in good time. The way that clan groups are initially encouraged to undertake the project is not through dollars and promises, but by realizing the importance of working with their own Elders and Country to do what they can, while they still can. With developing success and no definite promises, TKRP is working towards strengthening this resource and training component that supports the operations and implementation of TKRP into other areas.

The Traditional Knowledge Revival Pathways (TKRP) has developed direction towards the practical recording of Indigenous Knowledge and engaging with many communities to assist with the education project objectives. The aspirations that our indigenous Elders have in reapplying their invaluable traditional knowledge is developing into something really special for our community and environment to engage. It is the first time that our Elders have had the opportunity to undertake a leading demonstrative role towards mainstream educational issues by re-introducing values of their traditional knowledge. Supporting initiatives such as digital technology and practical research implementations, have shown demonstrative pathways in culturally reviving future generations and we aim to deliver cross-cultural collaborations.

While the project has taken time to develop the structure and build relationships to strengthen its capacity and direction, it now has the correct baseline structure in place for the next stages of development. TKRP now has many regions involved, along with the mention of many other clan groups being influenced by the process. The project has developed partnerships and allies in contributing assistance and resources to achieving this important educational initiative.

◊ ◊ ◊ ◊ ◊ ◊

Victor Steffensen, is a descendent of the Gulf People of Cape York, and is the project leader of the Traditional Knowledge Revival Pathways (TKRP) project in Australia. Victor, and two Kuku-Thaypan Elders, Dr Tommy George and Dr George Musgrave, began the project in 1999. The Project involves the recording of their traditional knowledge and re-applying the traditional methods back into community and environmental managment. This grassroots project was quickly noticed by other clan groups in Australia and is now involved with up to 16 traditional groups across the State of Queensland and growing well beyond. While working to save the knowledge with multi-media technology, the TKRP project is developing many components to support the recognition of Traditional knowledge into mainstream values, and to demonstrate the need to keep this program going, and to expand its scope. In order to save knowledge for the future generations before it is lost, this project understands that it is crucial for everyone to re-connect our responsibilities and spiritual connections to the environment. This Earth Day Conference marked the first time that the Project had ventured overseas to the United States.

Indigenous Response

Phil Bellfy

It would be wonderful to be able to say that all of the environmental problems we faced in 2007 at the time of our conference have been resolved, but, that is certainly not the case. In fact, the Great Lakes are under increasing threat, but the Indigenous response has been immediate and widespread.

Here's just a short rundown of the dire environmental threats we face in the Great Lakes:

- Tar-sands development
- Transport of that tar-sands "dilbit" through our territories via pipeline (Keystone XL, etc.), oil-tankers on the Great Lakes, or by rail
- Another Kalamazoo River (lower Michigan) "oil spill" that has permanently polluted several miles of this waterway and its tributaries –this is the biggest inland oil spill in US history –180,000 gallons of "dilbit" crude released into the environment
- The gutting of the "Sand Dunes Protection Act" by Michigan
- The abrogation of almost all "environmental regulations" by Michigan
- The approval of "mountain-top removal" for open-pit iron-ore mining in the traditional territory of the Bad River Ojibway in Wisconsin
- Nickel and copper sulfide mining in Michigan's Upper Peninsula, at Eagle Rock, a site sacred to the Indigenous people of the region
- A proposed limestone mining operation in the Eastern Upper Peninsula on Treaty land –the state of Michigan proposes to "sell" approximately 11,000 acres of land, but that land is under the jurisdiction of the Tribes of the area (see the "Consent Decree" discussion, below)
- The danger of a rupture in the 61-year old pipeline, carrying "light crude," that runs under the Straits of Mackinaw –it was designed with a 30-year lifespan
- The State of Michigan has leased over 700,000 acres of land for "oil and gas" extraction (this area equals the land mas of Rhode Island) – millions more acres are under this threat; most, if not all of this extraction will be done by "fracking." Michigan law *requires* the State to "foster the development of the [oil-gas] industry along the most favorable conditions and with a view to the ultimate recovery of the maximum production of [oil and gas]."
- The Mascoma/Frontier "cellulosic ethanol" project, proposed for Northern Michigan is projected to annually utilize 1400 tons of "feedstock," harvested from forests within a 150 mile radius of Kinross, the site of the proposed refinery. This refinery project is currently "on hold."

The Canadian government essentially abandoned its jurisdiction over most of the lakes and rivers in Canada in 2012 with the passage of Bill C-45. This "Omnibus Bill" removed 99.7% of Canada's lakes and 99.9% of Canada's rivers from federal oversight. Pipelines are also excluded.

This outrageous action by the Harper government in Canada gave rise to the Indigenous "Idle No More" movement, started by four aboriginal women from Saskatchewan (women are the traditional "keepers" of the water). From there, it has spread across North America and throughout the world –wherever Indigenous territories are being threatened. It's impossible to arrive at an exact number, but many (if not all) First Nations and Tribes throughout the Great Lakes have passed resolutions and/or held rallies in support of Idle No More.

But moving beyond rallies and resolutions, Indigenous Nations have been encouraged to assert their own "Indigenous Environmental Protection" rights throughout their Traditional Territories. One of the groups (in addition to the more general-focus Idle No More movement) is the "Article32.org" coalition.(1)

Article 32 – UNDRIP

Article 32 refers to that article of the United Nations Declaration on the Rights of Indigenous People (UNDRIP). The Article, in its entirety, is quoted below:

Article 32

1.   Indigenous peoples have the right to determine and develop priorities and strategies for the development or use of their lands or territories and other resources.

2.   States shall consult and cooperate in good faith with the indigenous peoples concerned through their own representative institutions in order to obtain their free and informed consent prior to the approval of any project affecting their lands or territories and other resources, particularly in connection with the development, utilization or exploitation of mineral, water or other resources.

3.   States shall provide effective mechanisms for just and fair redress for any such activities, and appropriate measures shall be taken to mitigate adverse environmental, economic, social, cultural or spiritual impact.

Of course, when presented to the United Nations for a vote, the US, Canada, New Zealand, and Australia all voted "no" (The final vote was 144 to 4). But, since that shameful act, all four governments have reversed their "no" votes, with varying commitments to the goals of the

UNDRIP. Of course, in a discussion of the Great Lakes, we need only concern ourselves with the US and Canada

Although Canada "endorsed" the Declaration on November 12, 2010, its support for the UNDRIP is still fairly nebulous, while the US response has been somewhat more forceful and supportive. While the US Senate has never taken up the issue, on December 16, 2010, President Obama directed all federal agencies to work with Tribes throughout the US to adhere to the Declaration through what can only be called a "Presidential Proclamation." The relevant section of that "Announcement" follows:

Announcement of U.S. Support for the United Nations Declaration on the Rights of Indigenous Peoples -- Initiatives to Promote the Government-to-Government Relationship & Improve the Lives of Indigenous Peoples

III. 2 — Protection of Native American Lands and the Environment, and Redress

The United States recognizes that some of the most grievous acts committed by the United States and many other States against indigenous peoples were with regard to their lands, territories, and natural resources. For this reason, the United States has taken many steps to ensure the protection of Native American lands and natural resources, and to provide redress where appropriate. It is also for this reason that the United States stresses the importance of the lands, territories, resources and redress provisions of the Declaration in calling on all States to recognize the rights of indigenous peoples to their lands, territories, and natural resources.

Consistent with its understanding of the intention of the States that negotiated and adopted the Declaration, the United States understands these provisions to call for the existence of national laws and mechanisms for the full legal recognition of the lands, territories, and natural resources indigenous peoples currently possess by reason of traditional ownership, occupation, or use as well as those that they have otherwise acquired. The Declaration further calls upon States to recognize, as appropriate, additional interests of indigenous peoples in traditional lands, territories, and natural resources. Consistent with that understanding, the United States intends to continue to work so that the laws and mechanisms it has put in place to recognize existing, and accommodate the acquisition of additional, land, territory, and natural resource rights under U.S. law function properly and to facilitate, as appropriate, access by indigenous peoples to the traditional lands, territories and natural resources in which they have an interest.

This is, of course, a very hopeful sign of the US federal government's commitment to working with Great Lakes tribes to insure their UN – DRIP "Article 32" rights are respected.

The Great Lakes—St. Lawrence River Basin
Water Resources Agreement

The Agreement gives further support to Indigenous Nations in their efforts to take control of the environmental protection functions abandoned by the government of Canada and Great Lakes states and provinces. Here's the relevant language from that Agreement:

Article 702 - Relationship to First Nations And Tribes

1. Nothing in this Agreement is intended to abrogate or derogate from treaty rights or rights held by any Tribe recognized by the federal government of the United States based upon its status as a Tribe recognized by the federal government of the United States.
2. Nothing in this Agreement is intended to abrogate or derogate from the protection provided for the existing aboriginal or treaty rights of aboriginal peoples in Ontario and Québec as recognized and affirmed by section 35 of the Constitution Act, 1982.

Of course, both the UNDRIP and the Water Resources Agreement are international agreements, and, as such, fall under the umbrella of "treaties," although they are not "officially" designated as such. But, in the context of the United States' Constitution, "Treaties are the Supreme law of the Land" (Article VI – quoted below. This, quite obviously, encompasses Treaties signed between the US and Indigenous Nations, as Article 702 makes clear.

Constitution of the United States — Article VI

... This Constitution, and the Laws of the United States which shall be made in Pursuance thereof; and all Treaties made, or which shall be made, under the Authority of the United States, shall be the supreme Law of the Land; and the Judges in every State shall be bound thereby, any Thing in the Constitution or Laws of any State to the Contrary notwithstanding.

As mentioned above, Section 35 (1) of the Canadian Constitution states that the "The existing aboriginal and treaty rights of the aboriginal peoples of Canada are hereby recognized and affirmed." Consequently, even a cursory review of international declarations, agreements, and Treaties all make clear that Indigenous people have the undisputed right to manage their "natural resources" to their benefit and in accordance with their own needs, and these rights are affirmed by Treaty.

On December 6, 2012, the Assembly of First Nations passed a **"Statement of Unity"** which said, in part:

> We unconditionally reject any Canadian or provincial legislation, policies, or processes that impact our lands, air, waters and resources which have not obtained our free, prior, and informed consent ... In order to ensure economic stability and protection of our environment, development projects or any other initiatives that may impact our Nations requires our full and inclusive participation and our free, prior and informed consent ... To protect the integrity of our treaty and inherent rights, we hereby put the Government of Canada on notice that any further imposition of legislation and/or policies will be met with appropriate measures.

It should be noted that the phrasing, "free, prior, and informed consent," is taken from Article 32 of the UN-DRIP (the phrasing can be found in several other Articles, as well).

2007 Inland Consent Decree

The US signed a Treaty with the "Ottawa and Chippewa" on March 28, 1836. Among the provisions of that "land cession" Treaty is this:

1836 Land Cession Treaty of Washington – Article 13

> The Indians stipulate for the right of hunting on the lands ceded, with the other usual privileges of occupancy, until the land is required for settlement.

The scope and validity of those "Article 13" Rights had been in dispute for more than a century, but the Inland Consent Decree "conclusively settled" those issues. The relevant language follows:

Findings And Order – 2007 Inland Consent Decree

> C. The Parties explored settlement of their respective claims regarding [the 1836 Treaty] Inland Article 13 Rights, reached an agreement in principle on the terms and conditions of such a settlement, and have now stipulated to the entry of this Decree, which is intended to resolve conclusively such claims, and to provide for the protection of the resources in the 1836 Ceded Territory.

Although the "1836 Tribes" (see map) have passed Resolutions asserting their opposition the State of Michigan's actions on occasion, they've not asserted their "Inland Rights" through the promulgation of "environmental protection" regulations, although the language of the Decree gives unquestionably them that right, especially Sections XXI and XXII, "Assessment" and "Restoration."

It should be noted that both the 1836 and the 1842 "land cession" Treaties contain nearly identical "Article 13" rights (in the 1842 Treaty of La Pointe, the relevant language is in Article 2).

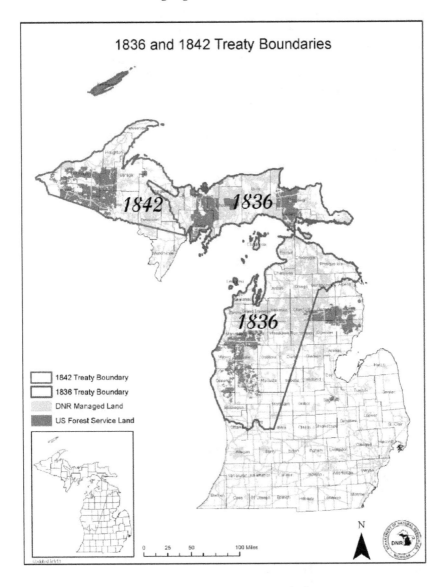

1836 and 1842 Treaty Boundaries
http://www.michigan.gov/documents/dnr/TCU_map_183629_7.pdf

State of Michigan & Indian Tribes Accords

Michigan and the Tribes resident therein have signed two "environmental protection" accords. In this, Michigan Tribes are rather unique; as far as can be ascertained, no other State has entered into such agreements with Tribes within "their" boundaries. The Tribal Water Accord was signed on May 12, 2004. Twelve Tribes signed the Accord, as did Michigan's Governor at the time, Jennifer Granholm.

The Tribal Climate Accord was signed on June 11, 2009. Again, all 12 Michigan tribes signed the Accord (Gov. Granholm, again, signed for Michigan). The language of the Climate Accord is relevant to this discussion, which says, in part:

> Whereas, the Tribal leaders of the federally recognized Indian Tribes in Michigan and the Governor of the state of Michigan recognize the vital importance of the health and quality of the Great Lakes, inland waters, air, geography, ecosystems, plants, and wildlife to the physical, cultural, and economic welfare and future of all of our citizens;

> Whereas, climate change poses a grave and immediate threat to the environment, quality of life, and economy for all of our citizens; ...

> Now, Therefore, the undersigned Tribal Leaders and the Governor affirm their joint commitment to combat global warming through reduction of greenhouse gas emissions and, in furtherance of this goal, agree to designate appropriate representatives of their respective environmental or natural resources pro-grams ... to address global warming through methods including but not limited to pollution control, alter-native clean energy technologies, and conservation. Because effectively addressing global warming is closely linked to the protection of our water resources, the Tribal-State Climate Change Forum may hold its meetings in conjunction with the bi-annual meetings being held under the Tribal-State water resources accord entered into on May 12, 2004.

EPA - Tribes as States, and Direct Implementation Tribal Coop-erative Agreements (DITCAs)

The final set of policy directives, at least as they apply to the US Tribes, are those of the EPA's "Tribal Environmental" initiatives. The first, "Tribes as States," authorizes the EPA to work directly with Tribes "in the same manner as states for implementing and managing certain environmental programs." Among those programs are the Clean Water, Clean Air, and the Safe Drinking Water Acts. DITCA, is "a funding mechanism for federally-recognized tribes and eligible intertribal consortia to carry out agreed-upon activities and to assist EPA with the implementation of federal environmental programs for Indian tribes in the absence of an acceptable tribal program."

Conclusion

As can be seen by the Treaties, Agreements, Consent Decrees, Accords, and policy statements and provisions outlined in this essay, Tribes and First Nations throughout the Great Lakes have the inherent right to provide for "environmental; protection" throughout their "traditional territories." Article 25 of the UN-DRIP makes this assertion explicitly:

Article 25 - UNDRIP

Indigenous peoples have the right to maintain and strengthen their distinctive spiritual relationship with their traditionally owned or otherwise occupied and used lands, territories, waters and coastal seas and other resources and to uphold their responsibilities to future generations in this regard.

Ours is a "Seven Generation" approach to our purpose on this planet – "future generations," indeed!

The struggle for justice (whether "environmental" or otherwise) is not a *choice* for Indigenous people, it is a *compulsion,* it cannot be ignored. It is true that our challenges are great, and it is also true that we are small in number, but, what we lack in number we make up for with commitment.

And, we have a number of things going for us, beyond those outlined in this essay. First, we need to look at the Canadian government's response to what they call "Aboriginal protest." To the Canadian government, this "protest" amounts to a "threat to Canada's resource agenda [which] poses a 'risk' to multi-billion dollar oil and mining plans."

And then we must couple this "risk" and "threat" with the very real threats and risks to extractive industry's profits and share prices. Aboriginal protests and other actions can and do affect a company's "bottom line." Consequently, Indigenous people can and do rec-ognize that their opposition to extractive activity on their traditional territory across North America is a very powerful tool –and gover-nments and the corporations recognize the power and effectiveness of "Idle No More" and similar actions in defense of the environ-ment, in defense of Aki.

Paraphrasing the conservative US politician, Barry Goldwater – "Extremism in the defense of the environment is no vice. And moder-ation in the pursuit of environmental justice is no virtue."

From the opposition to tar-sands and the XL Pipeline in the west, to the struggle of the Mi'kmaq people against fracking on their traditional territory, to the "fracktivist" fight against the destruction of the water and the industrializa-tion of Nature itself in Michigan, Indigenous people are standing side by side (sometimes, alone) with their non-Native sisters and brothers to fulfill their sacred duty to protect this earth. As was seen in Maaganiit Noodin's Preface, "aki" means "earth," but it also means "that which is sacred." And we take these "ancient instructions" to protect Aki very seriously, or we ignore them at our peril.

We don't fight the environmental fascists because we think we will win, we fight these fascists because they are fascists. I hate to sound melodramatic about this, but if we lose this fight, we are all dead.

NOTES:
1.   Article 32.org was established by this author. Links to all of the quotes and documents referred to in this essay, and more, can be found at that website.

◊ ◊ ◊ ◊ ◊ ◊

Conclusion

Phil Bellfy

A supportive, intact, viable, sustainable environment is essential to the survival of Indigenous people, as indigenous means "of the earth." And, Tribal and First Nations in the Great Lakes area are keenly aware of the stresses this valuable life-supporting region faces.

Our problem is two-fold. First, our nationhood is, quite obviously, based in the sovereignty we hold over our traditional territories. Secondly, our very lives depend on the sustainability of the environment in support of our way of life, and, again, quite obviously, the environmental crises the Great Lakes region faces have placed that sustainability in peril. The Spirit World has told us that as long as we take care of the land, the land will take care of us, so the environmental crises is a matter of life or death. Our relationship with Aki is one based on respect and reciprocity. So, in order sustain our lives, we must live in harmony and balance with the forces of the natural world.

The essays in this volume point the way, through our history, our current practices, and into the future, by a return to our languages, a return to our principles, a return to our responsibilities, a return to our spiritual practices, and a return to our commitment to Honor the Earth. So, although this may offend the sensibilities of some Tribal people, I encourage everyone to become an "Indian."

If being an "Indian" means developing an understanding and practice of our sacred relationship with the Earth, then "becoming an Indian" is simply the only way Human Beings can survive on this fragile planet. I hope the essays in this volume have encouraged you to become involved in this struggle, involved in repairing the earth, and our relationship with it. Our very survival --and that of the Earth, of Aki-- depends on it.

Miigwetch (thank you) for doing all that you do.

◊ ◊ ◊ ◊ ◊ ◊

Dr. Phil Bellfy is a citizen of the White Earth Nation. He is now Professor Emeritus of American Indian Studies at Michigan State University. His most recent book, *Three Fires Unity: The Anishnaabeg of the Lake Huron Borderlands,* won the University of Nebraska's North American Indian Prose Award for 2011. As Co-director of the Center for the Study of Indigenous Border Issues, Phil organized this Earth Day conference.

◊ ◊ ◊ ◊ ◊ ◊

◊ ◊ ◊ ◊ ◊ ◊

The Ziibi Press is the publishing arm of the Center for the Study of Indigenous Border Issues (CSIBI) which is incorporated in the State of Michigan as an educational non-profit organization.
(Ziibi is the Ojibwe word for "river" --as in Mississippi).

While the main focus of CSIBI is concerned with the *political/geographic boundaries* that often divide Indigenous Peoples, the concept of "border issues" for us is much broader.

Other boundaries that Indigenous people must often transverse are those that separate our cultures from that of the visitors. That is, we wish to explore what it means to be an Indigenous person in this era of mass consumption and environmental destruction.

This book explores the "environmental consciousness border" between Indigenous communities and the dominant culture. We are hopeful that the information in this book will help reverse the environmentally destructive patterns of the Visitor culture.

CSIBI Directors:
Phil Bellfy, Michigan State University, East Lansing
Karl Hele, Concordia University, Montreal
David McNab, York University, Toronto
Please visit our website for more information: http://csibi.org/

◊ ◊ ◊ ◊ ◊ ◊

CPSIA information can be obtained
at www.ICGtesting.com
Printed in the USA
BVHW04s1828050818
523625BV00009B/60/P